HOSPITALITY RECEPTION & FRONT OFFICE

–PROCEDURES AND SYSTEM

HOSPITALITY RECEPTION & FRONT OFFICE

–PROCEDURES AND SYSTEM

Dr. Jagmohan Negi

Gaurav M.J., Ritushka and Suniti

With the Assistance of
The International Culinary Foundation & Himalayan Tourism and Recreation in Mountains, India

S. CHAND
PUBLISHING

S. Chand And Company Limited

(ISO 9001 Certified Company)

S. Chand And Company Limited
(ISO 9001 Certified Company)
Head Office: D-92, Sector–2, Noida – 201301, U.P. (India), Ph. 91-120-4682700
Registered Office: A-27, 2nd Floor, Mohan Co-operative Industrial Estate,
New Delhi – 110 044, Phone: 011-49731800
www.**schandpublishing.com;** e-mail: **info@schandpublishing.com**

Marketing Offices:

Chennai	:	Ph: 23632120; chennai@schandpublishing.com
Guwahati	:	Ph: 2738811, 2735640; guwahati@schandpublishing.com
Hyderabad	:	Ph: 40186018; hyderabad@schandpublishing.com
Jalandhar	:	Ph: 4645630; jalandhar@schandpublishing.com
Kolkata	:	Ph: 23357458, 23353914; kolkata@schandpublishing.com
Lucknow	:	Ph: 4003633; lucknow@schandpublishing.com
Mumbai	:	Ph: 25000297; mumbai@schandpublishing.com
Patna	:	Ph: 2260011; patna@schandpublishing.com

First Edition 2013

Reprint 2024

ISBN : 978-81-219-3992-8 **Product Code:** H8HTM60HTRM10ENAA13R

PRINTED IN INDIA

By Vikas Publishing House Private Limited, Plot 20/4, Site-IV, Industrial Area Sahibabad, Ghaziabad – 201 010 and Published by S. Chand And Company Limited, A-27, 2nd Floor, Mohan Co-operative Industrial Estate, New Delhi – 110 044.

This project was supported by
The Himalayan Tourism and Recreation in Mountains
and
International Culinary Foundation

Project Coordinator and Executive Editor
Dr. Jagmohan Negi

FOREWORD

With travel increasing day-by-day, whether it is for business, pleasure or for any other reason, there is a mushrooming growth of hotels—big and small. At the same time there is a demand for people to work in these hotels. Most people working in smaller hotels learn on the jobs, which proves expensive. Hence there is a growing demand for trained persons who are able to perorm efficiently the basic front office operations in a hotel.

Front office is a business term that refers to a company's departments that comes in contact with clients, including the marketing, sales, and service departments.

In the hotel industry, the front office welcomes guests to the accommodation section: meeting and greeting them, taking and organizing reservations, allocating check in and out of rooms, organizing porter service, issuing keys and other security arrangements, passing on messages to customers and settling the accounts.

At the hub of the hotel-world is the reception desk where most guest transactions take place. It is here that the guest is received, registered and assigned a room. Information, mail, messages, complaints and room accounts are all dealt with here. Therefore, to a large extent, the reception team is the key to an enjoyable and problem-free stay for the hotel guest.

Combined with dealing efficiently with all customer needs, the receptionist's welcome can change an impersonal hotel building into a friendly place. To say that the receptionist gives personality to the hotel is not overstating the case - from welcome to leave taking, the receptionist reflects the hotel's response to its guests.

Due to the precise demands of customers, there is great potential in the hospitality industry for complaints. Poorly handled customer complaints may damage your reputation. Not only do the customers not return, they tell countless others of their bad experience. Complaints can occur regardless of the effort that you put into your service and the quality of the food and drink you serve. You need to develop a thick skin, and, where possible, turn negative complaints into positive experiences. Getting to know your customers and identifying their needs and preferences will ensure that you provide them with a personalized service to remember. In this book you will learn how to:

1. Develop and maintain product service and market knowledge.
2. Provide a quality service experience to customers.
3. Deal with complains and difficult customers service situations.
4. Manage and use information about clients and customers.

Upon successful study of this book the student should be able to:

1. Show how the hotel industry is part of the hospitality industry.
2. Describe the importance of good guest relations.
3. List the reasons people travel and choose a certain hotel.
4. Describe a hotel's mission statement and its importance.
5. Draw a hotel's and the front office's organizational chart.

6. List different hotel front office forms and equipment.
7. Describe the "guest cycle."
8. Demonstrate a typical guest account from check-in to settlement.
9. Process a night audit and discuss its relevance.
10. Explain the importance of front office security and list the different areas of concern.
11. Explain the importance of front desk selling.
12. Explain the importance of maximizing profits in establishing room rates, forecasting room availability, budgeting, and using revenue management techniques.

The book is divided into two sections. **Section I** deals with the hospitality techniques, guest relationship, communications and human relations, front office operations, reservation systems and procedures, determining room availability and rates, registration procedures, VIPs and group handling procedures, cashier and billing procedures, night audit procedures and telecommunication. **Section II** deals with important phrases in different languages as commonly used by tourist while traveling. An attempt has been made to incorporate all such pharasses which are generally used by the guests and the hospitality executives

Tables, figures, diagrams, photographs, and questions and assignments support the text. A comprehensive list of **Terms and Terminology of Hospitality- Reception** has been given in the form of an Appendix. For reference purpose there is selected **Bibliography** of the latest published literature available on the field.

Dr. Sunil Gulati
Chairman
Ellbee Hospitality Worldwide (P) Ltd.
Tourism & Hospitality Consultancy and
Academic Advisor & Formerly Hony. Secretary,
Federation of Hotel & Restaurant Associations of India

CONTENTS

SECTION–II

CONVERSATIONAL SKILLS: SOME ENGLISH, FRENCH, GERMAN AND HINDI COMMUNICATIONAL SKILLS

SECTION – I

Concept, Procedure, Skills and Techniques

1

The Concept of Hospitality

CHAPTER OBJECTIVES

After studying this lesson you should be able :

- To define the term 'hospitality'
- Understand the composition of hospitality
- Know the different terms related to hospitality.

Hospitality education traditionally has been oriented to the attainment of necessary survival skills in the industry. Now, it has exemplified instruction techniques and methodologies. Present hospitality education is technically qualified yet educationally (academic ability and methodology) unqualified. Changing societal trends coupled with wide varieties of experiential learning and the technological revolution force the need for today's hospitality education to address teaching in a highly organized, behaviorally objective, yet personal and sensitive manner.

'Hospitality' is the relationship between a guest and a host, or the act or practice of being hospitable. Specifically, this includes the reception and entertainment of guests, visitors, or strangers, resorts membership clubs, conventions, attractions, special events, and other services for travelers and tourists.

"Hospitality" can also mean generously providing care and kindness to whoever is in need. The act or practice of one who is hospitable, reception and entertainment of strangers or guests without reward, or with kind and generous liberality.

The hospitality industry consists of broad category of fields within the service industry that includes airlines, lodging, restaurants, event planning, theme parks, transportation, cruise line, and additional fields within the tourism industry.

The industry covers a wide range of organizations offering services. The hospitality industry is divided into sectors according to the skill-sets required for the work involved. Sectors include accommodation, food and beverage, meeting and events, gaming, entertainment and recreation, tourism services, and visitor information.

A view of a Hotel: Courtesy—Burj Al Arab Hotel, Dubai

Burj Al Arab Hotel, Dubai, which was opened in 1999, is unofficially billed as a 7-star hotel and is the world's most luxurious and tallest hotel. Designed to resemble a billowing sail, the hotel soars to a height of 321 metres, dominating the Dubai coastline. The hotel's own website describes it as the best in the world. With your chauffeur driven Rolls Royce, discreet in-suite check in, private reception desk on every floor and a brigade of highly trained butlers who provide around-the-clock attention, this hotel promises the finest the world has to offer.

The hospitality industry is a billion-dollar industry that mostly depends on the availability of leisure time and disposable income. A hospitality unit such as an airplane, a restaurant, hotel, or even an amusement park consists of multiple groups such as facility maintenance, direct operations (servers, housekeepers, porters, kitchen workers, bartenders, etc.), management, marketing, and human resources.

Usage rate is an important variable for the hospitality industry. Just as a factory owner would wish to have his or her productive asset in use as much as possible (as opposed to having to pay fixed costs while the factory isn't producing), so do airlines, restaurants, hotels, and theme parks seek to maximize the number of customers they "process".

In viewing various industries "barriers to entry" by newcomers and competitive advantages between current players are very important. Among other things, hospitality industry players find advantage in old classics (location), initial and ongoing investment support (reflected in the material up-keep of facilities and the luxuries located therein), and particular themes adopted by the marketing team of the organization. Very important is also the characteristics of the personnel working in direct contact with the customers. The authenticity, professionalism, and actual concern for the happiness and well-being of the customers that is communicated by successful organizations are a clear competitive advantage.

Hospitality industry is a major employer. The industry includes service sector work like tourism and food service. It suffers from more economic fluctuations compared to its peer industries.

Air India Flight

Landing of an Aeroplane

Nightclubs are entertainment venues where dancing is accompanied by light snacks and drinking. Apart from service personnel like waiters and cooks, nightclubs employ disc jockeys (DJs) and stand up comedians as part its varied attractions.

Fast-food restaurants now form a major part of the hospitality industry. These restaurants employ an optimal number of personnel for providing customer service. Food may also be sold from kiosks.

Hospitality industry is characterized by a large number of employees. Both white-collar employees and blue-collar workers may find gainful employment. Entry-level jobs usually require no formal education. Professionals in the hospitality sector are usually qualified with trade certificates and college degrees. Many hospitality schools offer specialized courses of study in one particular aspect of the industry.

A view of Bruj Al Arab Hotel

Another view of Bruj Al Arab Hotel

The hospitality industry is major service sector in the world economy. The industry encompasses an extensive variety of service industries that include food service, tourism and hotels. Hospitality industry suffers from fluctuations within an economy every year.

DEFINITIONS OF THE TERM 'HOSPITALITY'

'Hospitality' as a noun

1. *Cordial and generous reception of guests.*
2. Kindness to visitors: friendly, welcoming, and generous treatment offered to guests or strangers.
3. *According to the American Heritage Dictionary:*

   (a) Cordial and generous reception of or disposition toward guests.

   (b) An instance of cordial and generous treatment of guests.
4. *Century Dictionary:*

   The act or practice of one who is hospitable; reception and entertainment of strangers or guests without reward, or with liberality and kindness.
5. *GNU Webster's 1913 (1):*

   The act or practice of one who is hospitable; reception and entertainment of strangers or guests without reward, or with kind and generous liberality.
6. *WorldNet (1):*

   Kindness in welcoming guests or strangers.

'Hospitality' as an Adjective

From guests point of view the term is for the use of clients, guests, or visitors who are being entertained, especially by a company at a convention in a hospitality suite.

From business of catering and entertainment point of view it describes the business of providing services such as catering and entertainment in the hospitality industry.

Related Terms

Every visitor is overwhelmed by the hospitality of the people. Some related terms are:

1. Welcome
2. Warmth
3. Kindness
4. Friendliness
5. Sociability
6. Conviviality
7. Neighborliness
8. Cordiality
9. Heartiness
10. Hospitableness
11. Entertainment
12. Generous
13. Hospitable
14. Kind
15. Liberality
16. Reception
17. Reward.

Hospitality as commonly understood

1. *A Romance of Billy-Goat Hill*: A true Kentuckian may commit murder and still be a gentleman, but to fail in hospitality is to forfeit even his own self-respect.
2. The most important maxim in hospitality is to leave every one to his own choice and enjoyment, and to free him from an ever-present sense of being entertained.
3. *The Financial Express*: The luxury experience in hospitality is made (or unmade, as the case may be) by an understanding each team member that all interactions are vital.
4. *News wise*: Wehking received a bachelor's degree in hospitality from the University of Wisconsin and is a Certified Meeting Planner (CMP).
5. *Blisstree*: He has extensive experience in hospitality from a previous life, comes from a family who spends most of their time together talking about food and hanging out in kitchens.
6. Hospitality is the relationship between a guest and a host, or the act or practice of being hospitable. That is, the reception and entertainment of guests, visitors, or strangers, with liberality and goodwill.
7. The business of providing catering, lodging and entertainment service, the act or service of welcoming, receiving, hosting, or entertaining guests.
8. Constitutes a key ingredient of family life. Essential to hospitality is the ability to welcome people of diverse background and offering food and shelter. When hospitality is offered to a gathering of Baháis', the home becomes a "congress of the spirit".

9. This is the general term and designation employed to describe the efforts by a host unit at a bridge tournament in order to make the visiting players feel comfortable and welcomed.
10. As common social and cultural topic (a sub texture of social and cultural texture), hospitality is the welcoming of strangers as guests into one's home to dine or lodge.
11. Room or a service for coaches and officials working a meet. Coaches and Officials Meetings are normally held in the "Hospitality Room". The room is stocked with food and refreshments for coaches and officials during their breaks.
12. An event or gathering usually separates from the exhibit in which refreshments are served and exhibitors, personnel and invited guests socialize.
13. *Oxford Dictionary of Current English:*

    'The friendly and generous treatment of guests or strangers.'

Some selected quotations

1. *Bible: Hebrews:*

   "Be not forgetful to entertain strangers; for thereby some have entertained angels unawares".
2. *Ambrose Bierce The Devil's Dictionary:*

   "Hospitality: the virtue which induces us to feed and lodge certain persons who are not in need of food and lodging"
3. *Alexander Pope Imitations of Horace:*

   "Welcome the coming, speed the going guest"
4. *Max Beerbohm And Even Now:*

   "When hospitality becomes an art, it loses its very soul"
5. *According to Merriam Webster's Collegiate Dictionary* the word hospitality means:

   "Hospitable treatment, reception, or disposition."
6. *The word 'hospitable' means:*

   (a) Promising or suggesting generous and cordial welcome,

   (b) Offering a pleasant or sustaining environment.
7. *Readily receptive:*

   "Open (hospitable to new ideas)."
8. *When we look at the various Greek helps to determine the definition for hospitality in biblical times*, we find the word means basically the same thing. Vine's Expository Dictionary of Old and New Testament Words and Enhanced Strong's Lexicon give the following definition for hospitality:
   1. "Lover of strangers,"
   2. "Generous to guests."

9. *A look at some examples of biblical hospitality* and some of the customs of the Bible times enlightens us to the full scope of hospitality.
10. *A quote from The New Manners and Customs of Bible Times:*

    'Entertaining others to eat and to stay was important for the people of the Bible; the urge to give hospitality seems to have been rooted in their experience of nomadic life. Nomadic people are conscious of the loneliness of the desert and that the provision of food is often a matter of life and death. Because Esau was too weak to prepare a meal for himself after he had been hunting, his brother, Jacob, was able to extract the birthright from him. Even an enemy could not be allowed to die of hunger. Paul wrote, "If your enemy is hungry, feed him", and he was repeating what was always done among nomadic people.'
11. *The following is an observation from Kittel:*

    Strangeness produces mutual tension between natives and foreigners, but hospitality overcomes the tension and makes of the alien a friend. Historically foreigners are primarily enemies or outlaws who should be killed. It is then found, however, that hospitality is a better way to deal with strangers, and they thus become the wards of law and religion.
12. *Job, Abraham, the Shunammite woman and Martha* are just a few of the Bible characters who showed hospitality. Under the old law, the minimum care for a guest was to offer bread and water although many times the host would offer much more. The provisions offered many times included the best food; water to wash the dust from the guest's feet and overnight accommodations. It is true that during that timeframe hotels and restaurants were not readily available. The care of a traveler was dependent upon his fellow man. Times have changed. When traveling from point A to point B, multiple restaurants of varying types and hotel accommodations are readily available. We are not dependent on fellow man to provide a meal or a place to stay. However, that does not remove our responsibility to show our love and concern for others through hospitality. I can think of no better way to make a person feel at ease among strangers than to openly make him feel welcome as an honored guest in your home. Many times we feel we are being hospitable when we invite our friends and family members over for a meal.
13. *Greek-English Lexicon of the New Testament based on Semantic Domains* gives the following definition for hospitality.

    "To receive and show hospitality to a stranger, that is, someone who is not regarded as a member of the extended family or a close friend — 'to show hospitality, to receive a stranger as a guest, hospitality.'
14. As in every aspect of our service to God, we must have a proper attitude toward hospitality. It must be done in a kind, loving manner, but neither grudgingly nor done with a sense of duty or obligation. We should never grumble at the trouble or expense of showing hospitality toward others. Remember all that we have come from God and we need to use our abundant resources and blessings to the glory of God.

15. "I care about you and I want to teach you of God's love and concern for your soul." Making someone feel needed and welcome in our homes goes a long way to truly getting to know our brothers and sisters in Christ. Taking someone out to eat in a restaurant does not convey the same care and concern.

These few comments will inspire you to fulfill the God-given command that all show hospitality to one another. One of the qualifications of an elder is that he shows hospitality. I encourage each of you to make use of the modern conveniences available to each of us and open your home to others. Whether you prepare an elaborate meal, purchase sandwiches and cookies from a local sandwich shop or just offer a cup of coffee or a glass of water is not what will be remembered. What people will remember is that you took the time to think of them and invited them to your home. While there, you made them feel welcome and wanted. You made them feel at home. You became better acquainted with them and they with you.

Meaning of Hospitality

The word hospitality derives from the Latin 'hospes', which is formed from 'hostis', which originally meant to have power. The meaning of "host" can be literally read as "lord of strangers." 'hostire' means equalize or compensate.

In the Homeric ages, hospitality was under the protection of Zeus, the chief deity of the Greek pantheon. Zeus was also attributed with the title 'Xenios Zeus' ('xenos' means stranger), emphasizing the fact that hospitality was of the utmost importance. The family could invite a stranger passing outside a Greek house inside the house. The host washed the stranger's feet, offered food and wine, and only after the guest was comfortable could ask his or her name.

The Greek concept of sacred hospitality is illustrated in the story of Telemachus and Nestor. When Telemachus arrived to visit Nestor, Nestor was unaware that his guest was the son of his old comrade Odysseus. Nonetheless, Nestor welcomes Telemachus and his party lavishly, thus demonstrating the relationship between hostis, "stranger," and hostire, "equalize," and how the two combine in the concept of hospitality.

Later, one of Nestor's sons slept on a bed close by Telemachus to take care that he should not suffer any harm. Nestor also put a chariot and horses at Telemachus' disposal so that he could travel the land route from Pylos to Sparta rapidly, and set his son Pisistratus as the charioteer. These illustrate the two other elements of ancient Greek hospitality, protection and guidance.

Gourmet Buffet with Vintage Wine - Courtesy: Air India

Based on the above discription and its current meaning, *hospitality is about compensating/equalizing a stranger to the host, making him feel protected and taken care of, and at the end of his hosting, guiding him to his next destination.*

In the contemporary West, hospitality is rarely a matter of protection and survival, and is more associated with etiquette and entertainment. However, it still involves showing respect for one's guests, providing for their needs, and treating them as equals. Cultures and subcultures vary in the extent to which one is expected to show hospitality to strangers, as opposed to personal friends or members of one's in-group.

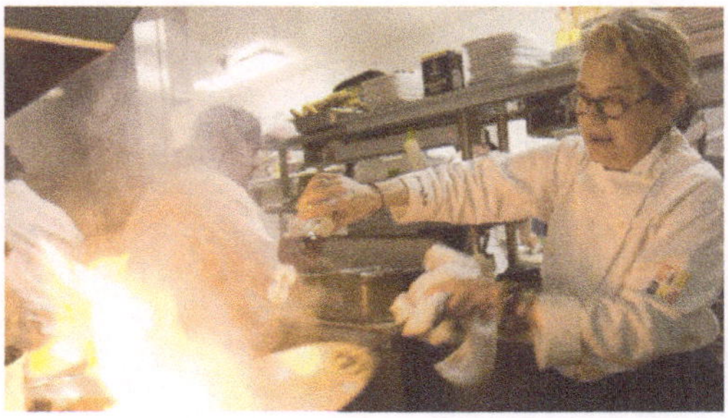

Guests Enjoying Hospitality

The hospitality service industry includes hotels, casinos, and resorts, which offer comfort and guidance to strangers, but only as part of a business relationship. The terms hospital, hospice, and hostel also derive from "hospitality," and these institutions preserve more of the connotation of personal care. Hospitality ethics is a discipline that studies this usage of hospitality.

In the western context, with its dynamic tension between Athens and Jerusalem, two phases can be distinguished with a very progressive transition: a hospitality based on an individually felt sense of duty, and one based on "official" institutions for organized but anonymous social services: special places for particular types of "strangers" such as the poor, orphan(s), ill, alien, criminal, etc. Perhaps this progressive institutionalization can be aligned to the transition between Middle Ages and Renaissance. An example of Hospitality would be, "I'm going to get you a pillow and make you feel real good." This is showing the guest hospitality

QUESTIONS AND DISCUSSIONS

Short Answer Type

Q.1. List main reasons for traveling.

Q.2. Name any ten terms related to the word 'hospitality'.

Q.3. List the different ways to classify hotels.

Q.4. Evaluate a hotel's mission statement.

Q.5. Describe a hotel's mission statement and its importance

Descriptive Type

Q.6. Show how the hotel industry is part of the hospitality industry.

Q.7. Describe the hospitality industry.

2

Hospitality Guest Relationship

CHAPTER OBJECTIVES

After studying this lesson you should be able :

- To describe the term guest relationship and guest satisfaction
- To know the significance of hospitality guest relationship.

Customer satisfaction refers to the extent to which customers are happy with the products and services provided by the hotel. Gaining high levels of customer satisfaction is very important in hospitality business because satisfied customers are most likely to be loyal and to make repeat hotel orders and use a wide range of services offered by the hotel.

In the hospitality industry, the one of the important strategy is to maintain current customers and attract new ones. As a result, most sellers attempt to deliver first-class service to customers, as high quality service is likely to enhance customer satisfaction. As one of the service industries, the hospitality involves a high degree of personal interaction between the hotel staff and customers; any miscommunication may lead to service failure.

It is estimated that the cost of gaining new customers is approximately five times that of retaining present ones. Service failure can put companies out of business if proper attention is not paid to this problem. Consequently, hotels cannot afford to lose guests who are the potential to become public relation makers for their hotels through positive word-of-mouth by referring others to use the company's product or services.

Once you know what customers want, you can then make it possible to tailor everything you do to please these customers e.g. providing the products and services that customers want, in the packing that they want, in outlets which are convenient to use and well placed. There are many factors that lead to high-level of customers' satisfaction including products and services that are customer focused and thence provide high levels of value for money.

Generally most customers are likely to appreciate the products and services of a hotel that they buy if they are made to feel special. This occurs when these customers feel that the products and services that they buy have been specially produced for them or for people like them. This relates to wide range of products such as accommodation facilities and services, food and beverages that are designed for ease of use and good quality finish products that are environmentally friendly and customized to meet the needs of particular type of customers.

Arrival of Tourists

In the hospitality business the loyalty of a hotel's customer has been recognized as the dominant factor in an organization's success. You need to understand the relationship between customer loyalty, customer satisfaction, and image. This is of considerable interest to both for partners and academics in the field of hospitality management. The objective is to identify the factors of image and customer satisfaction that are positively related to customer loyalty in the hotel industry. The hotel image and customer satisfaction with the performance of housekeeping, reception, food and beverage, and price positively correlated to customer loyalty.

For many years hospitality firms have believed that the goal of marketing is to create as many new customers as possible. While hoteliers believed it was important to satisfy the guest while they were on the house, the real goal was to continue to find new customers.

Customer satisfaction

For customer satisfaction to be high, promises and expectation must be met. This involves the hotel's ability to understand customer expectations and to do it right the first time.

The Indian civilization is one of the oldest on earth, and like every culture has it's own favorite stories including quite a few on hospitality. That of a simpleton readily sharing his meager morsels with an uninvited guest, only to discover that the guest is a God in disguise, who rewards his generosity with abundance. That of a woman who lovingly cooks up all the *Khichdi* she can afford, for everyone who is hungry... till one day when she runs out of food for the last hungry person to whom she offers her own share, and is rewarded by the god in disguise with a never ending pot of *Khichdi*. Most Indian adults having grown up listening to these stories, as children believe in the philosophy of "*Atithi Devo Bhava*", meaning the guest is God. From this stems the Indian approach of graciousness towards guests at home, and in all social situations.

A Growing Indian alcoholic drinks market

Wine Service

Hospitality Around the World

In Middle Eastern Culture, it was considered a cultural norm to take care of the strangers and foreigners living among you. These norms are reflected in many Biblical commands and examples.

The obligations of both host and guest are stern. The bond is formed by eating salt under the roof, and is so strict that an Arab story tells of a thief who tasted something to see if it was sugar, and on realizing it was salt, put back all that he had taken and left.

To the ancient Greeks and Romans, hospitality was a divine plight. The host was expected to make sure the needs of his guests were seen to. The ancient Greek term xenia, or theoxenia when a god was involved, expressed this ritualized guest-friendship relation.

An example of the importance of hospitality in the classical world is the tale of Baucus and Philemon. In this tale, the ancient gods Zeus and Hermes are visiting the town of Phrygia disguised as simple peasants. Their search for a meal and a place to stay for the night meets a lot of closed doors, until they arrive at the house of Philemon and Baucus. Though poor, the couple acts as good hosts by giving the little they have to their guests, and when they realize their guests are actually gods in disguise, they even propose to slay the one goose which guards their house. As a reward, the gods grant them one wish, besides saving them from the flooding of the rest of the inhospitable town.

Celtic societies also valued the concept of hospitality, especially in terms of protection. A host who granted a person's request for refuge was expected not only to provide food and shelter to his/her guest, but also to make sure they did not come to harm while under their care.

A real-life example of this is rooted in the history of the Scottish Clan Macgregor, from the early seventeenth century. The chief of Clan Lamont arrived at the home of the Macgregor chief in Glenstrae, told him that he was fleeing from foes and requested refuge. The Macgregor welcomed his brother chief with no questions asked. Later that night members of the Macgregor clan came looking for the Lamont chief, informing their chief that the Lamont had in fact killed his son and heir in a quarrel. Holding to the sacred law of hospitality, the Macgregor not only refused to hand over the Lamont to his clansmen, but the next morning escorted him to his ancestral lands. This act would later be repaid when, during the time that the Macgregor were outlawed, the Lamonts gave safe haven to many of their number.

The Champagne

Types of Hospitality

Hospitality industry can be empirically divided into two parts: entertainment areas like clubs and bars, and accommodation. Accommodation takes the form of public houses, resorts, inn, campgrounds, hotels, hostels, serviced apartments, and motels. The clubs and bars category include restaurants, fast foods, and nightclubs.

The hospitality industry also includes tourism support commercial activities like airline cabin staff and travel agents. Travel technology like applied information technology (IT) and its workers in hospitality, travel and tourism are also included in the hospitality industry.

A Tourist

A hotel is an establishment that renders lodging in lieu of payment. This lodging is usually given in exchange for a specified predetermined amount of money. Modern hotel rooms come equipped with climate control and attached bathrooms. Higher end hotels offer guests Internet connectivity within rooms and also throughout the premises. A combination of meals and accommodation comes as a package in most hospitality establishments. Professionally qualified managers usually manage hotels. Junior workers usually maintain the hotel. Functions like cooking is usually done by professionally trained chefs.

QUESTIONS AND DISCUSSIONS

Short Answer Type

Q.1. Write notes on:

(a) Types of Hospitality

(b) Customer Satisfaction.

Descriptive Type

Q. 2. Describe the importance of good guest relations.

Assignment / Activity Type

Q. 3. Demonstrate good guest service and guest relations.

3

Hospitality Ethics and Standards

CHAPTER OBJECTIVES

After studying this lesson you should be able :

- To describe the term hospitality ethics,
- To write hospitality standards,
- To identity the careers in airline and hospitality.
- To understand the aviation job market.
- To discuss the traits of hospitality employees.

'Hospitality' as a cultural norm or value is an established sociological phenomenon that people study and write papers about hospitality ethics. The term "Hospitality Ethics" is used to refer to two different, yet related, areas of study:

1. The philosophical study of the moral obligations that hold in hospitality relationships and practices.
2. The branch of business ethics that focuses on ethics in commercial hospitality and tourism industries.

Whereas Ethics goes beyond describing what is done, in order to prescribe what should be done, hospitality ethics prescribes what should be done in matters related to hospitality. Hospitality theories and norms are derived through a critical analysis of hospitality practices, processes, and relationships; in various cultures and traditions; and throughout history. Ultimately, hospitality theories are applied, and put to practice in commercial and non-commercial settings.

As a standard of conduct, hospitality has been variously considered throughout history as a law, an ethic, a principle, a code, a duty, a virtue, etc. These prescriptions were created for negotiating ambiguous relationships between guests, hosts, citizens, and strangers. Despite its ancient origins and ubiquity amongst human cultures, the concept of hospitality has received relatively little attention from moral philosophers, who have tended to focus their attention on other ethical concepts, e.g. good, evil, right, and wrong.

Yet hospitality as a moral imperative, or ethical perspective, preceded many other prescriptions for ethical behavior. In ancient Middle Eastern, Greek and Roman cultures, the Ethic of Hospitality was a code that demanded specific kinds of conduct from both guests and hosts. One example: Chivalry required men of station to offer food and lodging to any men of station that requested it.

In many ways, these standards of behavior have survived into the present day in the commercial hospitality industry, where descendents of the ancient ideas continued current standards and practices.

HOSPITALITY ETHICS IN PRACTICE

Ethics in commercial hospitality settings

Applied ethics is the branch of Ethics, which investigates the application of our ethical theories and judgments. There are many branches of Applied Ethics: Business ethics, professional ethics, medical ethics, educational ethics, environmental ethics, and more.

Hospitality Ethics is a branch of Applied Ethics. In practice, it combines concerns of other branches of Applied Ethics, such as business ethics, environmental ethics, professional ethics, and more. For instance, when a local hospitality industry flourishes, potential ethical dilemmas abound. There are some questions that Hospitality Ethics, as a version of Applied Ethics, might ask:

What effect do industry practices have on the environment?

On the host community?

On the local economy?

On citizens' attitudes about their local community, about outsiders, tourists, and guests?

The hospitality and tourism combine to create one of the largest service industries in the world. There are many opportunities for both good and bad behavior, and right and wrong actions by hospitality and tourism practitioners. Ethics in these industries can be guided by codes of conduct, employee manuals, industry standards (whether implicit or explicit), and more.

Though the UN World Tourism Organization has proposed an industry-wide code of ethics, there is presently no universal code for the hospitality industry. Various textbooks regarding ethics in commercial hospitality settings have been published recently, and are currently used in hospitality education courses.

Hospitality Standards

Consider the new employees. They are, typically, young, enthusiastic and just wanting to prove themselves. Let's say that they are working in banquets. On their first day of work they have a simple task of laying out tables for a conference.

They are teamed with an experienced teamleader. We will call Tarun's who shows them how to complete the task. Because they are bright and pretty much a self starter, when they are given the same task the next day and the new person they are paired with arrives late, they start laying out the tables as they are shown yesterday. They are surprised then when their new employee for the day arrives and says:

"Why are you doing it that way? That's not how we do it."

"But that is how I was shown", comes the reply.

"Oh that's Tarun's way of doing it. When I worked at The Hilton this was the way we did it. It's much better."

"OK, that's cool"

After a week, our young, still enthusiastic employee is setting up tables again and in walks the Banquets Manager on a get to know the new employees mission.

"Well, I can see you have settled in well. I've heard good things about your attitude. Can I ask you though, why you are setting up the tables that way? That's not how we do it."

After four weeks, our young enthusiastic self starter now waits for instructions on not only what to do but how to do it.

We have recounted this story to new starters who have had three to four weeks work experience at a popular five star destination and we get knowing smiles each time.

In a business which must be efficient and must set and then surpass customer's expectations, a lack of enforced standards is a drag on customer perceptions of service and hence, sales. A lack of enforced standards is also a drag on staff enthusiasm and empowerment which drags supervisors and managers closer to doing line duties all the time to make sure that things are done right.

Standards of operation

Most standard operating procedures in the hospitality industry have mix policy, process, standards, work instructions and occasionally key performance indicators or targets in one. They are, therefore, difficult to read, to understand, to what standard an employee must do something. In most cases they are text based, ignoring the communication preference of the majority of people.

The standards of operation may be separated into the following:

1. An overall process flows, to show you any relationships between what you are doing and others are doing.
2. Standards to show you WHAT you have to do, to what level of QUALITY and TIMING.
3. The competencies you should have to complete the task (optional).
4. Work instruction to show you HOW you should do some tasks that are no self-evident by the standard
5. Tools and references you may refer to from time to time.

Standards of Operation should also have as diagrams, pictures and screen shots as a default rather than text. Standards of Operation written this way are easier to read. Standards can be laminated and put up on the wall to remind people. Checklists can be made of more involved standards to make sure tasks have been done on time and to quality. Work instructions can be left with new employees to follow step-by-step instructions on how to do things. All of the components are built into one document, but in sections with each section having a separate purposes.

What should each standard of operation be about?

Most standard operating procedures are written around a department. The risk is that departments write standards, which work for them without consideration of other departments. The important point is not that other departments may have some difficulty, but that customers may have difficulty or at least experience great variations in service levels between departments.

We recommend, therefore, that standards be written around the customer's moments of truth, independent of departments. A responsibility matrix is all that is required to be clear for what each department has responsibility and accountability.

Do you want to offer your customers world-class service?

Unique Hospitality Etiquette Training courses may be started, aimed at a range of services within the hospitality industry such as airlines, hotels, caterers, restaurants, event organizers, corporate entertainers and tourist organizations. With the numbers of foreign guests traveling steadily rising, it is becoming more important that the hospitality industry becomes more aware of the way in which cross cultural differences can impact hospitality procedures.

Hospitality Across Cultures

The Hospitality Etiquette Training courses may provide personnel within the hospitality industry, such as managers and front of house staff, with key cross cultural skills to enable them to deal effectively with foreign guests.

Etiquette is perhaps one of the most fundamental skills hospitality staff must acquire. Meeting the cultural needs of foreign guests, dignitaries and/or V.I.P.s ensures that offense or costly cross-cultural blunders do not occur and helps raise the profile of an establishment. The training courses are tailored to meet the requirements of each of select clients. These courses cover a number of areas in relation to culture and/or nationality including:

1. Meeting and greeting
2. Use of names and titles
3. Body language
4. Touching
5. Proxemics
6. Eye contact
7. Dining/serving etiquette
8. Foods
9. Conversation
10. Hospitality and customer service expectations
11. Conflict resolution.

Tourists in a sunny beach

Careers in the Airline & Hospitality Industry

If you desire an enriching career in airline travel services, culinary arts or hospitality and restaurant management; then you will desire an education from the leading institute. If you are looking for travel agent schools or flight attendant schools you have come to the right place. You can learn the requirements to become a chef and fulfill your dreams of occupying chef jobs around the world or find out more about our hotel management-training program through our various specialized programs. From requirements for flight attendant training to pastry chef school, the educators and programs will give you the necessary skills to start your career.

A warm welcome by airline Hostess

Hospitality in the Sky/ Air

An airhostess or an airline stewardess is the face of any airline. Airhostesses, also referred to as air stewardess, airline stewardess or flight stewardess, are also one of the reasons that encourage people to travel by a particular airline. This is the reason that airhostesses (air stewardess, airline stewardess, flight stewardess) are expected to excel in customer service. Similarly, air stewardess or flight stewardess are expected to remain friendly and enthusiastic, as the smile of an airhostess tends to decrease the Jetlag of any passenger.

Being on the job of airhostesses, one has to face different situations, including unpleasant ones. This is the reason that airhostess or flight stewardess should be mentally as well physically tough. It has been noticed that air stewardess or airline stewardess uniform is according to the colour coding of the airline. Also, during the training of an airhostess or flight stewardess, the training of mental and physical toughness is an essential part.

Air India

British Airways

China Airways

Singapore Airlines

Air hostesses are expected not only to be a team player, but patient, as they say, is a virtue, should be an essential quality of an air stewardess or airline stewardess. Flight stewardess is also expected to be a problem solver.

Many young girls today are choosing to become **airhostesses.** Although there aren't too many strict requirements to become an airhostess, there are a few that are quite essential. One doesn't need to have a specific academic qualification, though most firms do prefer it if you have a basic graduation degree. Some airlines prefer to have candidates who have completed a diploma in the hospitality management or the tourism and hospitality management.

Air France

China Air

American Airlines

Koreian Air

If you are applying to become an airhostess, make sure that you are a people-friendly person and have the right kind of attitude sets in place. Almost all the airlines have a specific height requirement, which varies. Contrary to the popular myth, it isn't essential that an airhostess needs to be exceptionally beautiful or pretty. Nowadays, those interested in this industry can also join airhostess training schools, which provide special training and also recruit candidates in the top airline firms. If you don't wish to enroll for any of the training schools, keep an eye out for advertisements in the leading dailies and send in your application.

No matter where you live, India, Pakistan, China, Europe, USA, Asia the Philippines or anywhere around the world, you can become an Airhostess. The job of an Airhostess can have you traveling the world. This exciting flying job will have you flying with a first class attitude and staying in the finest hotels.

Airlines prefer to have poised, tactful, and resourceful people who can interact comfortably with strangers and remain calm under duress. Applicants usually must be at least 18 to 21 years old. Some carriers may have higher minimum-age requirements. Cabin Crew must have excellent health and the ability to speak clearly.

In order to become an airhostess you must have a certain level of knowledge. Becoming an air hostess is one of the greatest jobs in the world! Just imagine your new life ... travel, meeting interesting people, VIP's and make money as an airhostess.

Hospitality in the air is of utmost importance for employment of aspiring boys and girls as air hostesses also known as Cabin crew or Flight Attendant who are primarily on board an aircraft for the safety and welfare of the passengers and secondly for their comfort. If there were no services of food or drink during a flight, there would still have to be a minimum presence of Airhostesses or cabin crew for safety, which is a legal requirement.

Airhostess or flight attendant is the face of the airline hence they are expected to excel in customer service and always remain friendly, approachable and enthusiastic with a good sense of self-presentation. The role of airhostess or cabin crew can be physically demanding and one must be prepared to be flexible to work any day of the year. Hence there is a requirement of airhostess training to face the day-to-day challenges.

Airhostess can encounter many different situations whilst working on board an aircraft and must be an excellent team player with the ability to work on their own initiative using quick thinking and organizational skills.

Inner view of an Aeroplane

Inside view of a Conference hall

The Airhostesses or flight attendants are a very important element in the flying process. Airhostesses or Cabin Crew try to keep everything running smoothly on each flight, and they deal with the desperate situations that arise when things don't go according to plan. The airhostess training methodology instills in them the confidence and expertise required to make a mark for themselves in the aviation industry.

Air Hostess Hospitality

Airhostess jobs are one of the most sought after career in the aviation job market. As the airline industry continues to expand to meet growing consumer demand, more and more young people are taking up Airhostess jobs. To those workers who can stand the long hours and unpredictable lifestyle, there's nothing quite like flying through the air as an Airhostess for a living.

In an airhostess job the employees are expected to excel in customer service and always remain friendly, approachable and enthusiastic with a good sense of self-presentation. A flight attendant job can be physically demanding and you must be prepared to be flexible to work any day of the year. This does however give you a perfect opportunity to get away from the repetitiveness of a normal 9 to 5 job! Desire and even means to fly are growing in India as the galloping economy draws in more airlines, directly creating a huge demand for trained manpower.

TRAITS OF HOSITALITY EMPLOYEES

As the front office is a critical department in a hotel in view of its revenue generating capacity and influence in image building, the staff working in it assumes a special importance. Great care is taken in the selection of front office staff as they play a key role as:

1. They motivate the guest to spend more on the various hotel facilities.
2. Guests invariably approach the hospitality staff for help in case they have a problem or complaint. The staff has to be diplomatic and resourceful to solve the problem at the shortest possible time.
3. Guests who want information or want to pass on information use them for this purpose.
4. Since they are a reference point, the hospitality staff are required to coordinate with other departments, airlines, travel agencies and city tour offices to give the guest personalized service.
5. As an extension to their salesman's role, hospitality staff can certainly generate a good image for the establishment in their manner of dress, communication, personal conduct and efficiency.

In view of the important role they play, the hospitality staff must have the following essential attributes:

1. Uniforms must be clean and neatly pressed. Hair should be groomed well. It is preferable for ladies to tie their hair up in a bun. Nails should be manicured.
2. A soft cologne is preferable instead of heavy perfumes. Jewellery should be restricted to one ring and a necklace for ladies. In short, the front office staff must be seen at their best at all times.
3. As they are constantly exposed to hotel guests, a clean appearance helps to project a good image not only of themselves but of the establishment as well. This is necessary as front office personnel meet guests of different countries, statuses and cultures. They should be comfortable and feel at ease in dealing with these people.

4. It is preferable that front office staff knows more than one language. It helps in communicating with guests who cannot speak English or the local language.
5. Very often there are situations when a guest is irate over something; a diplomatic dealing helps in diffusing the explosive moment. It is quite common for a busy hotel to have no room to offer a guest who has come with a confirmed booking.
6. A diplomatic approach is the only way by which the guest can be pacified.
7. Being the nerve centre of the hotel, the front office is constantly in touch with guests and therefore invariably comes under tremendous pressure. The guests always expect personalized, priority treatment and the pressure of demand never ceases. Coupled with this are difficult guests who can unnerve a person. The hospitality staff should thus have a high degree of tolerance for pressure of work and be calm and composed at all times. This single attribute distinguishes the good from the average amongst the front office staff.
8. Every individual has an ego and his/ her name is most precious and personal to him. If the front office staff can call most guests by their names, this immediately flatters them and personalizes the guest experience. The guest begins to feel he is welcome as people recognize him by name.
9. As the hotel is a meeting place of social elites all the grace and etiquette associated with good society comes into play.
10. Guests of all status come to stay in the hotel and they are used to good manners and politeness. Wishing a guest the time of the day and saying "Thank you" are basic etiquettes shown.
11. Guests like to be handled by a cheerful staff at the desk. Their smile exudes cheer to the guests and puts them at ease.
12. The Front office operations require the staff to stand for long hours at a stretch. The staff must be sturdy, agile and active.
13. Guests often approach the Front Desk with problems and requests. Front office staff must be able to decide quickly a course of action that satisfies the guest, at the same time keeping the interests of the organization alive.

Possessed with the attributes mentioned above, the hospitality staff could make a fine team that is an asset to the hotel.

QUESTIONS AND DISCUSSIONS

Short Answer Type

Q.1. Differentiate between 'ethics' and 'standards'.

Q.2. Write notes on:

(a) Airline hospitality

(b) Airhostess.

Descriptive Type

Q.3. Explain the term 'hospitality cross-culture'.

Q.4. Explain and give examples of various ways hotel operations may be classified.

Q.5. In view of the important role of the hospitality, state essential traits and attributes required in a hospitality staff.

Q.6. Describe the various methods of ranking hotel organizations and the purpose each method serves.

4

Reception: Front of the House

CHAPTER OBJECTIVES

After studying this lesson you should be able :

- To understand and define the term 'reception',
- To draw organisation chart f a hotels,
- Describe the function and services of the front office.
- To discuss the guest cycle process
- To develop communication skills.
- To explain different front office systems.
- To demonstrate the bed-making
- To demonstrate the cleaning of bath rooms
- To discuss the duties of a receptionist.

At the hub of the hotel world is the reception desk where most guest transactions take place. It is here that the guest is received, registered and assigned a room. Information, mail, messages, complaints and room accounts are all dealt with here. Therefore, to a large extent, the reception team is the key to an enjoyable and problem-free stay for the hotel guest.

Combined with dealing efficiently with all customer needs, the receptionist's welcome can change an impersonal hotel building into a friendly place. To say that the receptionist gives personality to the hotel is not overstating the case - from welcome to leave taking, the receptionist reflects the hotel's response to its guests.

The front office is the key department of the hotel and it coordinates guest services with other department such as housekeeping for room status, food and beverages regarding charges and group meals, finance regarding cash, credit and billing.

Reception Desk

Font office also interacts with security, sales office, telephones and other departments providing services to the guest.

Hotel Reception Desk– Receving Guest

The front office is the first point of contact for the gust and is always at the centre of the guest service activities during the stay. The reception is the nerve centre of a hotel. From guest as well as and hotel point of view this area may be interpreted in two different ways:

From Guest Point of View

On arrival, the first contact of the guest is the front office. Here he gets the first impression about the hotel. The better the front office functions, the better his impression and opinion about the hotel. During his stay the guest receives and leaves his key at the front desk and it is where he receives his mails and information. When leaving, the billing section of the front office presents to him the bill and the guest pays it at the cashier's desk.

A Reception Desk

From the guest's point of view, the front office is not only an important part of the hotel, but he takes the front office as hotel and a responsible representative of the hotel management. In case he has any complaints, he will post them at the front office.

From Hotel's Point of View

The front office is one of the key point in the hotel organization The reservation department of the front office is responsible for the occupancies of the hotel. It is at the front office, where all the charges are posted, where the guest account are kept and where the money is cashed.

Hotel Organization

The Front Office in a hotel is the department responsible for the sale of hotel rooms through systematic methods of reservation, followed by registration and assigning rooms to customers. The term 'sale of rooms' may appear misleading to those unfamiliar with the industry. 'Sale' here means the use of hotel rooms at a price. A room is termed 'sold' for the day when a guest leases the room for stay in the hotel. "Room tariff" i.e. rate charged per room is computed for a "revenue day" which begins at noon of a particular day and ends at 12.00 hrs. the next day. In other words room charges are levied for a revenue day that is between noon and noon. Of course, a room may be sold for half-a-day as well, for which special rates are applicable. Such rates are referred to as "half-day" rates.

The front office in a hotel holds prime importance in view of the basic nature of business of a hotel, i.e. to sell rooms. Revenue collected from the sale of rooms contributes to more than 50 per cent of total hotel sales. The profit percentage from sales of rooms is very high. It has a complementary role of image building, which is the first and last point of contact of every guest. If one looks at each component of a front office role, one could have a better perception of this department. While the title Front Office is a generic term to include a number of activities, smaller hotels are satisfied to call it simply Hotel Reception.

A Guest checking in at the hotel reception desk

Thus the role of the front office is thus to reserve, receive, register, assign rooms to guests and act as a continuous source of information to guests during their stay at the hotel. A section of the front office is called the Reservation. This section is the hub of the department. Requests for reservation of rooms from various sources are received and the information is processed, properly documented, stored and retrieved at the appropriate time to ensure a guest his room upon arrival. Room, the chief product of a hotel, being a highly perishable commodity (as its sale is linked with a time element) the reservation department ensures that rooms are not allowed to "perish". The section called Reception handles this activity. The personnel in this section actually welcome and receive the guests and assign them a room after a few registration formalities.

Figure 4.1 Suggests organizational hierarchies for a typical large hotel, and the Figure 4.2 suggests hierarchy of a small hotel.

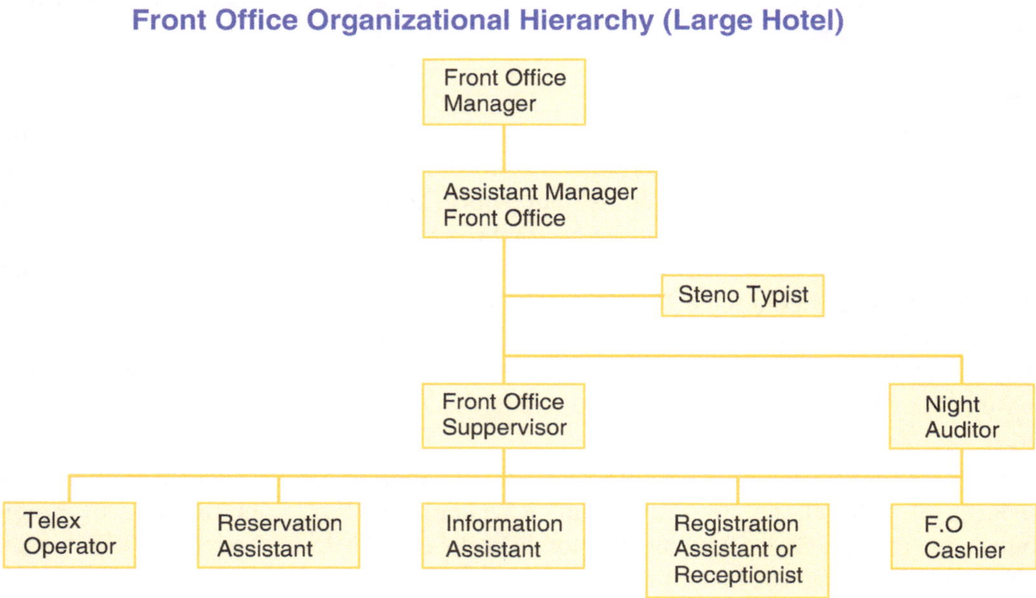

Figure 4.1. Front Office Organizational Hierarchy (Large Hotel)

Figure 4.2. Front Office Organizational Hierarchy (Small Hotel)

A view of the organization chart of a front Office of a hotel is depicted in Figure 4.3. As being key the department in the hotel organization, the front office has to depend on the other departments of the hotel. For example it would be not possible o sell the guest rooms when they are not ready as the rooms are to be released by the housekeeping department. A guest cannot be accommodated in case the restaurants and room service do not function. Similarly it is not worth keeping guest accounts when the charge invoices are not prepared and sent to the client by the credit section.

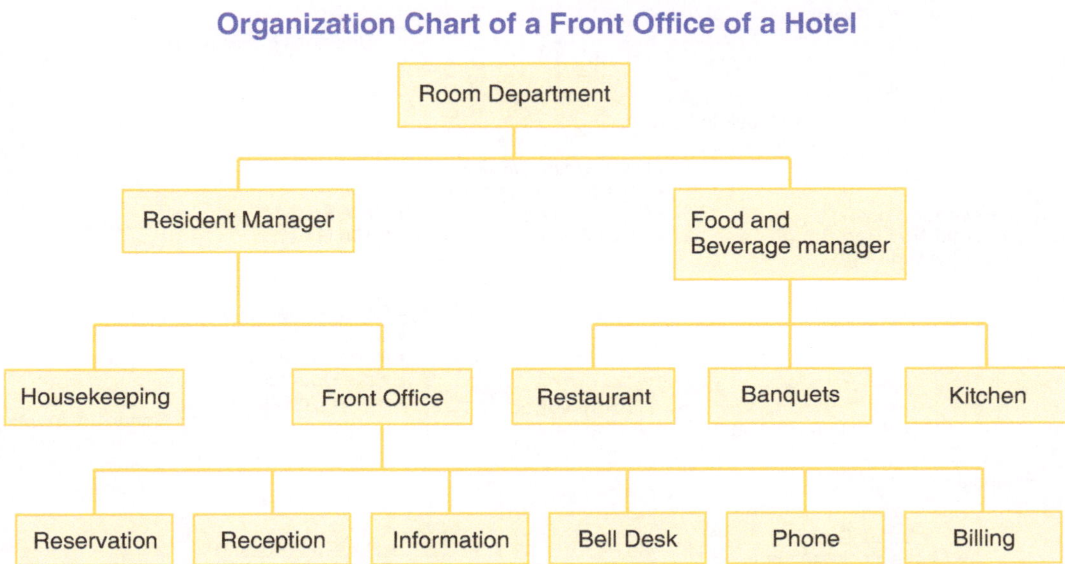

Figure 4.3. Organization of a Front Office in a Hotel

Functions and Services of the Front Office

The functions of a front office will depend on the type and size of a hotel. Some of the functions of the front office are:

1. To sell the rooms
2. To reserve the rooms, before the arrival of the guest
3. To register the guest
4. To assign the rooms
5. To coordinate with other departments
6. To provide the guest with the required information, as and when required
7. To maintain rooms status information
8. To maintain the accounts of the guests
9. To settle the bills.

Figure 4.4 shows the importance of the Front Office and its multifarious activities.

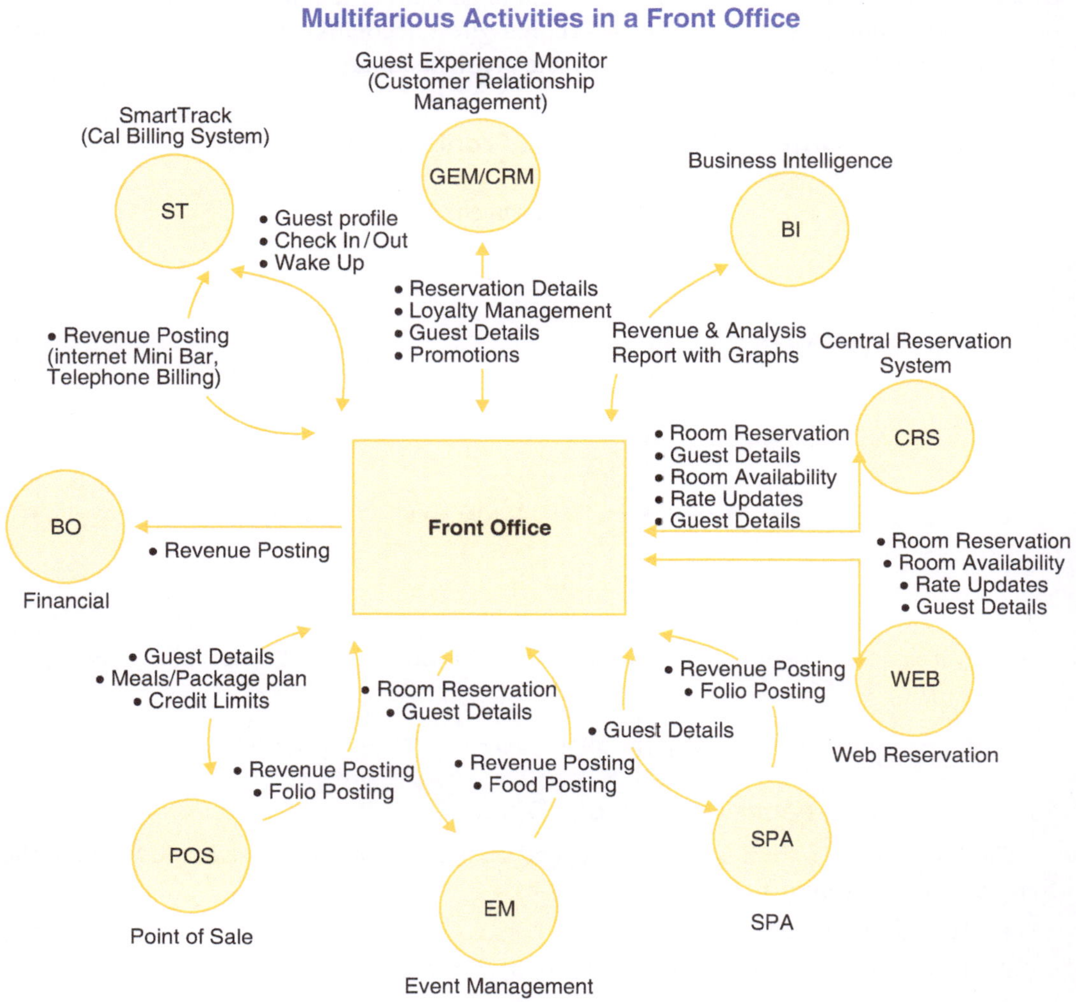

Figure 4.4. Multifarious Activities in a Front Office

General Duties of a Receptionist

The title "receptionist" is attributed to the person who is specifically employed by an organization to receive or greet any visitors, patients, or clients and answer telephone calls.

The title hotel receptionist is attributed to the person who is specifically employed by a hotel to greet visitors. He or she is responsible for welcoming guests as they arrive in a hotel premises.

A receptionist is an employee taking an office/administrative support position. The work is usually performed in a waiting area such as a lobby or front office desk of an organization or business.

The duties of a receptionist may be summarized as under:

1. To check the Housekeeping Report with the Reception rack and make out Discrepancy Report if necessary. Discrepancy Report is made 1 + 1 + 1, one for Bell captain and two for the file.
2. To make out Departure Lists for the next day for the next six days for the purpose of calculating room status.
3. Sort the mail, and those expected and forwarding addresses. If the guest is expected, mark "Mail" on the reservation Slip.
4. Packages and telegrams should be noted in the Register provided. If the guest is staying in hotel, he should be immediately informed about the telegram. Telegrams should be hold for three days and then returned if the guest does not arrive at the hotel.
5. Mail is held for one month and if no forwarding instructions are left at the information counter, it should be returned to the sender.
6. Receive all telephone messages in duplicate. Place in a copy in the pigeonhole and the other should be sent up to the room. If the message for a guest who is expected, it should be dealt with the same way ads his mail
7. If the guest leaves a message at the desk about his whereabouts, note it down on a message slip, inform the telephone operator and then place it in the respective pigeon hoe.
8. Hand over the key to the guest and put them in the key rack when the guest leaves them at the counter. Signed behind the lobby attendant Errand card, when a lobby attendant returns the key of guest who has checked out.
9. Complete and up date the knowledge of hotel facilities, tourist spots in the city, other attractions and other relevant information the guest may ask for.
10. To cross out the names of the guest who leaves the hotel and place these slips at the bottom of each section. These crossed slips are only to be removed by the Night Shift.
11. Keep checking the messages at short intervals to avoid any error e.g. a guest may have checked out and the message may be still in the pigeon hole in which case it is most likely that it will be handed over tot eh occupant of the room.
12. If the guest leaves a forwarding address, note it down on the card provided and arrange it in the forwarding address rack. When mail is forwarded, the details should be noted down in a Register.

FRONT OFFICE OPERATIONS

A brief description of the important front operations is given as under:

Guest Cycle

The guest cycle describes the activities that each guest passes by from the moment he/she calls to communicate a reservation inquiry till he/she departs from the hotel. In fact, the guest cycle encompasses 4 different stages, which are depicted underneath:

Four Stages of Guest Cycle

Pre-Arrival → Arrival → Occupancy → Departure

Each stage of the guest cycle is associated guest service, and guest accounting activity (ies).

1. Guest Services:

The four types of guest services are depicted as under:

Reservation → Registration → Occupancy services → Check-out and history

2. Guest Accounting:

The four stages of guest accounting are indicated as under:

Establishment of credits → posting charges → Night auditing → Settlement of accounts

Below is a brief description of the activities undertaken at each of the above stages of the guest cycle:

1. Pre-arrival:

(a) At the pre-arrival stage, the hotel must create for every potential guest a reservation record. Doing this initiates the hotel guest cycle. Moreover, reservation records help personalize guest services and appropriately schedule needed staff and facilities

(b) The reservation department should, then, complete all the pre-registration activities and prepare guest folios (applicable only for automated systems). Doing so will eventually maximize room sales by accurately monitoring room availability and forecasting room revenues.

2. Arrival:

(a) At the arrival stage, registration and rooming functions takes place and the hotel establishes a business relationship with the guest.

(b) The check-in clerk should determine the guest's reservation status (i.e. pre-registered guests *versus* walk-ins). Later, he/she shall prepare a registration record or make the guest sign the already-printed pre-registration record (under some of the semi-automated and all fully-automated systems).

The registration records shall include the following *personal* and *financial* information:

(a) Personal information:

1. Name and surname of the guest along with billing address, telephone number, and any other coordinates
2. Passport number, birth certificate, and/or driving license number (whatever applicable)
3. Any special needs or requests
4. Guest signature

(b) Financial information:

1. Date of arrival
2. Expected date of departure or length of stay depending on how the system in the hotel is designed
3. Assigned room number
4. Assigned room rate
5. Guest's intended method of payment

Registration records can be used for various purposes:

(a) Satisfy guest needs
(b) Forecast room occupancies
(c) Settle properly guest accounts
(d) Establish guest history records at check-out (personal & financial information)
(e) Assign a room type and a room rate for each guest
(f) Determine long-run availability (i.e. reservation information) versus short-run availability (i.e. room status)
(g) Satisfy special categories of guests such as disabled people through barrier-free designs

3. Occupancy:

(a) At the occupancy stage, the front office department shall coordinate guest services *in a timely and accurate manner*. Moreover, front office clerks should encourage repeat guests by paying a great attention to guest complaints. This is ensured by placing complaint and/or suggestion cards in every public place and revenue centers in the hotel. Moreover, the hotel shall, at least on a daily basis, collect comment cards, proceed with their analysis, and provide positive feedback to guest as soon as possible.

(b) In addition, the hotel shall design effective procedures in order to protect the funds and valuables of guests. This might be ensured through guest key control, property surveillance, safe deposit boxes, and well designed emergency panels and exits…

(c) Another activity at occupancy is to process posting of guest charges (i.e. post room rates, F&B charges, additional expenses, and taxes…) to various guest folios, master folios… While doing so, front office clerks shall continuously check for deviations from the house limit, and take corrective measures as to change the status of the guest to Paid-in-advance. Finally, front office clerks shall *periodically* review account balances in coordination with the night auditor.

4. Departure:

At the departure stage, the guest shall be walked out of the hotel. Moreover, front office clerks shall create guest history record. Finally, cashiers shall settle guest account outstanding balances (i.e.: balance the Guest Account to '**0**').

In general, a proper checkout occurs when the guest:

(a) Vacates the room

(b) Receives an *accurate* settlement of the guest account

(c) Returns room keys

(d) Leaves the hotel.

At departure, checkout personnel should encourage guests to consider returning to the hotel on any future date. That's why cashiers should act like a true sales person, and might eventually accept guest future reservations. That way, the stages of the guest cycle become really a cycle (i.e. start from where it ends).

If at departure, the guest account is not fully settled, then late charges accumulates. In such an undesired case, the responsibility of collection lies within the accounting department, however the front office department shall provide all necessary types of information to make this collection easier, quicker, and feasible.

EXERCISE 4.1

HOTEL CHECK-IN COMMUNICATION SKILLS

Structure

Making polite requests or suggestions to the guest :

Example 1

If you'd (just) like ...

If I could just ask you to...

The 'if' clause can stand on its own :

Example 2

If you'd like to fill in this form.

(This is enough as a request.)

But it can also be followed by a clause with WILL:

Example 3

If you'd like to fill in this form, I'll give you the key.

Responding to requests by guests

Yes, of course.

Yes, indeed.

Certainly.

No problem.

Expressions of Check-in

1. ***Phrases when the guest checks in***

Example 4

(a) What was the name, please?

(b) Ah, yes ...

(c) One moment, please.

Contd....

(d) Just a moment, please.
(e) Here we are.
(f) I've got it here.
(g) That's fine.
(h) I've put you in room (425).
(i) It's on the (4th) floor.
(j) The porter will take you up to your room.
(k) I'll get the porter to take your luggage up for you.

2. *Questions to help to fill in the forms*

Example 5

(a) Can I have your ...?
(b) How do you spell that and your ... ?
(c) Can you tell me your ... ?
(d) Where are you going after this ?
(e) How are you going to pay ?

3. *Some heading on the check-in forms*

(a) Surname
(b) Family name
(c) First name (forenames, prenames)
(d) Occupation
(e) Nationality
(f) Place of birth
(g) Next destination
(h) Method of payment
(i) Occupants (of a room).

Front Office Systems

Until the 1960's, nearly all hotels were operating under the manual system. At late 70's, with the introduction of computers, hotels shifted to semi-automated systems. Nowadays, most of the five-star hotels operate under the fully automated system. Below is a brief description of the three different systems under which hotels might operate.

1. **Non-automated (manual) systems:** This very system is the one characterized by the sole usage of hands. In fact, all formats, procedures, and different kinds of calculations are done manually.
2. **Semi-automated (Electro-mechanical) systems:** This system gets use of some electro-mechanical equipment. In fact, under the semi-automated system, each department might have its own computer system under which it handles all its operations.
3. **Fully automated (computer based) systems:** That's the best system ever used in the hotel industry. In fact, it is characterized by the excessive use of departmental software package programs integrated and connected to a main frame or terminal situated at the front office department.

EXERCISE 4.2

RECEPTION

Instruction:

Here are some inquiries and answers you could hear at the time of check-in.

1. **Match the parts of the receptionist's answers.**
2. **Match the answers of the receptionist with the inquiries of the guest.**

Receptionist's

A. Certainly. If you'd like to give me your passport. ... Yes.	You can get a light meal.
B. If you'd like to fill in this card, ... No problem.	He'll take you up.
C. If you'd like to hang a "DO NOT DISTURB" card on your details. door handle, ... Yes indeed.	I can fill in some of the details
D. If you'd like to go to the coffee shop, ... Yes.	She won't knock on your door.
E. If you'd like to fill in a request it will tell you all about to room service, ... our services.	Yes, of course.
F. If you'd like to follow, Certainly.	I'll give you the key to Porter, ...the room.
G. If you'd like to write the time on this slip	They can serve your breakfast in your room at any time.
H. If you'd like to look at this leaflet,	...The duty receptionist will give you a call.

Guest Queries

1. Can I go to the room now?
2. Can I check in now ?
3. Can you give me information about hotel services?
4. Can you give me a wake-up call in the morning ?
5. Can I get a snack before I go up to the room?
6. Can you fill in the registration form for me? I have to make a phone call ...
7. Can you tell me the room maid not to clean the room in the morning? I want to sleep late ...
8. Can I get an early breakfast? I have to catch a plane at 5.30 ...

GUEST CYCLE UNDER THREE DIFFERENT SYSTEMS

At this stage, it is essential to notice that the following stages of the guest cycle under the three different systems do not conflict with each other. In fact, the only differences are due to the nature of the system use. Therefore, what will be discussed above is not the repetition of the sequence; rather only differences will be highlighted.

Non-automated systems:

1. **Pre-arrival activities:** At the pre-arrival stage, reservation requests should be introduced in a loose-leaf notebook or index card. Moreover, only reservations up to 6 months horizons shall be honored. Lastly, it is not practical, under this very system, to issue reservation confirmation numbers, initiate pre-registration activities (at the exception of VIP and groups) and prepare occupancy forecasts. The reason is, time and money loss along with insufficient labor force to manually conduct all the above mentioned activities.
2. **Arrival activities:** At the arrival stage, guests shall either sign a page in the registration book or fill manually a registration record. Under this very system, the most widely used front office equipment is the room rack, in which registration records are inserted to serve as room rack slips. Moreover, registration books and records shall be time stamped as an internal control proving when the guest exactly came, who registered him/her…Lastly, guest folios shall be opened for each registered guest.
3. **Occupancy activities:** Under the occupancy activities, registration records shall be prepared with multi-copies. In fact, one copy shall be distributed to room rack, another stamped to the guest folio, another given to switchboard operators, and a final copy handed to the uniformed service personnel. Lastly, guests with charge privileges charges and payments shall be posted to respective guest folios.
4. **Departure activities:** At departure stage, cashiers should settle each guest account's outstanding balance and get room keys back from guests. Moreover, cashiers shall notify the housekeeping department that the room is no more occupied (i.e. room status change) to let this very department clean the room and prepare it for new arrivals. In addition, cashiers shall remove room rack slips from room racks to indicate departure. Lastly, these very rack slips of departed guests shall be filed in a cardboard box to serve as a guest history record.

Semi-automated systems:

This very system is less common in small and middle size hotels. For, these very hotels, financially wise, might not afford the huge investments associated with the installation of different hardware and software.

The main advantage of this very system over manual system is that various reports can *automatically* be generated. However, the major disadvantages associated with this system are various complexities of operating and controlling devices due to the fact that this equipment are not integrated with other systems and are subject to frequent maintenance problems.

1. **Pre-arrival activities:** At this very stage, guests can either call a national reservation network or directly contact the hotel. Moreover, reservation clerks can prepare pre-registration records, guest folios, and information rack slips.
2. **Arrival activities:** At this very stage, already reserved guests shall verify their pre-registration forms and have only to sign it. On the other hand, walk-ins shall complete a multiple copy registration record from the beginning.

3. **Occupancy activities:** At the occupancy stage, in order to track the different guest charge expenditures and all other possible guest transactions, hotels get an intensive use of various kinds of vouchers. Moreover, the most widely used equipment, under this very stage, is the mechanical cash registers and front office posting machines. Lastly, under this very stage, night auditor shall continuously resolve any discrepancy in guest accounts and efficiently reconcile guest folios.
4. **Departure activities:** At this very stage, cashiers shall relay room status information to the housekeeping department. Moreover, they should place registration records of departed guests in property's guest history files.

Fully automated systems:

1. **Pre-arrival activities:** Under this stage, the reservation department is equipped with a software package, which is interfaced and connected with one or more central reservation office(s). Moreover, the reservation department can automatically generate letters of confirmation, produce requests for guest deposits and handle pre-registration activities for all types of guests and generate daily expected arrival lists, occupancy and revenue forecast lists…

Looking at document

2. **Arrival activities:** At this stage, various reservation records can be transferred to front office department. Moreover, hotels might be equipped with an on-line credit authorization terminals for timely Credit Card Approval, self check-in / check-out terminals. Lastly, all guest charges and payments are saved in electronic guest folios.

   As far as walk-ins are concerned, all registration activities should be initiated from the very beginning.
3. **Occupancy activities:** Under this very stage, guest purchases at different revenue outlets are electronically transferred and posted to appropriate guest accounts. Moreover, the front office department can run and process continuous trial balances and, therefore, eliminate the tedious work for the Night Auditor.
4. **Departure activities:** At this very stage, cashiers can automatically produce bills to be sent to various guests with direct billing privileges and create electronic guest history records.

Front Office Forms

At different stages of the guest cycle different forms are used depending on which operating system a hotel chooses. Below are some of the common forms used:

1. Pre-arrival activities:
   (a) Reservation record or a reservation file
   (b) Letter of confirmation
   (c) Reservation rack and reservation rack slips
2. Arrival activities:
   (a) Registration card (or record) or registration file
   (b) Room rack and room rack slips
3. Occupancy activities:
   (a) Guest folio: This shall be of duplicate forms and pre-numbered for cross-indexing control purposes
   (b) Vouchers: These are support documents detailing facts of a transaction, but do not replace the source document (i.e. the invoice). Examples of vouchers might include charge vouchers, allowance vouchers, paid-out voucher, and correction vouchers...
   (c) Information rack slips
4. Departure activities:
   (a) Credit card vouchers
   (b) Cash vouchers
   (c) Personal check vouchers
   (d) Transfer vouchers
   (e) Guest history records.

Front Office Functional Organization

Whatsoever system and setting the hotel might use, it should reflect easy access to the equipment, forms, and supplies necessary. Moreover, the setting shall reflect position flexibility. Nowadays trend shows that traditional mail, message, and key racks are unnecessary at the Front Desk. Rather, they shall be stored in drawers or slots located under or away from the Front Desk. For, this would ensure security and safety of guests.

Hotel Reception Desk

Front Desk designed alternatives

1. Circular or semi-circular structure: This very structure provides an effective service to more guests and appears more modern and innovative but since guests will approach the Front Desk from all angles, more staff is needed.
2. Traditional straight desk: Under this very design, fewer staff is needed, but fewer guests can be served at the same time.
3. Deskless environment: Under this design, there is no Front Desk at all. This is usually replaced by a hostess, or steward welcoming the guest, seating him or her on a chair/sofa, and conduct registration activities there while, for example, having a cocktail or a drink.

In order to fulfill the responsibilities, the front office may be divided in to following sections:

1. Reservation
2. Reception
3. Telecommunication
4. Guest Relation Desk
5. Front Office cashiering
6. Lobby Desk
7. Concierge
8. Bell desk
9. Transport Section
10. Doorman
11. Valet Parking.

A Hotel Lobby: Caurtesy: Burj Al Arab
A lobby is designed to be a welcoming place... where you don't linger long.

Reservation

All kinds of demand for room reservations are to be handled at the reservation section of the front office. Immediately on receipt, each one of the demands is to be answered and filed. Every day a list is to be established, in which all arrivals expected for the next day are listed. It would be possible at any time to know the number of reservations being confirmed for any date (forecast).

Rooming

Rooming consists of distribution and rooming of walk-ins. In the morning rooming is distribution or allotment of rooms to the expected arrival i.e. confirmed reservations and the rooming of walk-ins i.e. the guests without reservations.

Atrium- Caurtesy: Burj Al Arab Hotel

Front Office Cashiering:

A front office cashier is a nerve centre of all guests billing. The front office cashier must have knowledge of accounting principles and basic front office accounting procedures of the hotel. He reports to the income accountant in the finance and Accounting department. He performs the following duties:

1. Requisition and maintenance of a cash bank for shift transactions
2. Post guest charges and credit into respective guest folios
3. Settle all guest bills at the time of departure.

The front office has to accumulate all charges made by guests during their stay in the hotel. These charges are announced to the billing section by means of vouchers issued by the different service centers of the hotel such as telephone, bar, restaurants etc. The guest accounts can be kept in handwritten form through a visitors' tabular ledger or with the help of machine or computer.

Key Handling at the Front Offices:

All keys for the guest rooms are stored at the front office. Usually, they are hanging in the appropriate pigeonhole in the key section of the front office. They are handed over to the guests when they arrive in the hotel or when they ask for it.

1. Two keys for each guest lock have to be handed over to the Front Office Manager. One key will remain on the tag and the other one will be on the rack in front Office manager's Office.
2. One set of duplicate keys will always be available with the Front Office Manger.
3. Bell staff and Front Office Cashier to ensure the return of the key when the guest checks out. This should be cross-checked by the desk clerk while signing for the keys.
4. Every time a new lock is fixed, two keys to be handed over to the front Office manager: one for the guest tag and one for key cupboard.

Information

The Information section is vital to front office operation. It controls the room keys, mail and messages. It is also equipped with all the information of the hotel facilities and the city. Though the major functions of the Front Office may seem simple, the actual mechanics to execute them successfully is complicated. The various systems and procedures on which the front office hinges shall be explained in detail later.

This section of the front office deals with the messages for guests, their mails, handling of their keys and any other information that the guest may ask such as sightseeing, shopping, etc. The information section is the centerpiece of a lobby. The first most interaction of a guest where he gets himself registered is the front desk and the last place where the guests clear their bills is again the front desk. The hotel pays lot of attention in making the front office attractive and clean with flower arrangements, brochure racks and other displays. During the display the due care is given to see that the counter top is clear so that all the formalities can be conducted. Manually the counter is handled in to two sections:

1. For the receptionist who registers guests into the hotel.
2. For information receptionist who stands at the guest alphabetical rack and controls the key rack.

It is important for the staff of this section to have telephones to coordinates with other relevant departments the telephones at the information section receives external calls from guest who wish to leave message for the guest who are staying in the hotel.

The guest expects the front office assistance to give them any information requested. The from office assistant should be prepared to answer all questions about the hotel, the company, the city for purpose of sightseeing, the country and the time tables of trains and airways.

The front office assistant must be able to answer all questions about plain, bus and train time tables, the own, the country, the hotel, other hotel s of the company, sightseeing places in the town etc. He should be in a position to recommend tours in the immediate surrounding and future distances. The front office assistant must know all about the restaurant, bars and other facilities and service he hotel offers.

There is no tangible profit in the information service, but it gives the customer the feeling that the hotel makes every possible effort to render effective service. A good information service ensures for the future.

In large sized hotels, the information services often have their own desks. It is, of course, not possible that an assistant has all these items required for good information service in his mid, but he should have enough material such as folders etc. and the knowledge how to use it.

Front Office Accounting

The front office cashier receives payments for a guest's stay in the hotel. This is the point where all the charge vouchers (bills) generated by the guest are received, to be included in the overall bill. Close liaison between the lobby staff and cashier is imperative. The Bell Captain must inform the cashier about the intended check out of a guest so that the

Guest's bills are updated and kept ready for presentation. Also, the cashier is informed of a new arrival by the Reception by opening and forwarding a new folio in the guest's name giving room number and time of check in, with defined billing instructions which the cashier places in the bill tray against the appropriate room.

The Night Auditor audits all guest bills received by the front office cashier and prepares and proves for the calendar day. This is the credit section that receives bills from front office that has extended credit as per previous arrangement between the hotel and the guest. This department follows up with the individual or company for the payment of the bills. The Room Service is kept closely intimated on arrivals and departures of guests. It is this department that provides food and beverage services to the room and must be informed as to the occupant in order to raise bills accordingly.

The front office informs room service through the Amenities Voucher and a List of the VIPs' expected to arrive in the hotel so that special service is extended. Also the room service provides a complimentary basket of fruit, liquor, cakes and pastries or whatever gesture the establishment wishes to extend to a VIP as per the policy.

Commissionaire

There are some special services to fulfill. Sometimes a customer wants on the bellboys to go into buying something for him etc. Most of the hotels give this service if possible. When such cases often happen, there should be commissionaire. Do not withdrawn staff during the rush hour when they are urgently needed elsewhere, unless the commission is really very important.

Complaints

Usually, a customer will post a complaint at the front office. Full consideration and attention should be given to such complaints. It is advisable to bring this to the notice of the supervisor. Answer politely. Investigate about the reason. Never blame other departments and employees.

Bell Desk

The bell desk is mainly responsible for luggage handling of the guests. It consists of a group of uniformed staff for guest services. In large hotel is section is has an independent status.

Reservation in Other Hotels

When a guest asks for a reservation in another town, the front office assistant should be able too propose and recommend good hotels. The general policy is that incase there is another hotel of the same company /chain in that town, the front office should name this hotel firstly and the reservation should be made there in.

Miscellaneous

There are many other services rendered at the front office. These include provision of airline, train and bus tickets and provision of cars etc.

General Understanding of Housekeeping

Briefing is that process at the beginning of a work shift which is provided by management to facilitate a two-way communication between management and staff. It is the one time during a shift that all housekeeping staff are together to share information and feelings before they disperse to their work areas.

Briefing is normally undertaken where all employees have to report on duty at the beginning of the shift. This is after the employees have formally clocked into the hotel at the time office and have already received their fresh uniforms, which they change into in their respective locker rooms. All employees must report for briefing properly attired and at the scheduled commencement of the shift or earlier.

In Housekeeping briefing is conducted at a prescribed common Housekeeping Lounge or at the Housekeeping Control Room. Ideally, the Executive Housekeeper must conduct the briefing; however, due to odd shift timings she may delegate this responsibility to her deputy. Here are some issues that should normally be covered in a briefing that should last no longer than 15 minutes.

A Receptionist on work

Housekeeping staff is mostly in guest visibility and contact areas. It is thus important that they are well-groomed and clean. While grooming projects the image and quality of the hotel, a guest also likes to feel that the people who clean his room are themselves very clean. It is thus important for the Housekeeper to ensure the following:

1. Personal cleanliness—fingernails should be clean and cut short; men should have shaved and should emit no body odour.
2. Hair should be clean and neatly combed/arranged. Hair nets are suggested but not essential.
3. Little or no make-up.
4. Careful use of lipsticks for maids.
5. No necklaces or bracelets—earrings, if worn, must be small and unobtrusive.
6. Uniforms must be clean and well pressed. They must be of the proper size and well fastened.
7. Stockings (if required) should be clean, of a permitted colour and free of holes.
8. Shoes should be dark in colour, low-heeled and clean.
9. Any new policies and procedures introduced by management must be made out and explained to the staff.

The names, room numbers and the importance of each VIP staying in the hotel must be communicated to all staff, especially those assigned to their floors.

At a briefing the duties of each staff member and the areas of accountability are explained. This would mean that maids are assigned a floor and allotted their number of rooms. The housemen, likewise, are told which floors or public areas they are assigned to for cleaning. They are also told which supervisor would be in charge.

The Executive Housekeeper must receive any professional or personal grievances of staff. It would help productivity if problems are resolved or at least heard with the intention of resolving them. This can also be an opportunity to test out whether policies and procedures already explained have been understood and implemented.

At a briefing the duties of each staff member and the areas of accountability are explained. This would mean that maids are assigned a floor and allotted their number of rooms. The housemen, likewise, are told which floors or public areas they are assigned to for cleaning. They are also told which supervisor would be in charge.

The Executive Housekeeper must receive any professional or personal grievances of staff. It would help productivity if problems are resolved or at least heard with the intention of resolving them. This can also be an opportunity to test out whether policies and procedures already explained have been understood and implemented.

Briefing is a time that can be used as a training opportunity. Simple tasks may be demonstrated so that they can be practiced under supervision at their work place. An Executive Housekeeper must constantly remind housekeeping staff of the standards expected by management. Standards could be the number of rooms to be completed by a maid in her shift or the time taken to complete a departure room etc. At a briefing, the housekeeping staff should get a first hand feedback on whether they are maintaining the required standards. Since all housekeeping staff on a given shift assembles for a briefing, it is the ideal time to give a word of praise or recognition to deserving candidates.

It is important to give information of a general nature, especially of the going-on in the hotel to staff. One normally shrugs off general information, as it does not concern staff—but all information is knowledge and brings in a feeling of pride and a team spirit to the totality of hotel operations.

Information like the gala functions in the hotel, the re-assignment of people in the hotel, promotions, increments, etc. must be shared. The sale of rooms constitutes approximately 50 per cent or more of the total hotel revenue. A 'sale' of room would mean the leasing of the room for occupation for 24 hours at a predetermined cost. A room not sold on a particular day has lost its opportunity to earn revenue for that day. Hence rooms are referred to as highly perishable commodities. The loss of an opportunity to sell a room can also be due to inefficiency of housekeeping in having a room ready when required. What does a room mean to a guest?

Hence, hotels spend efforts in ensuring the quality of beds, mattresses, weather, control, channel music, hot and cold water, attached baths, etc. The comforts must be regularly maintained and functioning. It is Housekeeping's responsibility to ensure this.

The primary security devise that hotels provide is to restrict entrance to the room/suite through only one door; a double locking system from inside; strict control on room keys and master keys; chain locking the door from within to further augment the door locking system; precautions in the room to ensure all electrical wiring is concealed and no equipment in the room is faulty; fire exit layout in the room, etc.

Room windows are provided with curtains. Superior hotels would have daylight curtains and heavy night curtains. Windows would normally overlook good scenic views, away from the prying eyes of others in the hotel or the outside public. The entrance into a room procedure is well defined to ensure guest privacy. Attached baths are also a measure towards privacy.

A guest is provided entertainment, food and beverage services, telephone services, etc. in his or her room. The guest is thus free to spend all the time towards fulfilling the purpose of his visit—be it a holiday or business. The House keeping Department should ensure such literature in the room as to enable a guest to know how to reach such conveniences and avail of them.

The Housekeeping Department has a pivotal role to play in this aspect. Hence he demands the highest standards in everything that the room stands for. In addition to the above, it is important for all housekeeping personnel to know the different types of rooms that hotels provide.

Royal Suite Hotel Room:
Caurtesy: Burj Al Arab hotel

The Royal Suite:
Caurtesy: Bruj Al Arab Hotel

The Royal Suite:
Caurtesy: Bruj Al Arab Hotel

The Royal Suite:
Caurtesy: Bruj Al Arab Hotel

Table 4.1. Different types of rooms in hotels

Sl. No.	*Types of Room*	*Description*
1.	Single Room:	Meant for a single occupancy. The room has one normal sized bed.
2.	Double Room:	Meant for double occupancy and has one large bed meant for two.
3.	Twin Room	Meant for double occupancy. The room provides two single beds. Hotels may reserve the flexibility to sell it on single occupancy as well.
4.	Studio Room	Meant for single or double occupancy. It has one normal bed and a sofa-cum-bed that acts as a sofa during the day and can be pulled out into a bed for the night.
5.	Single Suite	Meant for single occupancy. A suite is a two-room set—one room furnished with drawing-cum-dining facilities and the other as a bedroom with a normal bed.
6.	Double Suite	It is the same as a single suite in concept, except that the bedroom has a large double bed, or two normal sized beds to facilitate double occupancy.
7.	Cabana Rooms	Attached to the poolside for changing or resting. The room has one sofa-cum-bed.
8.	Duplex Suite Room	Built on two floors with an interconnecting staircase. Such suites normally have two bedrooms.
9.	Triple Room	Provided mostly for families. It has twin beds with an extra cot.

All the above rooms may be furnished with extra rollaway cots on the demand of the guest at an extra charge (Refer Table 4.2). All rooms normally have attached bathrooms. Exceptions would be in hostel where common bathrooms per floor are more economical for the guest and management for the low charges they levy on rooms.

Table 4.2:

Fresh bath linen and guest supplies in the room
(As per the number of person)

Linen	*Supplies*
One bath towel	2 toilet rolls
One face towel	1 bathroom tumbler per person
One hand towel	1 soap dish
One bath mat	2 soaps per guest (25 g each)
	1 candle stand with candle
	1 ash tray with a match box
	1 shoe mit
	1 soap sud satchel per person
	1 shower cap per person
	2 disposal bags
	1 blade dispenser
	1 face tissue box
	1 waste basket

Prior to commencing work, all housekeeping staff, especially room attendants, must follow some floor rules that lend an air of efficiency and least inconvenience to guests.

The floor and rooms are most private and personal to guests who are concerned by the people who frequent them. They lay a large trust in the management of the hotel through the room attendants who are privy to their rooms and belongings. To uphold this trust the following rules must be strictly observed:

1. Speech amongst the floor staff must be restricted to a minimum. In case communication is necessary, this must be done in low tones even when guests are not in sight.
2. Unnecessary movements like running or jumping must be avoided.
3. The passageway must be kept free of equipment, trays or trolleys.
4. The floor telephones must be attended to promptly.
5. Room attendants must greet all guests according to the time of the day.
6. Staff must be helpful and readily give required information. Misleading a guest through misinformation must be avoided.
7. Alertness to guest movements is necessary so as to report anything suspicious.
8. Remember the guest is always right. Arguing with a guest is prohibited. If a guest is being unreasonable refer him/her to the next superior.
9. It is prohibited to enter rooms, which display a "Do not disturb" sign outside. If a DND sign is on for a long time, this may be reported to the floor supervisor.
10. The door of the room in which the attendant is cleaning should always be kept wide open.
11. If the guest returns when the room is being cleaned the room attendant may ask the guest if she can continue or come later.

12. In spite of following the procedure for entering a room, if the guest is inside either sleeping or awake, quickly withdraw, apologizing if required and shut the door softly.
13. Always follow the procedure of entering a room even if the room is seemingly vacant.

The maid's cart is a trolley meant to stock a given number of linen items, supplies and equipment to service an allotted number of rooms. Each maid, after receiving her room assignment, should check her supplies against a standard list to avoid needless trips. The maid is responsible for the condition, cleanliness and appearance of her cart.

The lower shelf of the cart is used to carry heavier items like mattresses, protectors and bed sheets and night spreads. The middle and top shelf stock pillowslips and bath linen. Linen will include:

1. Night spreads	1 for each bed
2. Sheets	2 for each bed
3. Pillow cases	2 for each bed
4. Bath towels	1 for each guest
5. Face towels	1 for each guest
6. Hand towels	1 for/each guest
7. Bath mats	1 for each bathroom
8. Mattress protectors	few to replace as necessary.

These terms should be arranged in neat stacks, the heavier items below and the lighter ones on top.

The top tray should be neatly arranged with the following guest room supplies and cleaning agents:

Supplies and cleaning agents

There should be supplies of such promotional material as the management of the hotel may from time to time prescribe. In any event, this material should include:

1. Room service menu
2. Room service beverage list
3. Tent cards for special promotion

In addition, the cart may carry cleaning equipment such as feather brush, dustpan, mops, sponges, dusters, carpet brush or vacuum cleaner, clean scrub bucket, scrub brush on the same end of the maids cart as the trash bag. The exact location is below the trash bag. The cleaning material will include:

Disinfectants:

Dettol, Deodorizer.

Cleaning agents:

Vim, Sanitizer (sanifresh), Liquid soap (teenopol), Naphthalene balls, Room freshener and Anol.

Polishing material:

Brasso, Wax polish.

Room cleaning

After securing all the supplies and equipment outlined above, each maid should proceed to her duty station and begin the cleaning procedure on the assigned number of rooms with room checklists.

Maid carts are to be placed along the corridor wall on the same side of the corridor where rooms are being serviced. The cart should be so positioned as to service a minimum of two rooms without much movement of the room attendant to minimize trips to the cart and thereby reduce the fatigue factor. When designing maid carts consideration must be given to the fact that the cart should be lightweight to ensure easy mobility by the maid. Heavy carts also pucker corridor carpets. The wheels of the cart

Table 4.3. Contents of a Maid Cart

S. No.	Content	S. No.	Content
1.	A.C. Operation	33.	Luggage chest
2.	Lining paper	34.	Shoe shine card
3.	Wall paper	35.	Vestibule celling
4.	Dresser and stool	36.	Ash tray
5.	Matches	37.	Candle and candle stand
6.	Tent card	38.	Portfolio
7.	Guest house rule	39.	Writing material
8.	Telegraph form	40.	Guest comment form
9.	Room service menu	41.	Breakfast knobs
10.	Laundry and Valet list	42.	Sewing kit
11.	Plsdyiv bags	43.	Waste paper basket
12.	TV and TV programme	44.	TV comments form
13.	Mirrors	45.	Chairs and tables
14.	Heavy curtain	46.	Sheer curtain
15.	Window operation	47.	Window cleaning
16.	Safety	48.	Safety bar
17.	Headrest	49.	Bed and mattress
18.	Bed cover	50.	Studio bed
19.	Wall plaques	51.	Bedside table
20.	Bedside lamp	52.	Lamp shade
21.	Telephone	53.	Message pad
22.	Service directory	54.	Pen
23.	Thermos flask	55.	High ball glasses
24.	Telephone	56.	Gita
25.	Bible	57.	Light switch
26.	A.C. switch	58.	Message light
27.	Music operation	59.	Carpet
28.	Skirting	60.	Walls & Ceilling
29.	Cobweb chicking	61.	Toilet door
30.	Toilet door latch	62.	Bolt
31.	Robe hook	63.	Bottle opener
32.	Wshbasin and counter	64.	Mirror

must be of a good standard and well oiled periodically to ensure smooth movement (Refer Table 4.3).

Prior to reporting on a floor the room attendant already knows the status of a room in her given lot of rooms. The room attendant can prioritize rooms to be attended to first on the basis of immediate needs; however, the normal practice is to attend to vacant rooms first, then departure rooms, "Clean my rooms," and finally occupied rooms.

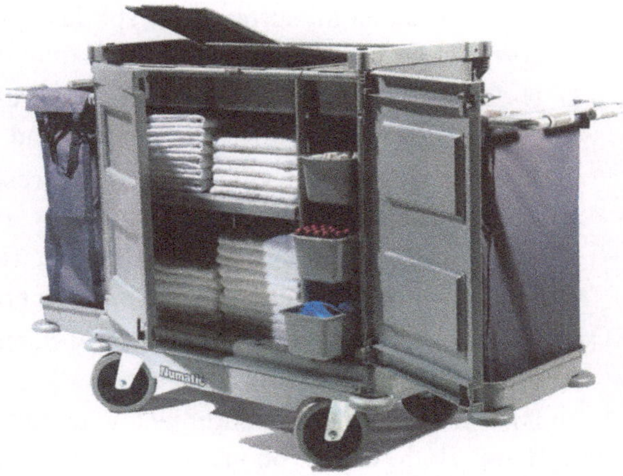

Housekeeping Trolley

For occupied rooms look whether the room has a "Do not disturb" card on the doorknob. If it does, then go to a room that does not. Knock at the door firmly with the index finger knuckle announcing clearly "Housekeeping." When there is no answer, repeat the knock after 10 seconds announcing yourself as before. If there is still no answer open the door with the floor master key. Push the door again, knock announcing inside the room "Housekeeping." When there is no reply and one is relatively sure that there is no one in, open the door wide and keep it that way till the entire cleaning cycle in the room is complete.

Room Cleaning Procedure

1. Switch off the room air-conditioner or heating. Draw all curtains and open the windows for airing the room.
2. Remove soiled linen from beds and bath. Shake out the linen to ensure that no guest articles are lost in the folds of linen. Put the soiled linen in the linen hamper provided in the maids cart.
3. Check for maintenance requirements and report the same to the control desk and enter in room check-list.
4. Check for lost and found in departure rooms and report to supervisor desk.
5. Contact Room Service to remove used trays.
6. Turn the mattress side-to-side on succeeding days followed by end-to-end turning. Smooth out mattress to air it.
7. If a vacuum cleaner is not available, brush the carpet first to enable the dust to settle while doing the next task.
8. Clean bathroom.
9. Empty all ashtrays into the waste paper basket in the room. Collect other loose trash on tables and floors and throw them in the waste paper basket.
10. Pick up guest clothes and hang in closet or place in dresser.
11. Collect all loose papers or magazines and stack them neatly on the desk.

12. Clean all the surfaces in single circular motions with a dry cloth. Use a hand dustpan to collect any unwanted matter on the surfaces without lifting dust in the air. Ensure that all surfaces are spotlessly clean. Pay special attention to nooks and corners especially those points that may not obviously be visible to the guest eye.
13. Use a stiff upholstery brush or vacuum cleaner (with the appropriate attachment) on upholstered furniture arms, backs and seats.
14. Replace, if necessary, stationery as prescribed by management. The number of items must exactly be as per standard.
15. Dust and replace each item on dressers, bureaus and desks. Special attention must be given to the display of publicity material as prescribed by the management.
16. Clean lamp shades with a clean dry duster. Lift lamps and clean under the base. Replace lamp and adjust the shade.
17. Disinfect telephone mouthpiece with dettol. Wipe balance of the telephone with a damp cloth. Check phone for the dial tone.
18. Clean mirror with a dry cloth first and then with a damp newspaper to make it sparkling.
19. Dust closet, shelves, hangers and rods. Brush the closet floor. Supply new laundry bags and replace missing hangers and drawers/shelf with plastic or paper liners.
20. Dust both sides of all room doors, baseboards, window sills, inside and out, bottom and centre sashes or windows, sash rails and tops of radiators and air-conditioning units.
21. Close windows.
22. If a vacuum cleaner is available then vacuuming of carpet should be done at this stage as against brushing the carpet.
23. Arrange furniture if necessary.
24. Switch on the air-conditioning or heating on the minimum temperature for a departure room and at the same temperature the guest has left it for an occupied room.
25. Have a last look at the room referring to the checklist for completion of work.

Making a Bed

Housekeeping in a hotel is a very physically demanding job that includes many, varied tasks. Typically, in this case study, housekeepers were responsible for cleaning 16 rooms per shift. The actual amount of work depends on the size of the room and the number of beds. A housekeeper needs between fifteen and thirty minutes to do one room.

A housekeeper carries out the following tasks:

1. Remove soiled sheets and pillow cases and shake out individually.
2. Turn out mattress as previously described.
3. Shake out mattress protector and relay it on the mattress. Change the protector if soiled or smelling.
4. Open out fresh lower sheet evenly and tuck it securely at the head, foot and sides.

Figure 4.5: Making beds

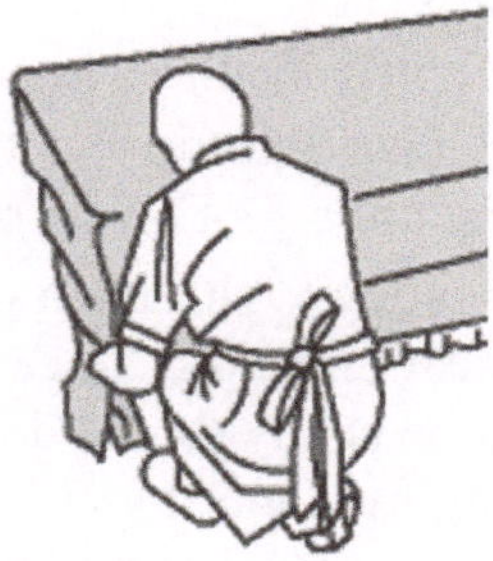

Figure 4.6: Making beds

Figure 4.7: Making beds

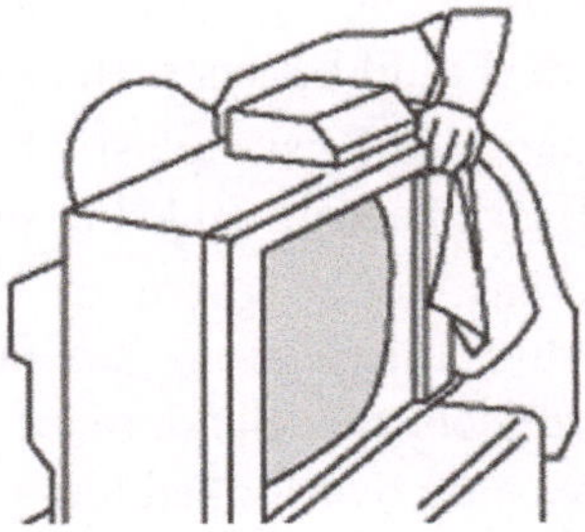

Figure 4.8: Tidying a room

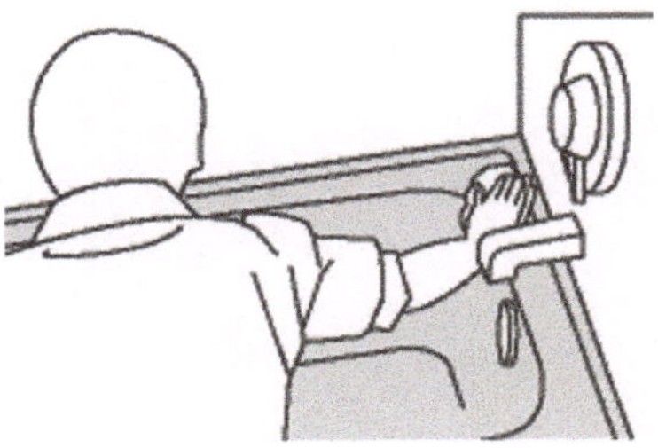

Figure 4.9: Cleaning

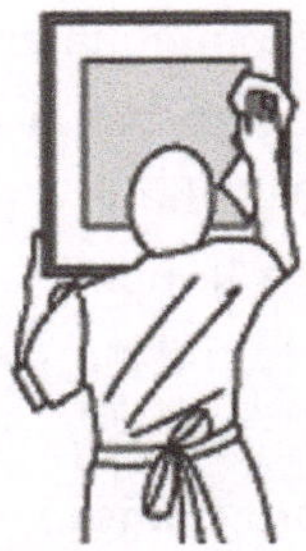

Figure 4.10: Cleaning

(a) Making beds (Ref. Figures 4.5, 4.6, 4.7),
(b) Tidying rooms (Ref. Figure 4.8),
(c) Cleaning and polishing toilets, taps, sinks, bathtubs and mirrors (Ref. Figures 4.9, 4.10),
(d) Washing floors,
(e) Removing stains, and
(f) Vacuuming.

5. Open out fresh top sheet and distribute it evenly over the lower bed sheet. Ensure that the laundry crease is in the same line as the inner sheet for even distribution. The sheet hem should be evenly pulled up to the headboard. Tuck this sheet at the foot.
6. Open out blanket and distribute it evenly on the top sheet using the crease as described earlier for even distribution. Ensure that the blanket labels are at the foot. Pull the blanket four inches from the headboard.

7. Fold top sheet, at the head of the bed, over the blanket and fold the sheet and blanket once again.
8. The blanket and top sheet are together tucked uniformly on both sides while the corners at the foot of the old are mitred.
9. Cover pillows with fresh pillowslips. Fluff the pillow and even out pillowslips to look neat and tidy. Since pillowslips are larger than the pillow the excess slip should be neatly folded downward. The side of the pillow that has the fold should be away from guest view.
10. Cover completed bed with the bedspread ensuring it is right side up and falling evenly all around the bed. Keep extra bed spread towards the headboard to crease in between the pillows so as to make the bed look appealing. The bedspread corners should be aesthetically done.
11. Put spare blankets in plastic bags in the uppermost or lowermost shelf in the guest closet. Blankets are folded in such a manner that the hotel insignia appears on the top.

Certain areas in the room or bathroom elude the maid's attention and tend to accumulate dust. Such areas are normally hidden from a guest's eye. However, its cleanliness reflects the standard of cleaning of the hotel. Experience shows that the following areas are overlooked and appropriately called the "dirty dozen":

1. Top of door edges and ceiling.
2. Air-conditioning ducts and diffuser grills.
3. Under bathroom counters.
4. Beneath the grab-bar and dresser table.
5. Behind the WC bowl—the Strap.
6. In the toilet roll niche.
7. Faucet nozzle filter.
8. Toilet vents.
9. Top of picture frames.
10. Area above pillow racks.
11. Rear surface of doors.
12. Interior surfaces of drawers.

Cleaning a Bathroom: Basic principles

(a) Cleaning activity starts from the ceiling downward to the floor.

(b) Floors are cleaned from the wall farthest to the door to the exit.

   1. Open all windows and exhaust vents.
   2. Shake out all soiled bathroom linen, e.g. towels, bathroom mats. etc. and deposit in the linen hamper of the maids cart.
   3. Collect all trash in bathroom wastebasket and deposit in trash hamper of the maids cart.
   4. Clean the ceiling and air-conditioning vents for cobwebs.

5. Wipe off light bulbs and shades with a dry clothe. Check that all bulbs are working.
6. Wipe down the walls using a sponge or damp cloth. Follow with a dry cloth ensuring that tiles are free of watermarks.
7. Clean mirror first with dry cloth, then with damp newspaper and finally with dry clothe. Ensure that the mirror is smudge and scar-free. Clean the medicine cabinet.
8. Wipe dries the shower curtain with a sponge.
9. Scrub dry the area next to the washbasin.
10. Scrub and clean dry the bathtub ensuring that the water faucets and shower are sparkling and in working condition.
11. Scrub the toilet bowl and bidet using the special brush or mop and the prescribed sanitizer. The inner rim should be cleaned. Ensure it is dry and spotless inside. Clean the WC from the outside with a sponge till it is sparkling and dry. Clean the lid and toilet seat of the toilet bowl dry and close them by placing the disinfectant label.
12. Replenish fresh bath linen and guest supplies as per the number of persons in the room at the following number per person.

    Place advertising material as prescribed.
13. Scrub the floor with the prescribed mops and ensures it is dry.
14. Finally close the windows, shut all lights and close the bathroom doors.

In occupied rooms, when cleaning the counter around the washbasin, collect all guest belongings onto one side and clean the other. Shift the belongings to the other side to clean the surface they were occupying. Finally replace all belongings as the guest had left them.

QUESTIONS AND DISCUSSIONS

Short Answer Type

Q.1. Name the functional managers who report to the executive assistant of a hotel.

Q.2. Give examples of hotel departments within the back-of-the-house area.

Q.3. List the job titles for hotel employees who are assigned to back-of-the-house departments.

Q.4. List the different ways a hotel is classified and why.

Q.5. List the reasons people travel and choose a certain hotel.

Q.6. List different hotel front office forms and equipment

Q.7. Draw a hotel's organizational chart.

Q.8. Outline some of the Front Office procedures that can be implemented to ensure customer satisfaction.

Q.9. Explain the different duties of a receptionist.

Q.10. Write notes on:

(a) Rooming

(b) Bell Desk

(c) Key Handling.

Q.11. Give an organization chart of a front office for a medium sized hotel.

Q.12. Define the terms as they apply to front office operations.

Descriptive Type

Q.13. Compare and contrast the job title organizational chart of a full-service hotel with professional levels organizational chart for the same or similar hotel.

Q.14. Show how the hotel industry is part of the hospitality industry.

Q.15. Draw a hotel's and the front office's organizational chart.

Q.16. Describe the "guest cycle."

Q.17. Explain the importance of front office security and list the different areas of concern.

Q.18. Explain the importance of front desk selling.

Q.19. Explain the importance of maximizing profits in establishing room rates, forecasting room availability, budgeting, and using revenue management techniques.

Q.20. Explain the concept of revenue management, its techniques and pros and cons.

Q.21. Give examples of hotel departments, which are within the front office area.

Q.22. Describe hotel functions that are involved in the guest service cycle.

Q.23. Design an effective front desk.

Q.24. Define the terms front-of-the house, back-of-the-house, guest services trilogy, concierge, chain-managed, franchise, MOD, and MIS as they apply to front office to front office operations.

Q.25. Discuss the importance of front office security.

Q.26. Describe the role of the general manager of a hotel.

Q.27. Describe the role of the executive assistant of a hotel.

Q.28. Describe the role of the rooms' division manager and name the job titles that report to this level.

Q.29. Compare and contrast the position of rooms' division manager with the manager on duty for typical hotel operations.

Q.30. Describe the role of the front office manager and name the job titles of employees that report to this level.

Q.31. Describe the basic functions of a hotel desk clerk.

Q.32. Discuss the responsibilities of a hotel desk clerk.

Q.33. Describe the basic functions of a hotel concierge.

Q.34. Discuss the responsibilities of a hotel concierge.

Q.35. Describe the basic functions of a hotel bell attendant.

Q.36. Discuss the responsibilities of a hotel bell attendant.

Assignments / Activity Type

Q.37. Demonstrate a typical guest account from check-in to settlement.

Q.38. Read the conversations given below:

(a) The parts are not in the correct order.

(b) Which parts are spoken by the guest ?

Mark the parts with a "G"

(c) Which parts are spoken by the receptionist?

Mark the parts with an "R"

(d) Write numbers on the lines. Then act out the conversations with a partner.

Conversation 1

.... : That's fine. Here's the key-room 485, on the second floor. If you would just fill in this form, the porter will take your luggage up to the room. ( )

.... : Good morning madam. May I help you? ( )

.... : Yes. I'd like to check in. ( )

.... : Yes, I'd made a reservation by telephone. The name is Lalita-Lalita. I made a reservation for myself and my sister. ( )

.... : That's right. ( )

.... : Ah yes. One moment. I've got it here. Lalit. A twin room. ( )

.... : Do you have a reservation? ( )

Conversation 2

.... : Er ... the name is Sunil. I have a reservation. ( )

.... : Yes, a single room, with bathroom. ( )

.... : Yes of course. I'll get the porters to take it up for you. ( )

.... : Right. Just moment till I find it. Yes ... here we are ... Mr. Sunil, single room. ( )

.... : Right. Just a moment till I find it. Yes ...here we are ... Mr. Sunil, single room. ( )

.... : O.K. now, we've put you in room 417, which is on the fourth floor, overlooking the hotel gardens. The rate is Rs. 10, 000. ( )

.... : Can I help you sir ? ( )

.... : Well, that sound fine. ( )

.... : O.K. I'll do that. By the way, I've got some heavy luggage in the car. Can you get someone to help me with it ? ( )

.... : Good. And before you go up, if I could ask you to fill in the registration card. ( )

Q.39. Take turn to be the receptionist and the guest. Ask for and give personal information for the registration card.

A. *Pre-reading*

Discuss the following questions :

(a) When does the check-in take place ?

(b) What is the role of the check-in in the hotel business?

(c) What is the important information needed in the check-in?

(d) What departments in the hotel are needed to corporate with the front office ?

(e) What is the most important factor to make the check-in service impressive to the guest?

B. *Reading Practice*

Guest Registration

One of the first opportunities for face-to-face contact with a hotel occurs when the guest registers. At this time, all the marketing efforts and computerized reservation systems should come together.

Will the guest receive what has been advertised and promised ?

The front desk clerk who is well trained in the registration process must be able to portray the hotel in a positive manner. This good first impression will help ensure an enjoyable visit.

The first step in the guest registration process begins with capturing guest data such as name, address, zip code, length of stay, company affiliation, etc., which are needed during his or her stay and after departure. Various departments in the hotel require this information to provide service to the guest. The registration process continues with the extension of credit, room selection, room rate application, opportunity to sell hotel services, room key assignment, and folio processing. Continually efficient performance of the registration process is essential to ensuring hospitality for all guests and profitability for the hotel.

Lalita is front office manager of the JP Hotels, Mussoorie. She has held the positions as front office agent, night auditor, night supervisor, relief night manager, night manager, and assistant day manager. Ms. Lalita says that the first contact any guest receives is Very critical to their overall stay. If a guest receives a warm reception from the beginning experience on the front drive, followed by a smooth and friendly check-in, more than likely the overall stay will be memorable and pleasant. The result of this encounter will be positive, free publicity from this guest and a loyal repeat customer.

She states that employee training in conflict resolution and customer service is important to ensure that the first guest contact experience is positive.

Feedback from guest is also an important part of providing quality guest services. Corporate guest surveys can yield information on specific areas as well as overall stay satisfaction. In-house guest surveys provide more immediate feedback from guests and highlight areas for improvement. Telephone surveys are sued to provide information on guest satisfaction.

Ms. Lalita feels that customer service issues are very critical to the overall business. Each person who checks in will tell two people who will also tell two people. One of the most important elements of a guest's stay is the service received in the first ten minutes of arrival.

Based on the above decide whether the following statements 'true' or 'false' :

(a) When the guest registers, only the front office deals with the registration process.

(b) The staff at the reception needs good training to offer impressive services at the first meeting.

(c) All the guest data was already recorded when the guest made the reservation.

(d) The hospitality for all guests and profitability for the hotel are guaranteed with the efficient registration process.

(e) The hotel needs to make surveys to get the feedback from the guests to ensure quality guest service.

5

Reservations

CHAPTER OBJECTIVES

After studying this lesson you should be able :

- To describe the different sources of reservation.
- To draw a Guest Reservation Form
- To understand the various terms related to reservation.
- To explain various methods of reservation.

The reservation section in the front office is a nerve centre for the of the department where all requests of reservations are received and processed. Request for reservations may come by various modes, such as:

1. Letters
2. Telex
3. Telegrams
4. Cables
5. Telephones
6. Person
7. Computer/internet.

Reservation

The reservation of rooms is done through various sources and the required information is retrieved at the appropriate time to ensure the availability of room to the guest at the time of their arrival. Most of the hotel bookings are done through reservations, and the walks in revelations are very few. For this purpose a skilful reservation assistant is required in the hotel. In large sized hotels, a reservation manager heads this section. It responds to request for a room reservation quickly, maintains records of all data regarding reservations, and reservation charts with dates of arrival and departure (including information on type of rooms, tariff and special requests). These are then forwarded to the front desk on the day of the guest arrival. This section also forecasts future occupancy statistics to help management in further planning.

Reception-front desk

The main functions of the reception in a hotel are:

1. Welcoming the guest
2. Register the guest after identification
3. Rooming the guest
4. Issuing a room key to the guest
5. Provide necessary information to the guest as and when required.
6. Maintain guest bill and settle their accounts.

This section is responsible for receiving the guest on his arrival, ascertaining status and confirming the details before assigning room to him. The reception staff also informs the guest about various facilities available in the hotel like parking, safe deposit, and other house rules and some times it has to cash the checks. The reception area is the front desk. Guests on arrival are greeted by receptionist and receive the first impression of the hotel, its staff and it service. The receptionist helps the guests to register and assigns them their rooms. Form 'C' is used for registration of the foreign guest. The work and preparation of this section starts early in the morning, when the employee of the eight hours shift on the registration desk report for duty.

Thus the registration of the guest and assigning him the appropriate room is the work of the reception. The staff receives and welcomes the guest. The issuing of the room key, controlling it during the time of guest stay and receiving them back is also the work of the reception. The key control is a vital activity because a room key lost means changing the lock. The main activity of the section is to complete registration formalities, like the billing information for the cashier to process during the guest stay and on his leaving the hotel. In small hotels the work of the receptionist gets widened, as he acts as constant source of information, mail and message. The front office assists in multi-task the reception, telephone operator, information assistant and cashiering. Once a guest is registered in the hotel, it is then the duty of the hotel to look after his safety and security. The act of registration also helps government in keeping track of foreign travelers during their stay in the country.

When answering positively a demand for reservation, always note clearly the following points:

1. Types of rooms
2. The name of the person
3. Number of persons
4. Arrival date
5. Departure date
6. The price of the room.

Confirmation

Never repeat the customer's expressions such as twin-bedded room and double-bedded room. This often causes a lot of trouble when the customer arrives. For example, in the guest opinion, the 'confirmed double bedded room' may have only one large room with two separate beds. Such confusion can easily be avoided when confirming only by saying 'one room for two persons' or 'double room'.

Overbooking

Many a times a hotel is completely booked out however a certain amount of 'overbooking' is accepted. These clients will receive a normal confirmation and have indeed a full valuable reservation. According to experience ascertain number of guests do not arrive (no show). It is, of course, not possible to established fixed rules, as this depend on the reason of booking and the profession of the client, e.g., a businessman, who reserved for a fair must probably will arrive, but a businessman, who reserved for a normal business visit may not arrive. The hotels accept over bookings in order to have the maximum number of guests possible to accommodate. A basic need for overbooking is a fixed arrival time.

Waiting List

When the hotel is booked out and the limit for acceptance overbooking is reached, you can only suggest to the clients to be put on a 'waiting list'. This means that his reservation will be confirmed in case there are rooms vacant. In all such cases the overbooking is to be taken into consideration first. When a client get 'wait listed', he usually will contact for reservation in some other hotels and will not inform you, when he gets a reservation there. Therefore, never hold a room for wait-listed reservations when you can sell it otherwise.

General Rules regarding Reservations

When confirming reservations, some basic rules should be observed:

1. Fix arrival time: For example, **'we will only hold the room until 6.00 pm unless a deposit of Rs.... is sent'.**
2. When a guest announces that he arrives late in the evening, ask for his estimated arrival time and hold the room only till one hour later. Without deposit this, of course, is only done for well-known customers.
3. When the guest intends to arrive at 6.00 pm or earlier and wants the room ready, inform him, that in this case he will have to pay for the preceding night also.
4. While dealing reservations for unknown guests, always ask for an advance deposit.

Written demands

When receiving a written demand, you must read it carefully and underline with thick color-pen the desired type of room, name, and number of persons, arrival and departure dates. Write on the right upper corner the arrival date and the first letter of the customer's name again. This helps the secretary in filing the letter.

The person incharge simply writes down on the letter 'Yes' or 'No' and hands it over to the secretary who writes to the customer.

Letters

When receiving letters, letters should answer them. Ordinary reservations can also be answered by filling in preprinted confirmation form. A letter always should accompany confirmations for larger parties.

Telex

Telex-written demands should be answered at once as long as you are still connected with the customer. As this answer is at the expense of the customer, it is an exigency of courtesy to only write the most necessarily and not to allow the telex operator to 'chat' with the counterpart. In case the customer has clearly stated what he wants, it is enough to write 'confirm the reservations' and give the automatic sign of the hotel.

A basic need for immediate confirmation is, of course, a schedule at the telex where all days, which are occupied, are crossed out. The operator then can see at once whether or not be can accept the demand for reservation.

Incase the customer has disconnected after having posting his demand; the confirmation should be given by ordinary letter, if there is enough time. As the minimum charge for the telex put through by INTELEX is at least three minutes, there is no sense at all to sell the room. The charge for the confirmation may be higher than the estimated earning out of the business. The further away the customer is located, the higher is the rate for the telex.

Telegrams

Confirmations for demand for reservations are usually given by telegram, when the customers have prepared the answer. As the charges for the telegrams are very high, the same procedure as mentioned for telex is too applicable. When the answer is not paid, the confirmations sent by ordinary letter if the delay until the customer arrives allow it.

Otherwise, of if no address as been given, no confirmation would be sent. Exceptions: even if the confirmation given by the telex or telegram is very expensive and often makes the business unprofitable, there might be some cases to do so. In case the customer is regular and good client, or it is in an interesting order for the party, the person is charge often will take the risk and answer by telex or telegram.

Phones

A great number of reservations are demanded for the confirmation at once at the phone. The employee must be enabled by a good and up-to-date forecast to know immediately whether or not he can confirm the reservation, In addition to the rules mentioned under general rules above you should never forget the following tips:

1. Ask for full and complete name of expected guest. If necessary, have it spelt.
2. Ask for full and complete name and address of the person or establishment who places the order.
3. Repeat arrival and departure dates.
4. When a gust wants a written confirmation, ask him to send you written demand FIRST.

5. When the customer says on the phone that the bill is to be charged to a company, immediately inform him that this only can be done after having received a written (letter or telex) confirmation by his company, that they will accept their bill.
6. Hen accepting or confirming a reservation request by phone, a special form should be filled in, where in all the above mentioned points, if applicable, are specified. This form is the handled and filled in confirmations are not usually sent. They are only valid and binding if they are based on a written demand.

Hotel.........................

GUEST RESERVATION FORM
(To be completed for confirmation of reservation)

Guest's Name:

Initials: ____________________ Title: ______________________________

Phone no. - work: ______________________

Phone no. - home: ______________________

Fax number: ______________________ Cell number: __________________

Postal address:

____

____

____

E-mail address: ____________________________________

Arrival date: __________________________ No. of nights: __________________

Departure date: ______________________ No. of guests: __________________

Estimated time of arrival: ____

Room description: Single Double

Special requests:

____

____

____

Method of Payment: ____

Credit card no.: ____

Expiry date: ____

Credit card type: ____

(Contd. ...)

Cardholder's signature: ______________________________

Date: ______________________________

Credit card holder: ______________________________

Last three digits at the back of the card: ______________________________

I confirm that I am the legal and rightful holder of the above-mentioned credit card and hereby authorize the (hotel name) to debi the above credit card account with a 50% deposit of the total accommodation cost indicated in this credit card authorization.

In the event of this reservation being cancelled less than seven days before my arrival date. I understand that hotel management will retain the 50% deposit. A further 50% will be debited to my credit card account if the reservation is cancelled less than 12 hours before my scheduled date of arrival.

Account
Instructions: ______________________________

Reservation made by: ______________________________

Date of confirmation: ______________________________

Company details:

______________________________ Account to:

Tick correct block: To be confirmed ☐ Confirmed ☐

Deposit details:

____

Please fax your confirmation and/or bank deposit slip to us at .... within 48 hours.

Thank you for your support.

Figure 5.1: Specimen Guest Reservation Form

Special instructions are recorded regarding billing, preference in rooms, additional requirements. Mentioned the name of person and organization who made the reservation

Mention also how reservation was made e.g.,

L- (letter), what date- 10.4, A (answered), 12-4 (on 12th April) by S. Sudershan.

Standard abbreviations may be used to show how reservation was made:

L	:	**Letter**
PHN	:	**Phone**
TEL	:	**TELEGRAM**
DEK	:	**OVER THE DESK**
UNCF	:	**Unconfirmed**
TELEX	:	**TELEX.**

Additional information may be added or on the reserve slip. In the later case, P.T.O. should be typed on the face of the slip in the lower right hand corner.

Multiple Reservations

When multiple reservations is made for two or more names, a cross reference will be typed as follows:

ANIL S. N. JAN 29

SEE ANIL SWRUP

The duplicate of the reservation slip is then stamped to the reservation request to show that it has been dealt with. The original is fixed on an aluminum carrier that is placed on the Reservation rack. The reservation request is then filed in the filing cabinet on the respective date.

All letters requesting accommodation must be answered promptly. The Reservation Forms and letters are filed in date order. Group reservations should be filled on top on the day of arrival.

The night receptionist in the racks provided on the reception desk places all reservations for the following day. The morning shift receptionist blocks out rooms by writing all necessary details on a small white card known as Blocking Slip and placing this into the Room Rack. At the same time, the number of the rooms blocked out must be entered no the Reservation Slip so that the receptionist receiving the guest bill know which room has been blocked. Reservation slips are mounted on a reservation rack-wise and in alphabetical order. They are then arranged under respective months, dates, alphabetically.

Group bookings are placed right on top of the section for any respective date.

These reservations are entered in the Room Reservation Status Chart indicate the number of rooms reserved for each date.

Advance Payments

There are two types of advance payments:

1. Advance payment received for a future reservation.
2. Advance payment received over the counter.
3. The advance payment received by cheque. The cheque is entered and recorded by the General Manager's secretary in it usual course. And sent to the front office manager which is credited to the customer's account on city ledger and also notations are made on eh advance reservation slip.

Record of Reservation

Depending the stage of the hotel we may use any of the following methods for recoding of reservations:

1. Register or Book System
2. Reservation Sheets
3. Whitney System (Slip System).

Register or Book system

Average sized hotel and city hotels mostly use this system. These books are maintained wherein all confirmed reservations are recorded. For each day one or more pages are reserved. The best method is use a ring book with interchangeable pages. In this case, only one or two books are needed, as additional pages can be added. Otherwise it would be necessary to reserve for each day the maximum space possible needed, which could result in the need of one book for each month. The handling of different books of course is not so easy as is the handling of one book only.

Each reservation letters even before their confirmation will be recorded at once. For this important work only one person per shift should be responsible.

The procedure to be followed is as under:

1. Take the appropriate page for the arrival date and fill in all statement needed.
2. Record the name and first name of the customer.
3. Record the number of persons.
4. Mention number and type of rooms enquired.
5. Record the rate, if confirmed.
6. Record the arrival time, if known.
7. Write the first letter of name, which is written on the demand for reservation. This helps to fasten the finding of correspondence when the guest arrives.
8. State the mode of reservation: letter, telex, phone etc.
9. Special remarks such as waiting list, not confirmed, etc.
10. Initial of the reservation assistant when using a ring book, this page can be taken out from the Arrival List (current reservations) of this day.

After recoding the above information, the letters are to be answered. All other proofs are filed immediately. Letters are filled together with a copy of confirmation when they are received back.

Reservation Sheets

This method is popular among the resort hotels. The method is applicable when letter makes major pat of reservation and the average duration of stay is several days. The system consists of a big sheet with small, about one cm. wide with vertical columns, numbered 1 to 31 and about one cm. high horizontal columns numbered accordingly to the room numbers. The size of the sheet depends on the number of rooms, and how many months (usually 3) are shown on one page. When working with this system, for each reservation the appropriate room is immediately specified and marked on the letter.

The names of the client is then entered on this sheet in the horizontal column on the room, starting in the appropriate column of the arrival date and marking the duration of stay with a line drawn to the appropriate vertical column for the departure date.

The advantage of this system is that you are always able to see which rooms are available during a special period. This is necessary because customers who intend to stay for longer period often ask for a very exact type of room and are not willing to change for example, second floor, overlooking the gardens, near the elevator etc.

The great disadvantage of this system is the difficult handling case of alterations. The disadvantage disqualified the system for hotel with a short average duration of sty like city hotels.

Whitney system

The Whitney Duplicating Check Company, New York, provides this system. Several firms have copied this system. Under this system Whitney Advance Reservation Rack consists of separate frames, which hold the carriers. The frames are mounted vertically on a wooden wall in manner, that they can be shifted to the left and to the right and also can be resolved very easily. The carriers can slide in the frame up and down, so that it is possible to insert a carrier between two others.

There are special guidance for the names of the months and the days 1 to 31. In practice, you will have only one set of month's carriers and two sets of day carriers.

For each reservation, instead of recording in a book, a special form is filled in. This form is then inserted in the frame. Then posting a reservation for the next two months, the carrier is inserted under the date of arrival in alphabetical order. Other reservations are inserted under the appropriate month carrier in numerical (day of arrival) and alphabetical order (with in day of arrival). If the frame is full and no more carrier s can be inserted, another frame can be installed. As this continues, at last all arrivals or the next day will be held by one or two frame only, in alphabetical order. These frames are then given to the reservation section, forming automatically without any further handling the current reservations for this day.

The advantage of this method is the easy handling and transparencies. As it is always up to date, it allows to know roughly with one glance is sold out. However a detailed forecast is needed.

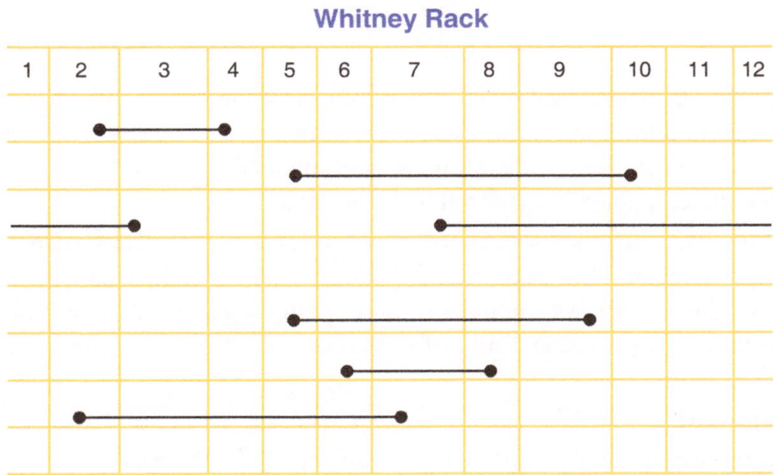

Figure 5.2. Specimen Whitney Rack

Whitney Rack

12								
Suite – 48								
~~48~~	~~47~~	~~46~~	~~45~~	~~44~~	~~43~~	~~42~~	~~41~~	
~~40~~	~~39~~	~~38~~	~~37~~	~~36~~	~~35~~	~~34~~	~~33~~	
~~32~~	~~31~~	~~30~~	~~29~~	~~28~~	27	26	25	
24	23	22	21	20	19	18	17	
16	15	14	13	12	11	10	9	
8	7	6	5	4	3	2	1	
–8	–7	–6	–5	–4	–3	–2	–1	
Standard double – 18								
~~18~~	~~17~~	~~16~~	~~15~~	~~14~~	~~13~~	~~12~~	11	10
9	8	7	6	5	4	3	2	1
–9	–8	–7	–6	–5	–4	–3	–2	–1

13								
Suite – 48								
~~48~~	~~47~~	~~46~~	~~45~~	44	43	42	41	
40	39	38	37	36	35	34	33	
32	31	30	29	28	27	26	25	
24	23	22	21	20	19	18	17	
16	15	14	13	12	11	10	9	
8	7	6	5	4	3	2	1	
–8	–7	–6	–5	–4	–3	–2	–1	
Standard double – 18								
~~18~~	~~17~~	~~16~~	15	14	13	12	11	10
9	8	7	6	5	4	3	2	1
–9	–8	–7	–6	–5	–4	–3	–2	–1

Figure 5.3. Specimen Whitney Rack

Room Racks

The most important tool when registering guest is the room rack. No matter which system is chosen and how the room rack is constructed, it should always show the state of the rooms. For example, if the room is occupied, blocked, vacant or assigned and whether or not the customer is expected to leave today.

The Whitney rack consists of one or two frames for each floor with printed room numbers. There is a slot for each room. Where the room slips can be inserted. The exposed part of the slip shows the guests name, plan, departure date and room rent. For further information, transparent flags of different colors can be inserted as explained under:

1. **Transparent Green Flag:**

   Room is assigned, but assignment can be changed if necessary
2. **Transparent Purple Flag:**

   Room is assigned to a VIP guest. Assignment cannot be changed.
3. **Transparent Red Flag:**

   VIP guest occupies room.

4. **Transparent Yellow Flag:**
   Light luggage.
5. **Non-transparent Red Flag:**
   Room is blocked (the reason may be specified on the flag, such as renovation etc.)
6. **Room Slip is folded into half:**
   The guest is expected to leave today.
7. **Room slip without ant transparent Flag:**
   Rom is occupied.
8. **No slip and no Flag in a slot:**
   Room is vacant and can be sold.
9. **Room slip is folded into half and inserted vertically:**
   Guest has paid and left, but room is not ready.

There may be additional flags in different colors and shapes to announce group or permanent reserved room for air companies etc.

Filing of correspondence

All advance reservations are to be filed according to the date of arrival. The best method is to use hanging files, where the letters are slipped in. The files are numbered from 1 to 31 representing the days of the month. It is possible to use only one set of those files. The correspondence is then put in to the files, without regard of the month. This facilitates that all reservations are looked through during the month. The correspondence of the current reservations should be given to the front desk, that it can be checked when the customer arrives. Billing instructions then are given directly to the billing section.

After the guest arrival the correspondence is filed alphabetically, month wise. Special files should be used for government booking, travel agencies, and groups. Cancelled reservations should be taken out of the files immediately and put in a specific file 'cancellations' in the alphabetical order.

Arrival List

In the evening list of expected arrivals for the next day is to be written. Special conditions (e.g.: AP, EP or MAP) are to be specified. Copies of this list are to be distributed to the following:

1. Housekeeping
2. All Restaurants
3. Restaurant cashier
4. Billing section and
5. Management, for information.

In a special paragraph of the arrival list all expected groups are to be mentioned. Writing VIP behind the name in the arrival list specifies expected VIP guests. The arrival list should be prepared in alphabetical order.

QUESTIONS AND DISCUSSIONS

Objective Type

Q.1. Choose the correct answer from the following questions :

(a) A unit that has been reserved for a specific arrival date, but not for specific guest:
   (i) Booked room (ii) Blocked room
   (iii) Advance reservation (iv) None of the above

(b) The refusal and subsequent placement of guest with a reservation at another hotel is called:
   (i) Bumped reservation (ii) Bounded reservation/walking the guest
   (iii) Cancellation (iv) Blocked room.

(c) A guest that comes to the hotel as a non-affiliated group member is known as:
   (i) Group incentive travel (ii) Company guest
   (iii) VIP (iv) Free independent traveller.

(d) A guest who makes a reservation and then neither cancels or registers with the hotel:
   (i) Turnways (ii) Walk-in
   (iii) No show (iv) None of the above

(e) A reservation that becomes void due to the guest's failure to register with the hotel at a time prior to the cancellation hour:
   (i) Cancellation (ii) Time cancelled reservation
   (iii) Bounced (iv) Bumped.

(f) The number of persons denied accommodation at the hotel:
   (i) No shows (ii) Turnways
   (iii) Over-booking (iv) Walking the guest.

(g) During the reservation process the following form (s) is / are normally generated:
   (i) Reservation form and confirmation notice
   (ii) Reservation log
   (iii) Cancellation record
   (iv) All of the above

(h) The document (s) normally generated during the registration process is (are):
   (i) Reservation card
   (ii) Room rack slip and information rack slip
   (iii) Bell captain's slip and room change slip
   (iv) All of the above.

(i) Two rooms in a hotel that have a common connecting door way:
   (i) Adjoining room (ii) Adjacent room
   (iii) Double room (iv) None of these

(j) An adjacent room that has an insided connecting doorways:
   (i) Adjoining room (ii) Double room
   (iii) Adjacent room (iv) None of the above.

[Ans.: (a)(ii) (b) (i) (c) (iv) (d) (i)
(e) (ii) (f) (ii) (g) (iv) (h) (iv)
(i) (ii) (j) (i)]

Q.2. Choose the correct answer from the following questions:

(a) Which is the odd one out. Please cross out:

(a) Hard Key (b) Plastic Key
(c) Magnetic Key (d) Computerised Key.

(b) The other word of Doorman / Carriage Attendant is —
....

(c) There are 9 copies of Arrival Notification Slip, distribution of which is as follows :
1 in Room Rack,
2 to G.M.'s office,
1 to F & B Manager's office,
1 to Telephone,
2 to Room Service,
2 to Housekeeping
How many copies are there ....
Give the correct distribution ....

(d) Single occupancy formula is

$$\frac{\text{HC} - \text{No. of rooms sold}}{\text{No. of room sold}} \times 100$$

Is the question correct ? Yes / No
Correct the question ....

(e) How is the Approximate Room Rate calculated ? Is the question correct? Yes/No.
If no, correct the question ....
Give the correct answer.

(f) SPA stands for Special Protection for Animals. Is the answer correct?
Give the correct answer.

(g) What is the difference between move central and Movement Slip?
Is the question correct? Yes / No
If no, correct the question ....

(h) There are 6 types of reservation system: Diary, American Express, Visa, Whitney, Computer.
How many types are there ....
Delete the incorrect ones.

[Ans.: a. Computerised Key;
b. (i) Commission (ii) Linkman;
c. 6, 1 Room service, 1 HK, 2 Telephone, 1 Room Rack, 1 Information Rack.
d. No, What is double occupancy percentage ?
e. No, How is the average room rate calculated ?
f. SPA is a resort hotel for health faddists.

g. No, What is the difference between movement control and movement slip?, The first is related to arrival and departure and the second with room charge.

h. Three, Diary, Whitney, Computer.

Short Answer Type

Q.3. Identify different front office systems.

Q.4. List different types of reservations.

Q.5. List different reservation reports

Q.6. Explain the importance of front office security and list the different areas of concern.

Q.7. Write notes on:

(a) Confirmation

(b) Overbooking

(c) Whitney system

(d) Reservation Sheet.

Q.8. Draw a Performa of a Reservation Form.

Q.9. Give examples of hotel departments within the back-of-the-house area.

Q.10. List the job titles for hotel employees who are assigned to back-of-the-house departments.

Q.11. Give examples of special rates and discuss their application in hotel operations.

Q.12. State the formula used to find percent of occupancy.

Q.13. Name the forms and charts, which aid front desk personnel in full-house management.

Q.14. Give examples of special rates and discuss their application in hotel operations.

Descriptive Type

Q.15. Describe the procedure used to determine the expected number of no-shows, cancellations, and stay-overs, and discusses their impact on the number of reservations, which may be accepted.

Q.16. Discuss hotel policies concerning guest negotiating room rates.

Q.17. Describe the factors that are considered when establishing the rack rate for specific rooms within a hotel.

Q.18. Describe the factors, which influence the percent of occupancy for a hotel operation.

Q.19. Apply a knowledge and understanding of reservation systems for processing guest reservations using appropriate industry examples

Q.20. Identify and explain some Front Office procedures that can be implemented to ensure customer satisfaction

Q.21. Communicate using precise industry and enterprise terminology providing a cohesive response

Q.22. Apply knowledge of reservation systems for processing guest reservations using possible industry examples.

Q.23. Outline some of the Front Office procedures that can be implemented to ensure customer satisfaction. Communicate using general industry terminology

Q.24. Explain the basic outline of reservation systems and/or Front Office procedures that can be implemented to ensure customer satisfaction. Make use of industry terminology.

Q.25. Describe manual reservations systems for hotel operations.

Q.26. Discuss the types of hotel operations that use manual reservation systems.

Q.27. Describe automated reservation systems for hotel operations.

Q.28. Discuss the types of hotel operations that use automated reservation systems.

Q.29. Compare and contrast the economic factors of manual andautomated reservations systems as used by various types of hotel operations.

Q.30. Describe the functions of a hotel central reservation office.

Q.31. Discuss the various routes to reserving a room that are available to potential guests.

Q.32. Discuss the classifications of individual guests identified by hotel reservation systems.

Q.33. Discuss front desk procedures for informing walk-in guests of room availability and room rates.

Q.34. Discuss front desk procedures for verifying reservations upon arrival of guests holding reservations.

Q.35. Describe the procedure a desk clerk uses to determine the number of over bookings.

Q.36. Discuss the practice known as walking the guest and describe a situation that called for its use.

Q.37. Give examples of questions guests typically ask desk clerks about room accommodations and hotel services.

Q.38. Discuss the procedures used to inform a guest of a full-house condition.

Q.39. Give examples of various hotel policies concerning an obligation to find alternative lodging when a potential guest arrives during a full-house

Assignments /Activity Type

Q.40. Demonstrate an understanding of Front Office reservations systems and procedures

Q.41. Demonstrate an in depth understanding of Front Office reservations systems and procedures

Q.42. Demonstrate a basic understanding of Front Office reservations systems and/or procedures.

Q.43. Demonstrate superficial understanding of Front Office reservations systems and/or procedures. Communicates using non-industry specific terms.

Q.44. Demonstrate the procedures a desk clerk uses to matchavailable hotel accommodations to guests' expectations.

Q.45. Demonstrate the desk clerk's techniques for informing guests of types/classes of rooms' available and applicable rates.

Q.46. Demonstrate the registration process including the key security issue.

Q.47. Demonstrate the procedures a desk clerk uses to match available hotelaccommodations to guests' expectations.

6

Reception And Registration of Guests

CHAPTER OBJECTIVES

After studying this lesson you should be able :

- To describe the guest registration procedure,
- To assign the rooms.
- To fill up the Registration card and 'C' Form
- To explain the methods of payments
- To descrete the arrival procedure
- To handle the mail
- To understand the paying system
- To prepare the Discrepancy Reports.

The title "receptionist" is attributed to the person who is specifically employed by an organization to receive or greet any visitors, traveller, patients, or clients and answer telephone calls. The title 'hotel receptionist' is attributed to the person who is specifically employed by a hotel to greet visitors. He or she is responsible for welcoming guests as they arrive in a hotel premises.

A receptionist is an employee taking an office/ administrative support position. The work is usually performed in a waiting area such as a lobby or front office desk of an organization or business.

Job Interview and Examination Questions

The hotel industry is currently one of the most promising and lucrative sectors in an economy. It is rapidly developing and adapting to the requirements of our modern lifestyle. Nowadays there are wide range of employment opportunities in this field.

On arrival of the Guest, the Reception Assistant brings out the Reservation Rack containing reservations for the day and places it on the Reception Desk. He checks each reservation for any special request or preference and deals with it prior to the arrival of the guest. If the request is for a suite or a particular room, enters the details in the card provided and blocks the accommodation accordingly. He enters the room number on the reservation slip for ready reference for the person who attends that guest on his arrival at the hotel. All V.I.P., and special request rooms must be blocked in advance.

Immediately on arrival, the guest requires help in carrying his luggage to the reception desk and then to his bedroom. It is in the reception that the guest is registered, assigned a room and given the keys. He obtains information, messages or lodges his complaints here. This is also the last point of contact for the departing guest, as he settles all his account here.

The reception of guest sand rooming should be as fast as possible, keeping in mind, that the client comes from a long journey and is tired. Because he is tired, he easily gets angry about delays in getting his room. When he is angry, his bad impression will remain and be adapted to the whole hotel.

Guest Registration Procedures

1. Receive the guest with a smile, and wish according to the time.
2. Check if she/he is holding reservation.
3. If there is reservation there is no problem, otherwise check for availability of room.
4. Get the Guest Registration Card (GRC) and fill it up.
5. Fill up the Key and Welcome Card.
6. If the guest is a foreigner, get the C - Form and fill it up.
7. Allot the accommodation.
8. Fill the Arrival Register.
9. Make in the Information Slips and send them to telephone, room service, and housekeeping (if the hotel has PMS then not required).
10. Open Guest Folio.
11. Incase of VIPs, CIPs etc., inform all departments.
12. Lastly inform the Bellboy to carry the luggage and escort the guest to the room and wish a comfortable stay in the hotel.

Registration begins when Front Desk Assistant extends the sincere welcome to the guest.

Guest registration procedure

A warm greeting sets the tone for every thing that follows. Front Desk Assistant moves to the registration process after determining the guest's reservation status. To a great degree registration relies on the information contained in a reservation record. Front office personnel will finds registration simpler and smoother when accurate and completed information has been captured during the reservation process.

The registration process can be divided into six steps:

Step 1. Pre-registration activity

Step 2. Creating the registration record

Step 3. Assign the room and the rate

Step 4. Establishing method of payment

Step 5. Issuing the room key

Step 6. Filling the special requests.

Pre-registration Activities

Through the registration process, a guest provides nearly all the information needed to complete registration. In other words, guest who makes reservation will likely expect a more rapid check in. Pre- registration activities (registration that occurs before the guest arrives at the hotel) accelerate the registration process. Typically pre-registration guests' only need to be verifying information collected by the reservation assistant during reservation process. Typically pre-registered guest only need to verify information entered on to a Reservation Card and provide a valid signature in the appropriate place on the Registration Card.

Pre-registration involves room and rate assignment and creation of Guest Folio apart from producing Registration Card. However, some hotels are reluctant to do room assignment, if there are some last minutes cancellations then they may create an imbalance in the status for vacant rooms. Pre-registration tasks are done in non-automatic and semi- automatic Front Office System also. But in many such hotels the pre-registration services may be limited to specially designated, VIPs and groups.

Pre-registration helps plan for special requirement of guests as well as of the hotel. For example, frequent guests may have special requests. And guest with disability may need room out-fitted to their special needs. By pre-registering these guests, the Front Desk Assistant can be sure to satisfy them. In addition, pre-registration helps managers when they know that the hotel will be full occupancy in the next several days.

At the semi and fully automated systems, guests with reservations (*i.e.* expected arrivals) experience a more rapid check-in due to the information collected by reservation clerks during the reservation process. However, at the manual system, it is inconvenient to pre-register guests with the exception of VIPs and groups. For, VIPs, even under the manual system, needed to feel different than other guests. Moreover, group reservations, even though time consuming, might create time benefits at the arrival stage. Lastly, whatsoever operating system the hotel opts for, all walk-ins shall be registered at the arrival stage of the guest cycle.

The Registration Records

After a guest arrives at the hotel, the Front Office Desk Assistant creates a Registration record, a collection of important guest information. Registration Card facilities the registration process and the require guests to provide his/her names, address, telephone number, company affiliated and other personal data. The registration card usually contains a space for guest signature. Generally, this is a legal pre-requisite to establish guest's relation with the hotel. In automated hotel, the Registration Card can be pr-printed wherein the guests can verify and then sign. At the time of check in, the Front Desk Assistant need to reconfirm the pre-assigned rate and the planned departure date. The registration Card is either filed in the room rack or attached with the Guest Folio.

In an automated system the details will automatically get communicated to the required departments herein otherwise it need to be passed on so that the guest is able to do credit purchases against the room count.

At check out, the information captured on the Registration Card may be used as the primary source for creating a Guest History record. This record may then become part of the data base to be used in the future by the hotel's sales and marketing efforts. The information contained in a guest history database can be analyzed to assist management in developing market strategies, marketing lists and detailed reports.

The registration record is a collection of important personal and financial guest information. A typical registration record includes:

(a) Guest name and surname
(b) Guest address and telephone number
(c) Company affiliation (if applicable)
(d) Expected arrival date
(e) Planned departure date or length of stay
(f) Required room rate
(g) Required room type
(h) Room number
(i) Method of payment
(j) Special requests
(k) Signature.

A Guest checking in at the hotel reception desk

In the semi and fully automated systems, most of the registration activities are handled at the pre-arrival stage while in the manual system they are conducted at the arrival stage. Registration encompasses the following major activities:

1. Creating the registration record
2. Assigning the room & rate
3. Fulfilling special requests.

Assignment of Rooms

Assignment of rooms means to distribute the rooms to the confirmed reservations. This important work has to be done in the morning by the chief receptionist.

Before starting to assign the rooms the room rack must be looked through. All room slips of guests expected to leave today are folded and put back in to the rack.

In the meantime the assistant looks through the guest file and takes out the guest history cards of all guests who have been in the hotel before and expected to arrive today. He sticks those cards to the correspondence and hands it over to the chief-receptionist.

HOTEL HARSHIL HEALTH RESORT
Uttranchal, India

REGISTRATION CARD

Number ....
Date ....
Time ....

Name of the Guest ....
Address (permanent)
....
....
Telephone Number ....
Arrived from .... Proceed to ....
Date of Birth ....

For Foreigners only	**For Office use**
Passport Number	Date and time of arrival ....
Date of Issue	Expected date of departure ....
Place of Issue	Time of departure ....
Valid up to	Type of accommodation ....
Type of Visa	No. of Pax ....
Date of Issue	Room No. .... Rate..............
Proposed duration of stay in India	Plan .... Booked by .... Billing instructions:
Registration Number if any	....
Date of registration	....
Valid up to	....
Whether employed in India....	Special remarks ....
	Advance if any ....
	Date of advance ....
	Receipt No. ....

The management does not take responsibility for the loss of guest valuable.

Lockers are available.

I take he gone through the terms and conditions fo stay in the hotel and I agreed to abide by the same.

....

Receptionist Signature Guest Signature

Fig. 6.1. Specimen Guest Registration Form

The chief-receptionist goes through the reservation list (typed list, frames with carriers or detached sheets of reservation diary, accepting the system) and assigns appropriate rooms. First to the VIP guests and then to the others. Whilst assigning the, the chief receptionist pays attention to the wishes of the client expressed in their letter or recorded on the guest history cards. A transparent green or purple flag is slipped in to the slot of the room racks to show that this room is assigned and then corresponding room number is written on the current reservations record. Incase there are rooms left where the room slip is folded, but no transparent flag is inserted, they can be sold to 'walk-ins'.

As the name suggests, the registration is done on the card form. Normally three copies are made with carbon papers/ the original copy along with the C- Form is send to the police department, second copy is for the hotel's records and then the third one is kept along with the Guest Folio. But many times C- form is a separate document.

Guest Arrival Report (C-Form)

Under the rules C-form is to be filled up for all foreign residents of the hotel. The purpose of C-Form is to furnish certain information to the police department to check to the movements of foreign nationals visiting country. The C- form has to be filled in duplicate for all individuals including the husband, wife and all the chidden. Naturally passport numbers, date and place of issued, purpose of visit, address, duration of stay are all main details found in the C-Form (Ref. Fig. 6.2).

HOTEL ....

HOTEL ARRIVAL REPORT
(Form-C)
(To be completed in duplicate)

1. Name of hotel. ....
2. Full name of foreigner visitor (in block capitals, surname first.)
   ....
3. Nationality. ....
4. Number, date and place of issue of passport ....
5. Address in India.
   ....
   ....
   ....
6. Date of arrival in India. ....
7. Arrived from. ....
8. Whether employed in India - yes/No.
9. Proposed duration of stay in India. ....
10. Number, date and office of issue of Passport/ Certificate of Registration, if any.
    ....
    ....

....
(Manager's signature)

Fig. 6.2. Format of a C-FORM

When a group is staying only one C- Form is made for the whole group. The Group Rooming List, which consist of all group members' names along with their nationality, passport number, date and place of issue are printed. The group rooming list along with the C- form prepared for the group is sent to the police department. C- Form have to be sent to the police department within 24-hours of arrival of the guest.

Guest registration information items flow to different areas and functions of the hotel as given in Figure: 6.3.

Fig. 6.3. Flow chart showing flow of guest registration information

Room and Rate Assignment

The hotel shall identify and allocate an available room from a specific required room category (*i.e.* type & rate). That's why, under semi and fully automated systems, reservation and check-in clerks shall be sales minded while negotiating room and rate assignment with guests. This fact applies for registration clerks under the manual system. Moreover, while assigning rooms, check-in clerks shall keep an eye on hotel's future reservation commitments and not assign a room to a guest, while that very room is pre-assigned to some other guests at the same period of time.

Room rates

While pricing rooms, the hotel shall keep in mind that rate should be between a minimum (determined by cost structure) and a maximum (determined by competition structure) boundary as depicted below:

1. Minimum (Hurdle Rate): Room Rate: Maximum (Rack Rate)
2. Cost Structure: Room Rate: Competition Structure

Front office department shall finalize room rates with guests during the registration process. Moreover, rack rates shall only be applicable for walk-ins especially during the high season. Lastly, room rates might be affected by:

1. Seasonality
2. Variations in the number of guests assigned to rooms
3. Service level
4. Room location
5. Type of Guest and/or usage (ex. commercial, corporate, complementary, group, family, day, and package-plan)

Room status

1. At registration, check-in clerks shall contact the housekeeping department to be informed about the last status of hotel rooms so that they can assign only clean and available for salerooms to their guests. That's why; the Front office, Housekeeping and Reservation department shall maintain a high degree of collaboration between them.

2. The front office and housekeeping department shall continuously update the status of each single room. Below is the typical housekeeping room status flow of any single room:

   Occupied → On-change → Clean and Available for Sale.
3. The front office and housekeeping department shall frequently reconcile and compare their updated reports (especially under the manual system) for any possible room status Discrepancy. The aim is to detect these very discrepancies before it's financially and timely too late and correct them.
4. Room characteristics: In order to be sales minded and convince potential guests to accept the highest priced rooms, the front office clerk shall be aware of the characteristics of each room type, the differences within the same room category (*i.e.* furnishings, amenities, and location...).

Methods of Payment

Guests, at the registration stage, shall communicate or confirm their intended method of payment. Hotels accept some of the common methods of payments as given below:

1. Cash

Guests intending to settle their accounts by cash shall have no in-house charge privileges and, hence, all their purchases should be paid in advance (i.e. PIA status), which means that as guests purchase any kind of service or product, they shall pay for it immediately. In accordance to cash payment, registration clerks shall prepare lists of PIA guests and communicate them to all Point of Sales outlets. On the other hand, paying immediately might not suit some guests (even though intending to settle their accounts by cash), that's why hotels might give guest charge privileges, at the condition they provide an imprint of a valid card or an approved direct billing privilege at registration.

While handling cash payments, all cashiers shall be aware of counter-feats and short cash change situations! Moreover, cashiers shall be trained as to accept so many cash equivalent tools that are legally accepted as cash payment such as cashier checks, traveler checks, and money orders...

2. Personal checks

Nowadays, very few hotels still accept personal checks as a method of payment due to the high probability of fraud associated with this method. In fact, in order to accept personal checks, most hotels necessitates that these very checks be supported by a credit card with a check-cashing guarantee, that the amount to be cashed against checks shall be within the hotel's established limit, and preferably accept personal checks only during standard business hours where banks are open. If personal checks are to be accepted, front office personnel shall imprint the credit card on the backside of the guest personal check and record the Guest ID card or driving license certificate along with the guest's address and telephone number on the face of the check.

3. Credit cards

Credit cards, nowadays, become a preferable method of payment for guests and hotels. In accordance to this very method of payment, front office clerks should check the following items before accepting the credit card as a method of payment:

(a) Expiration Date

(b) Invalid Credit Card: This can be checked either by on-line authorization systems, or comparing the card across some cancellation bulletins.

(c) Credit card floor limit.

4. Direct billing

Some guests (especially VIP) do not prefer to wait at checkout queues like other guests before departure. They, rather, prefer only to sign their guest folios, go to their homes, and later receive a certain invoice detailing their charges while they were staying at the hotel to be settled by payment to hotel bank accounts. In order to satisfy the needs of this category of guests, hotels created the direct billing process.

To be eligible for a direct billing privilege, guests shall at pre-arrival stage or maximum at the arrival stage fill a hotel credit application form along with the provision of an imprint of a valid credit card. This very form is sent to the Front Office Manager, or Rooms Division Manager for approval. If not approved, guests are requested to pay with any of the other methods of payments.

Special Programs

Special programs are any form of vouchers, coupons, or any special incentive awards received from businesses, airline companies etc.

Issuing Room Keys

With the issuing of room keys, the rooming process gets to an end. However, concerning room keys, front office clerks shall respect hotel's written policies governing guestroom key control. As an illustration, front desk agents shall only handle the room and key to the guest without announcing and/or spelling out the room number. This is a vital requirement to protect and ensure guest safety and privacy.

After guest is handed his/her room key, front office clerks shall offer bellboy assistance.

Fulfilling Special Requests

1. The Front Office department shall watch for any guest special requests and try promptly to satisfy them. This may creates a good and professional relationship with the guests and increases the probability that the hotel will receive these guests for another time in the future (*i.e.* repeat guests).
2. Guests' requests are usually grouped under the following categories:
   (a) Room type
   (b) Bed type
   (c) Location

(d) View

(e) Amenities.

Creative Options

Some of the following innovations are nowadays commonly used while registering a guest:

1. Eliminating the front desk structure (*i.e.* deskless environment).
2. Having a hotel greeter register guests at a special lobby location.
3. Creating a unique and separate registration area for VIP guests.
4. Simplification of room process for corporate gatherings, tour, and convention groups.
5. Self-registration (*i.e.* self check-in terminals).

When a guest arrives, greet him and ask, if you can help him. Usually he will say: **'I am Mr..........., you are holding a reservation for me'**, or similar. If he only says that he wants a room, ask him whether or not he has a reservation. In case he has not, he is treated as a **'walk in'**.

Present the registration form to the guest and ask him politely to fill in. Help him when he does so. Be patient when the guest especially foreign guest gets angry at the sight of all questions he has to answer on this from. Check the form if all statements are filled in. It is most important for the hotel to know the client's home address in order to send mail, lost property or charges not figuring on his bill and that have arrived after his departure only.

On arrival the following procedures are worth following:

1. The guest completes the registration card that must be carefully checked for address and name (surname first) by the receptionist. When a lady signs in and does not mention Miss or Mrs., you have to clarify it and write it accordingly on the card. It is imperative that each guest must be asked to confirm the exact length of stay while he is still at the desk, in order to avoid any possible difficulties, which might arise later regarding the date of his departure.
2. Make sure that all details pertaining to the passport are filled out in the Registration Card.
3. During the busy seasons ask the guest if he has a reservation before having him fill the Registration Card. When the hotel has room available, the Registration Card is placed before the guest so that they type faces the guest. Read the guest name before he has finished filling in the card, so you will not have to ask him if he has reservations. If he has done, the slip is taken out of the rack and room assignment is made. If there is no reservation, the assistant has the opportunity to affect a room sale by offering a suite of a higher priced room.
4. The assistant should make sure that all the particulars of the registration card are filled in, especially those required by the government. An entry is then made in the Arrival/ Departure Register.

5. Make a Temporary Arrival Slip wherein you may enter the room number in upper left hand corner and the name in the middle of the first line of the slip. This slip contains 5 copies, the first of which is placed in the slot corresponding to the room number allotted to the guest. The others are distributed after the guest leaves.

The distribution of these slips is done as follows:

(a) Information rack
(b) Room Service
(c) Telephone department.

These slips will be replaced by permanent Arrival Slips and distributed in the same way as the distribution of Temporary Arrival slips as explained above.

The above procedure is carried out only after the guest has been attended to at the desk and he leaves the desk.

6. The Lobby Attendant Errand Card is filled in with room number and the guest name. Receptionist should assign and put the date on the errand card. The Lobby attendant is summoned, informed of the room number and handed over the Lobby Attendant card along with the room key. When there is a crowed at the Reception Desk, the guest must be pointed out to the lobby attendant discretely.
7. Every guest is given a Guest Welcome Card on check-in. Fill this card with the room number, date and rate charged, hand this card over to the guest. This Welcome Card contains some information regarding the hotel facilities, which may be helpful to the guest. All these procedures must be so quick that the guest is not kept 'Waiting' at the desk after if there is any mention of any mail or message on the Reservation Slip and dispense accordingly.
8. All V.I.P. arrivals are to be conducted to the room by the Lobby Manager on duty.
9. Any person joining a registered guest (except Mr. & Mrs.) is asked if the room rate is to be divided equally or the joining guest pays the difference. Also the assistant should inquire from the occupant of a double accommodation (other than Mr. & Mrs.) whether they desire the room rate divided equally. If not, which of the two will be charged the full rate. In this case, no room rate is indicated in the other card.

Scanty Baggage Check (SB)

In case of guest without baggage/ scanty baggage who walk in the hotel following registration procedure may be followed:

1. No walk in is to be taken in the hotel without consultation of Lobby Manager if Front Office Manager is not available to avoid any suspicious person check-in. Whenever an 'SB' check in takes place, the handling bell boy will inform the front office assistant with a signal that the guest checking has no baggage. When the front office assistant is aware that a scanty baggage is checking in he will let the guest fill in the registration card completely. Then check as how the guest is setting his bill.

2. If it is noticed that he is setting his bill with a credit card discretely ask him to show you the card and get the slip signed. Following procedure may be followed:
   (a) Check it and see if it is acceptable in your hotel.
   (b) Check the expiry date in the card and not the number and expiry date on the Registration card.
   (c) Most credit cards have the holder's specimen signature on the card. Check the signature with the signature on the Registration Card.
   (d) Have a blank charge from signed by the guest if he is a walk in.
3. If the reservation for the guest has been made by a reputed or known organization then make a note of the credit card number and the date of expiry (mentioning the credit card number and eh date of expiry (mentioning the credit card issuing company). On the Registration Card correctly.
4. If is found that the guest is settling the bill through a travel agent ask him if he has s a voucher from the travel agent. The voucher you should check thoroughly and see that the period of stay incorporated on the voucher coincides with the period of stay the guest has mentioned on registration card, also check the plan (AP, MAP or EP). Ask him you could keep the hotel's copy of the voucher with you. Attach this copy to the Registration Card.
5. If on cash payment, advance of three nights has to be taken. Other services on cash basis only.
6. If the guest is settling his bill in cash on travelers' cheque, excuse yourself for a minute and call the Lobby Manger and explain the situation without the guest knowing what is happening. One thing must be noted that the guest should never feel offended and you should do it very discretely.
7. Now it is Lobby Manager who will check and see whether any credit can be given to the guest or not, it's a normal procedure to ask guest for a deposit which would normally cover his entire stay (room and meals etc).

The above procedures are to be followed very strictly in order to save the hotel from bad debts.

After the Guest has registered

As soon as the guest registration is complete following procedure may be followed:

1. The assistant would make four carbon copies of the Temporary Arrival Sip, showing the guest ' name, room number and the rate of the room. These copies would be sent as under:
   (a) One copy to the Telephone Department
   (b) One copy be placed on the Room Rack
   (c) One copy is sent to the Room service, and
   (d) The fourth copy is placed in the Information Rack.

   Temporary Arrival Slips must be immediately distributed. Under no circumstances they are to be kept in the front desk for any length of time. These are to be written legibly and in the proper sequence.

2. Enter the details in the Arrival /Departure Register.
3. The Reservation Slip is then stamped to the left hand top corner on the front of the Registration Card.
4. The Registration Card is then passed to the Reservation Assistant to type the Arrival Slips, and the registration card number should also be typed on the Guest Folio. Five copies of the Arrival slips are required for purpose of:
   (a) Room rack
   (b) Telephone Exchange
   (c) Information
   (d) Room Service.
5. The Registration Card and Folio goes to the Lobby Manager for signing and then to the Front Office cashier and Arrival Slips are distributed as stated in Item No. 4 above.

HOTEL ....

Arrival Slips

551 ANIL MRS TARUN	1/400	11/12
NATIONALITY ADDRESS	Plan	1/12
Re. Murcury Travels, New Delhi		KU/KP
Reason for discount (if any)..		
Registration Card Number:		

Fig. 6.4. Specimen Arrival Slip

The Arrival Slip contains the following information:

1. Top Line:
   (a) Room Number
   (b) Name (last name first)
   (c) Number of person Rate Departure date
2. Second line:
   (a) Nationality
   (b) Address
   (c) Plan
   (d) Date of arrival
3. Third line:
   (a) Reservation made by initials of the person who takes the check in and also the person who typed the folio
4. Last line:
   (a) Reason for discount, if any, and
   (b) Bill Number.

When two or more people are sharing a room, sharing with "X" should be on the card and folio of "Y" and vice versa and two separate slips should be made and placed together in the Rom Rack and separately in the Information Rack alphabetically.

Arrival procedure

Lobby:

The bellboy escorts guests from the main door with their luggage to the front office. After the guest has been registered the front office informs the bellboy of the room number so that the guest may be escorted to his room and his luggage placed in the room.

Step 1: When a guest arrives, the doorman buzzes the Bell Captain Desk for a bell Boy.

Step 2: The bellboy should wish the guest and collect his baggage and bring it into the lobby via the baggage entrance and place baggage at the bell desk that is located normally opposite the Reception counter. The bellboy should wait for the guest to register at the front office. If the hotel has tags to identify baggage these should be attached to the baggage. Inform scanty baggage to the lobby manager or front office.

Step 3: The Information counter at the front office will indicate that the guest has been allotted a room by handing over the errand card that mentions the room number. The room key is also handed over with the errand card. Bring to the guest's attention any baggage damaged to protect the hotel from blame.

HOTEL ....
Guest Arrival Errand Card

Bell Boy No. .... Date ....
Room No. .... Name ....

Suit Case	Brief Case	Hand Bag	Packets	Others

Remarks:

Bell Boy Sig. Capt's Sig.

Fig. 6.5. Guest Arrival Errand Card

Step 4: Lead the guest to his room along with his baggage. Some hotels have separate baggage elevators.

Step 5: The bellboy should open the door of the guestroom and let the guest enter first. After positioning the baggage at the allotted rack in the room, the guest must be told where the floor-lights are located, channel music, air-conditioning/central heating thermostat control, internal locking system, etc. are located.

Step 6: Offer any other help and if not required, wish the guest a pleasant stay. Do not solicit for tips.

Step 7: Report back to the bell desk.

Note: *A hotel may have different coloured errand cards for arrival and departure of guests.*

The Bell Captain, one of his primary functions is to control bellboys. This control is necessary as bell boys are subject to many errands that take them to all corners of the hotel and even outside. To be able to optimize the productivity of the team within a given shift the Lobby Control Sheet is constituted. The purpose of this sheet is to keep a record of and check on the movement of bellboys.

The control sheet above is sell-explanatory. The bellboys are given code numbers to easily record their activities. Alternatively, the bellboy's names may be also used. For an arrival, the room number is filled in after the front office has intimated the same. The "room changed to" column would indicate the number of the new room a guest has been allotted. His old room number is mentioned in the first column. Through this sheet the workload per bellboy is ascertained and the bell captain is able to distribute workload uniformly. He gets a chance to find out who the lethargic members of the team are through the time control. Of course, the bellboy should know in advance a reasonable time that an errand would take to fill his remarks in the last column.

HOTEL ....

Lobby Control Sheet

Captain.. Sheet No. ....

Date ....198.................. Shift - from.................................... To ....

Room No.	Attendant No.	Arr	Dep.	Room	Service Change To	Call	Time		Comments
							From	To	

Fig. 6.6. Specimen Lobby Control Sheet

Services and duties during the stay of the Guests Changing of Room

There are several reasons that a guest changes his room, such as

1. He expressed the wish to do so, as he is not satisfied with the room he occupies.
2. When the customer arrives, appropriate accommodation was not available. To not loose the customer, the front office promised to move him to a better room the next day.
3. Installations in the room fell out of order and cannot be repaired immediately.

4. A customer wants to prolong his stay, but the room is needed for a VIP guest. The customer is asked to change the room.

The Procedure

After the customer had agreed to be changed, the housekeeping department is informed to get the new room ready. When the room is ready, the housekeeping department helps the customer to move over to the new room. In case the customer wants it, the housekeeping can do this without the customer being present, but under the supervision of a housekeeper.

When guest changes room, a bellboy is sent with a change slip, together with the key. After completing the room change the bell boy gets the Room Change Slip asigned by the Telephone Exchange, Room Service, Laundry, Housekeeping, the Front Office Cashier so that all these department are informed about the room change and they take necessary action.

Immediately after changing, the front office is to be informed, who distributes this information immediately tot eh phone operator and the billing section. Room rack, information rack and guest file are to be adjusted. The change had to be recorded in the arrival and departure book.

Guest Mail and Information

The concierge section of the front office is responsible for the mail arriving for the guests. This mail is put into the guests' pigeonholes. If the guest is yet to arrive these are put in to an ABC Box. For special mail special records are maintained in a separate register.

Business people working together at table

Arriving Mail

All incoming mails are first divided in to three main categories:

1. Hotel Mail; **2. Staff Mail;** **3. Guests' Mail**

1. Hotel Mail: Usually given to the manager's office and sent from there to the respective departments to be dealt with.
2. Staff Mail: This may be directed to and distributed by the staff office, a staff housekeeper or some other person appointed for the purpose.
3. Guest Mail: In this case there are three possibilities which will affect the manner in which the mail is handled:
   (a) The guest stays in the hotel
   (b) The guest has left, and
   (c) The guest is yet to arrive.

Mail for Resident Guests

Whilst the mail and information sections do not produce revenue it performs a very important service for the guest. It is here that the mail, messages and enquiries are handled. Therefore, the of information rack must be kept as under:

1. The rack should be maintained in alphabetical order.
2. Up to the minute with temporary slips.
3. Message slips left by guest at information counter giving his where about for a specified time, where he can be located. The Front Office Information Assistant should inform the Telephone Exchange. The Telephone Operator number to be noted on the slip, this is to be countersigned by the receptionist receiving the message.

The assistant who is in charge of the mail goes through the mail with the aid of the information rack (alphabetical index) to ascertain whether the guest is resident and if so, to write down the room number in pencil on the mail. The individual pieces are then placed in the key and mail rack. The mail that is not disposed of in this way should, therefore, be that of a past or future guests. On this mail the date of the delivery must be stamped. (As a matter of principle, this stamping is very often is done for all incoming mail).

Mail for Past Guests

The assistant then goes through the remaining mail with the aid of the Mail Forwarding Card indeed. In this index all, cards on which guests gave their forwarding address. On the reverse side of the forwarding card notice can be give about the type, number and date of mail forwarded. On the forwarding card an expiry the guest writes date. The index must be looked through regularly send the expired cards can be taken out. They are then stored for a period of 6 to 12months before they are destroyed.

Mail for future Guests

After scrutiny the mail for the past guests only the mail for future guests is left. This mail is stored alphabetically. Every day the clerk must go through it with the aid of the list of the expected arrivals of the day. Appropriate notice of waiting mail is given on the reservation record (current reservations). Incase any mail stored for future guests is not delivered with in 10 days of delivery to the hotel; it is handed over to the front office manager who will decide further handling. If the mail will be forwarded to the address given on the Guest **History Card** (last known address) or returned to the sender. The same is applicable when the time limit of the forwarding address has expired.

The advance reservations have to be checked whether or not the hotel is holding a reservation for his customer.

Registered Mail, Telex, Telegrams, Parcels

For all kinds of special mail a list must be kept in which the name of the receiver and the kind of mail is recorded. The guest is asked to assign in this list when the mail is handed over to him.

Guest Mail to Be Posted

A customer may give mail to the front office to be posted. For this purpose a good, precise letter-balance as well as charge schedules are necessary in order to avoid under- and over charges of postage. This schedule should be visible to the customer. On all letters handed over by guests to be mailed the stamps have to be stuck in the guest's presence.

A list for registered outgoing letters and outgoing parcels should be kept. The customer is requested to sign here when the receipt is handed over to him.

Message Handling

All messages whether over the phone or given in person are taken in duplicate. One copy (duplicate) is kept in the guest key hotel on the key rack and one copy (original) is sent to the guest through the message register. The bellboy, who takes the message, enters in the message register and then slips the message under the door of the guest.

Rates, size and location of accommodation and the carrying out the service form the basis for most complaints brought to the front desk. Listen very attentively to the guest, don't interrupt him. When he is right, do your utmost to adjust the grievance he reported.

Never blame other department or employees. In case it really is the fault of another employee, say to the client that you will enquire about it in order to avoid ' such things' in future.

All complaints must be reported to the front office manager. Serious complaints should be reported in writing to the manger.

When the complaint is not justified, explain the fact to the guest, but do not argue and do not insist that you are right. You win the argument, but lose the customer.

Paging System

In most hotels, a guest wishing to check out of the hotel calls the bell desk for a porter to carry his luggage down. The bell desk informs the front office of the intentions of the guest so that the cashier can prepare his bill. It is only after the front office is satisfied regarding the payment of bills and retrieval of room key will they allow the bellboy to remove the luggage outside the premise of the hotel.

Often, a guest requests the front office for a change of room. The front office intimates the bell desk to send bellboys to help in the shifting of luggage.

"Skippers" are those guests who leave the hotel without paying their bills. This is made possible because the "skipper" comes with little luggage to avoid bringing the attention of the bellboys to his "secret" check out. Alternatively, if he has just a briefcase, he may leave the hotel under the pretext of a business call. The bellboys have to be alert to notify the front office about guests with scanty baggage so that a necessary advance is taken from them and a close watch is kept on them.

The information section of front office alerts the bellboys to deliver messages received by them for guests in the hotel.

"Paging" is the system of displaying the name of a guest on a small board with a long handle. The board is held above the head of the bellboy and has small bells that are rung to draw the attention of customers to the board.

When a phone call is received for a guest in a specified location, this paging system is used to contact guests. The bellboy does the paging in most public areas especially the lobby.

To keep a tight control on rooms, the housekeeping and front office have to closely coordinate. One way is through the room report whereby the housekeeping staff checks each room on every floor and advises their status through a report.

Discrepancy Report

The front desk on receiving the Room Report from the Housekeeping prepares a discrepancy report. The front office compares it with the Room Rack for reconciliation of room status. Discrepancies noticed between room rack and housekeeping room report are noted down on a separate report called the "discrepancy report" which is then handed over to a bell boy for physical check and reporting back of the room under discrepancy. After a physical check of the room the bellboy notes down the correct status that is accepted by the front office and room rack and reconciled accordingly.

HOTEL ....

DISCREPENCY REPORT

Room	Per Room Asstt.	Per House Keeper	Investigation Remarks
			Asstt. Manager

Fig. 6.7. Specimen Discrepancy Report

QUESTIONS & ASSIGNMENTS

Objective Type

Q.1. Number the following steps in the correct order :

(a) Guest registration procedures.
(b) Front desk clerk assigns room rate.
(c) Front desk clerk discusses sales opportunities for hotel products and services with guest.
(d) Front desk clerk makes room selection.
(e) Front desk clerk processes folio.
(f) Front desk clerk provides room key.
(g) Front desk clerk inquiries about guest reservation.
(h) Front desk clerk makes room assignment.
(i) Front desk clerk projects hospitality toward the guest.
(j) Front desk clerk reviews completeness of registration card.
(k) Front desk clerk verifies credit.
(l) Guest completes registration card.
(m) Guest requests to check into the hotel.

Q.2. Fill in the Blanks

(i) How do you calculate full house count ? Yes / No.
Is the question correct. ....
If no, correct the question ....
Give the correct answer ....

(ii) The following are the Credit Cards. Cross out the incorrect ones.

(a) Morgan Stanley (b) Mckenzie
(c) Visa (d) Master Card
(e) Bob Card (f) Diners.

(iii) Calculate double guest per room.
Is the question correct?
If no, correct the question ....
Give the correct answer ....

(iv) How do you calculate 100% room occupancy?
Is the question correct. Yes / No
If no, correct the question ....
Give the correct answer..................

(v) Free phone stands for ....

(vi) What is paging?
....

(vii) A telex machine consists of cross out the incorrect ones.

(a) Key board (b) Display
(c) Line Box (d) Printer

(e) Visual (f) Dial
(g) Perforator (h) Memory.

(viii) Give the abbreviations for
(a) Did no stay .... (b) Distinguished guest ....
(c) Special attention guest .... (d) Charges from a no show guest ....

(ix) A bell boy control sheet controls the movement of doorman and valets. Yes / No.
Is the question correct ?
If no, correct the question ....
Give the correct answer..................

[**Ans.** (i) No, How do you calculate Housecount ? Previous day HC + Departure + Arrivals.
(ii) (e)
(iii). No Calculate double Company ?
(iv) No, How do you calculate company percentage?
(v) ?
(vi) Paging is to locate a person. Can be done by pagers, beefs, page boys, public address systems.
(vii) All
(viii) DNS, DG, SPATT, Retention charges.
(ix) No, A Bell Control Sheet controls the movement of bell boys.

Short Answer Type

Q.3. List types of reservations.

Q.4. List different reservation reports.

Descriptive Type

Q.5. Discuss reservations' sales techniques

Q.6. Take a room reservation, from inquiry to confirmation

Q.7. Discuss reservation maintenance and different considerations

Q.8. Discuss the issues of room and rate assignment and fulfilling special requests.

Q.9. Discuss option when guests cannot be accommodated.

Q.10. Describe a typical guest registration card/form and discuss the legal and managerial functions it serves.

Q.11. Distinguish between terms :
(a) Did Not Stay (DNS),
(b) Did Not Arrive (DNA), and
(c) Registered but Not Assigned (RNA) .

Q.12. Describe the procedures used by the hotel bell attendant when "rooming" a guest.

Q.13. Explain the basic outline of reservation systems and/or Front Office procedures that can be implemented to ensure customer satisfaction. Make use of industry terminology.

Q.14. How will you deal guest with Scanty Baggage Check (SB) ?

Q.15. Discuss the purpose and contents of the hotel housekeeping report and its use by the desk clerk.

Q.16. Distinguish between terms as they apply to registering guest by front desk personnel:

(a) Did not stay (DNS),

(b) Did not arrive (DNA),

(c) Registered but not assigned (RNA)

Q.17. Write short notes on:

(a) Changing of room

(b) Arrival Slips

(c) Arrival of a guest.

Assignments/Activity Type

Q.18. Demonstrate the techniques used by desk clerks to identify guest payment methods.

Q.19. Demonstrate processing of credit cards when guest is registering at a hotel.

7

Group Handling

CHAPTER OBJECTIVES

After studying this lesson you should be able :

- To understand the pre-arvival procedure of a group
- To deal with the arvival, departure procedure of a group

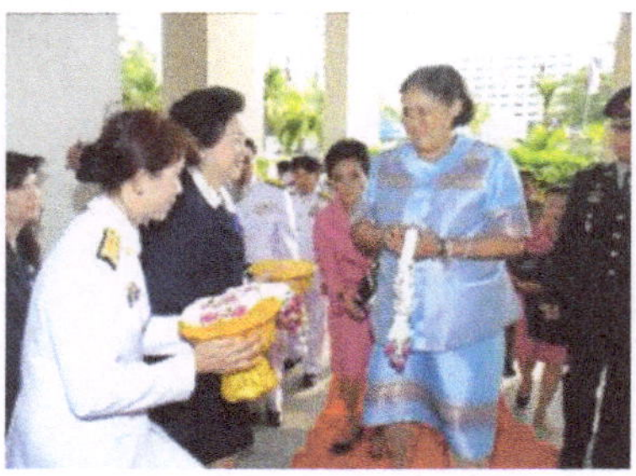

Handling groups requires special procedure from arrival to the departure. This may be described under three heads:

1. Pre-arrival of group
2. Arrival of group
3. Group departure.

Pre arrival of a Group

Following procedure may be adopted:

1. Fill out the Group Information Sheet and circulate the copies to all departments indicated on the sheet. This should be circulated at least a day or two before the group check in.
2. Make advance copies of the Rooming List indicating the doubles and single rooms separately and the occupants of each type of room under these headings. Mention the room numbers, as the rooms should be blocked prior to arrival of the group. Distribution of the copies is as follows:
   (a) Group Leader
   (b) Group File
   (c) To be attached to registration card
   (d) Room service
   (e) Telephone
   (f) Housekeeping
   (g) Laundry
   (h) Lobby Manager
   (i) Bell captain.
   (j) For 'C' form

3. If the group is booked on AP or MAP, the necessary meals coupons should be made out and placed in individual envelops with the room key. The envelope should indicate the name of the guest and the room number.
4. **Check the mail against the names of the group numbers.**

Arrival of a Group

On arrival of group the procedure would be:

1. As mentioned before, only the group leader fills out a Registration Card.
2. The respective envelopes are handed over to group members. Hand over any mail for the group members.
3. Now Lobby Attendant Card is made.
4. Guest Folios and Permanent Arrival Slips are to be made
5. Prepare the **'C" Forms.**
6. Once guest folio is opened in the name of the group leader where all the regular room and meal charges will be posted in the individual guest folios of the group members.

Departure of a Group

When the group is leaving the hotel the most important job of the Receptionist is to check the keys against the group rooming list and see that no keys are missing. When he receives the Departure Card duly signed by the Cashier as " Clear" the slips on the reception rack are folded to indicate the departure rooms. A subsequent entry is made in the Arrival /Departure Register. Finally the group departure is announced over the phone to housekeeping, room service and telephones and the same entries are made in the Departure Intimation Sheet. When the rooms are given as " clear" by Housekeeping you can remove the folded slips in the Reception Rack. Now the room can be resold.

QUESTIONS AND DISCUSSIONS

Short Answer Type

Q.1. Explain the procedure of group handling.

Q.2. Write notes on:

(a) Departure of a group

(b) 'C' Form

(c) Pr-arrival of a group.

Descriptive Type

Q.3. Visit a deluxe hotel, and note down the procedure of group reservations handled by the hotel front desk.

8

Very Important Persons (VIPs) in a Hotel

CHAPTER OBJECTIVES

After studying this lesson you should be able :

- To describe the polices and procedures of we learning and registration of different class of VIP guests,
- To handle the aminities for VIP guests,
- To understand the procedure of arrival and departure of VIP guest.

A V.I.P. is escorted directly to his room without stopping at the front office by the Lobby Manager. Afterwards a bellboy or the assistant should go to the guest's room and have the Registration Card filled and signed. The Lobby Manager escorts all VIP guests to their rooms without exception. So the Lobby Manager should be informed as soon as VIP guests arrive in the hotel.

The VIP guests who visit the hotel regularly must be pr-registered i.e. all details of the Registration Card should be filled in before the guest comes to the desk so that the VIP guest has to sign the Registration Card.

GENERAL GUIDELINES: POLICY AND PROCEDURE

In conjunction with the hotel recognizes VIP guests who are of commercial importance to the establishment and, the owner of the property.

PROCEDURE VIP1 (VIPS)

1. Presidents of state
2. Prime Minister
3. National Leader
4. Ambassador
5. Leader of VIP delegation
6. Presidential suite occupant.

Amenities /Expression

1. Welcome letter with General Manager/ Resident manager's signature

2. Fruit basket with finger bowl (daily replenish)
3. Welcome tea and hand towel with tray.
4. Pastry
5. Deluxe flowers in room
6. Champagne
7. Full bar set up
8. Complementary best quality spring water
9. Deluxe turndown cookies
10. Newspapers (daily) and special newspapers in guest mother tongue.
11. TV set in guest on mother tongue
12. Garland upon arrival
13. General Manager/ Resident Manager welcome and farewell
14. Free from upgrade subject to availability
15. Special security attention
16. Give away gift.

Guest receiving a warm greeting

Registration Card

No Registration Card, method of payment or signature required (all this information should already be on the guest profile). In-room check in.

VIP2 (HIGH LEVEL VIPS)

1. Governor
2. Mayor
3. Hotel Owner
4. Council General

5. CEO
6. Chairman
7. President of Key Account,
8. Senior Corporate Executive (international),
9. Domestic Celebrities,
10. Full paying Club suite occupant.

Amenities /Expression

1. Welcome letter with General Manager/ Resident manager's signature
2. Fruit basket with finger bowl (daily replenish)
3. Welcome tea and hand towel with tray.
4. Pastry
5. Deluxe flowers in room
6. Imported Red Wine
7. Complementary best quality spring water
8. Turndown cookies
9. Newspapers (daily)
10. TV set in guest on the mother tongue
11. General Manager/ Resident Manager welcome and farewell
12. Free from upgrade subject to availability
13. Special security attention
14. Give away gift.

Registration Card

No Registration Card, method of payment or signature required (all this information should already be on the guest profile). In-room check in.

VIP3 (NORMAL LEVEL VIPS)

1. Corporate Account VIP
2. Multinational Corporate VIP
3. Domestic/ overseas TA VIP
4. Tourism Trade VIP
5. Owning Company VIP
6. Other Sister Hotel Owner
7. Journalist /Media
8. Honeymooners.

Amenities /Expression

1. Welcome letter with General Manager/ Resident manager's signature
2. Fruit basket with finger bowl (daily replenish)

3. Welcome tea and hand towel with tray.
4. Pastry
5. Deluxe flowers in room
6. Imported House Wine
7. Complementary best quality spring water
8. Turndown cookies
9. Newspapers (daily)
10. TV set in guest on the mother tongue
11. DOSM/ FOM welcome and farewell

Registration Card

Normal check in

Conferring method of payment and registration card detail.

VIP4 (SPECIAL ATTENTION)

1. Owning company management
2. Hotel Staff
3. Hotel Privilege Golden Cardholder
4. Gust with complains
5. Repeat Guet+10
6. Normal Hotel Club Occupant.

Amenities /Expression

1. Welcome letter with General Manager/ Resident manager's signature
2. Fruit plate
3. Newspaper
4. Front Office Manager (Assistant Front Office Manager) and /or Assistant Manager welcome and greeting

Registration Card

Normal check in

Conferring method of payment and registration card detail.

PRIVILEGE GOLDEN CARDHOLDER ONLY

1. In addition to silver privilege guest.
2. D-3 available guarantee- any reservation made before 07.00pm at least 3 days before arrival date using rack rate, in the event of the hotel is full, alternative accommodation will be found for the guest in the nearest sister hotel/or hotel of the same standard. If the guest is accommodated outside own network, the hotel will incur any extra cost of the hotel room for the first night, as well as transfer costs to the alternative hotel.

3. Reservation guaranteed in case of late arrival. If the guest is delayed, the room will be guaranteed until mid-day the following day. The Reservation Manager will advise the Assistant and reception Manager / supervisor of their arrivals and where possible, pre-allocate room.
4. Early Check in: A room will be made available before mid-day on request at no extra cost, subject to availability. The Reception Manager /Supervisor will allocate the arriving room by 09.00, then forward the list of rooms to the Housekeeping Supervisor. All rooms should be ready, for arrival and check in by 11.00 am (subject to hotel availability).
5. Upgrade: An automatic upgrade to the next room is offered, subject to availability. The Reception Manager/Supervisor will coordinate this.

SILVER PRIVILEGE CARDHOLDER ONLY

1. Receptions will handover a 'Welcome Drink Voucher' for two upon check in.
2. Automatic late check out of 16.00 will be made at the time of check up to 16.00. Any time thereafter, fees will apply.
3. Receive Complaints Points for each stay at the sister hotels, which can be converted to 'Complementary Gift Voucher'. Receptionist is to advise the guest on check in that they have the chose of receiving frequent flyer point on valid rates and program only/or Hotel privilege Points. Not both.

VIP Code Practiced in the Hotel's System

Sl. No.	*Guest Categories*	*Code*
1.	Normal Guest	0
2.	VIP1 (VIPs)	1
3.	VIP2 (High level VIP)	2
4.	VIP3 (Normal level VIP)	3
5.	VIP4 (Special level VIP)	4.

Fig. 8.1. VIP codes

Some examples of giving away gifts are:

1. Long Jing Tea
2. Chinese Silk
3. Paradise Umbrella
4. Chinese Seal Cutting
5. Chinese Painting
6. Chinese Pen Craft.

Amenities Voucher

The front office informs housekeeping to be alert to attend to rooms occupied by groups or VIPs. Service has to be quicker and efficient. Housekeeping provides "flowers" for VIPs in the room on receipt of the Amenities Voucher issued by the Front Desk (Ref. Fig. 8.2).

Hotel ....

Amenities Voucher

Day Date

- Please Send Complimentary
- Flowers
- Full—Single ( )—Double ( )—Special ( )

• ....

To .... Arriving ....

Room No. ....

....

Authorised by ....

Copy of Auditor MAURYA—FO—021

Fig. 8.2. Specimen Amenities Voucher

Amenities Handled by:

1. Welcome letter with General Manager/ Resident Manager signature prepared by GM's secretary, delivered with welcome amenities by Room Service
2. Fruit basket with finger bowl (daily replenish), prepared by Food and Beverage, delivered by Room Service.
3. Welcome tea and hand towel with try, prepared and serve by Guest Relation Officer.
4. Pastry prepared and delivered by Food and Beverage
5. Deluxe flower in room prepared and delivered by Housekeeping.
6. Champagne, prepared and delivered by Food and Beverage
7. Full Bar set up- prepared and delivered by Food and Beverage
8. Complementary best quality spring water - prepared and delivered by Housekeeping
9. Deluxe turndown cookies- prepared by Food and Beverage and delivered by Housekeeping.
10. Newspaper (Dailey) and special Newspaper in guest mother tongue – prepared by Front Office, delivered by Housekeeping during turn down service.
11. TV set up in guest mother tongue- handled by housekeeping.
12. Garland upon arrival, prepared by Housekeeping, service by Guest relation officer.
13. General Manager/ Resident Manager welcome and farewell - By GM/RM.
14. Fee room upgrade subject to availability – handled by Front Office Manger.
15. Special Security an Attention- handled by Security department.
16. Give away Gifts - chosen by General Manager/ Resident Manager during turn down service.

Procedure

1. Reservation Department should key in the right VIP code in the reservation according S & M's reservation order. And arrival time is very important for VIP handling.
2. Front Office Room Controller should print the 'Next day VIP Arrival List' at 03.00 pm daily. submit to General Manager's Secretary to prepare the welcome letter.
3. Front Office Room Controller should print the 'Next Day VIP Arrival List' at 03.00 pm daily, submit it to Food and Beverage to prepare welcome amenities of next day.
4. Room Controller must make VIP room assignment on priority before 09.00 am daily.
5. After room assignment, Front Office Room Controller must inform it to some department concerned, present the ' Today VIP Arrival List' with room number and submit it to Room Service for amenities delivery
6. Regarding same day VIP booking, Front Office Room Controller should inform to each department concerned at first time and present the Amenities Request Form to Room Service
7. Room inspection must be done one hour before by Guest Relation Officer and Assistant Manager, all welcome amenities must be delivered in to the room one hour before also.
8. Welcome tea and hand towel must be prepared 30 minutes before by Guest Relation Office and Assistant Manager.
9. All members of welcome team should stand by in hotel lobby 15 minutes before arrival in hotel lobby 15 minutes before arrival especially Guest relation Office who serves the garland
10. Check in process accordingly to the different treatment of each VIP level.
11. Guest Relation Officer serves the welcome tea and hand towel in guest room.
12. The turn down cookies and give away gifts should be put into room during turndown service
13. The departure time should be collected to advance for farewell.

QUESTIONS AND DISCUSSIONS

Short Answer Type

Q.1. Answer the following questions:

(i) What is Mail Forwarding slip?

(ii) What is VPO ?

(iii) What is the name for a collapsible tray used for keeping guest folio ?

(iv) 'A group rooming list gives flight details'. Is it correct? Yes / No Give the correct answer.

(v) Are the following terms correct? If no, correct the terms.

(a) Stay over Yes / No

(b) Stay over Yes / No

(c) Out of sleep.

(vi) Correct the following corresponding with the abbreviations.

(a) Friendly Individualistic Traveller (FIT)

(b) Public Air System (P A System)

(c) Unilateral Selling Proposition (USP).

(vii) What is Adds?

[**Ans.:** (i) Mail forwarding slip is one which is filed by a guest who is to leave and his formal address is written on it.

(ii) Visitors paid out. Charges like taxi etc. are charged here.

(iii) Cashier's Bucket / well.

(iv) Yes.

(v) No, under stay.

No, sleep out.

(vi) Free individual traveller, Public Address System, unique selling possession.

(vii) Adds are the last minute reservation which are added to the reservation list.

Descriptive Type

Q.2. Discuss the guest designations as used in the hotel:

(a) Very important person (VIP),

(b) Special attention guest (SPATT), and

(c) Distinguished guest (DG).

Q.3. Explain the following term:

(a) Amenities and Expressions

(b) Privilege Golden Card Holder

(c) VIP Codes.

Q.4. Write notes on handling of amenities for VIPs and explain the full procedures generally used in hotel.

Q.5. Explain the procedure of registration and reception procedure of VIP.

Q.6. Write a note on Very Important Person.

Q.7. Discuss the guest designations very important person (VIP), special attention guest (SPATT), and distinguished guest (DG) and when they are used.

9

Guest Leaves the Hotel

CHAPTER OBJECTIVES

After studying this lesson you should be able :

- To describe the procedure of departure of guests,
- To understand the handling of departure of guests,
- To prepare the Departure Intimation Control sheet.

Generally a guest is never questioned regarding his date of departure except at the time when he is filling in his Registration Card. But during the busy season, the reception assistant must contact the guest in the morning of the date indicated by the guest when he intends to leave the hotel.

Following points are worth noting incase of departure of a guest from the hotel:

1. The Reception Desk is not involved in checking whether the guest has settled his bill or not before leaving the hotel as the **Lobby Attendant Errand Card** is signed by the Front Office Cashier indicting the clearance of bills before this card is handed over to the Reception desk.
2. The Lobby attendant hands over the Lobby Attendant Errand Card with the Registration card at the Reception Desk. This indicates that the guest has vacated the room. This information is entered in the Arrival / Departure register in the departure column.
3. At the same time this information i.e. room number and the guest's name is noted in a duplicate sheet which is known as the Departure Intimation Sheet.
4. The white slips is filled in half and placed back in the Room Rack. This is removed only when the Housekeeping Department informs the reception Desk that the room is cleaned, ready for reallocation.

5. Housekeeping is informed of the departure rooms immediately so that they can be attended to it and get it serviced.
6. When the registration Card of the guest who has left the hotel is red turned to the Reception Desk by the Front Office cashier, any further details necessary are entered against the entry already made in the Arrival/ Departure Register.

Departure Procedure

Step 1: The bell desk will receive a phone call from the guest about his intention to check out. Write the room number carefully on the errand card, a stack of which is kept at the bell desk itself. Inform the Bell Captain and proceed to the room.

Step 2: Knock on the guest's door and announce yourself. Look around the room for any guest articles left, any damaged hotel property and switch off the air-conditioning/ heating, lights, etc. Collect the room key and depart from the room letting the guest led the way. Ensure that the guest room is locked. If the guest wants to carry the room key himself, permit him to do so.

Step 3: Place the baggage at the bell desk. Stick on any hotel stickers or publicity tags. Hand over the room key to the Information counter and errand card to the Front Office Cashier. Wait for the guest to pay the bill.

Step 4: The bellboy will receive an authorization to take the baggage out of the hotel only after the Front Office cashier Has signed that the guest has paid his bills, and the Receptionist That the room key has been received.

Step 5: Take the baggage to the car porch and load it to the transport.

Step 6: Report back to the bell desk and hand over the Errand card with the authorization signatures.

Departure Intimation control sheet

When a guest checks out, the front office has to immediately inform the housekeeping desk (which is the central point of information for housekeeping) or the floors, to clean the room so that it is ready for sale again. This information is controlled on Departure Intimation Control Sheet. Housekeeping in return would have to inform the front office immediately after a room has been cleaned and prepared for sale to a guest. In technical parlance when the front desk informs the housekeeping desk about a check out room, it is referred to as giving a "departure room" to housekeeping and when housekeeping informs the front office about rooms that are ready for sale, it is known as "cleared rooms" (Ref. Fig. 9.1).

HOTEL ....

DEPARTURE INTIMATION CONTROL SHEET

Date ______________ RECEPTION

ROOM NO.	NAME OF GUEST	NAME OF PERSON INFORMED AT			TIME	BY
		House keeping	Telephone Dept.	Room service		

Figure 9.1. Specimen Departure Intimation Control Sheet

QUESTIONS AND DISCUSSIONS

Objective Type

Q.1. Do the following abbreviations stand for ? If no, give the correct answer.

(a) B & B – Bread & Breakfast

.... Yes / No

(b) CRS – Control Railway System Yes / No

....

(c) GRE – General Reception Executive

.... Yes / No

(d) VTL – Value Traveller Ledger

.... Yes / No

(e) PYP – Planning Yearly ProspectiveYes / No

....

(f) MAO – Modified American Order

.... Yes / No

[**Ans.:** (a) No, Bed and breakfast.
(b) CRS No, Central Reservation system.
(c) No, Guest relation executive.
(d) No, visitors tabular ledger.
(e) No, perpetual year planner.
(f) No, real and accommodation order.]

Short Answer Type

Q.2. Write notes on Lobby Attendant Errand Card.

Descriptive Type

Q.3. What points are to be taken in consideration when a guest leaves a hotel?

Q.4. Describe departure procedures and checkout options.

10

Front Office Accounting (Billing)

CHAPTER OBJECTIVES

After studying this lesson you should be able :

- To draw and prepare Guest Bill
- To understand the system of posting of vouchers,
- To know the procedure of presentation of bill to the customer
- To acquire the basic knowledge of establishing room rates
- To calculate daily operational ratios,
- To forecast Room Availability

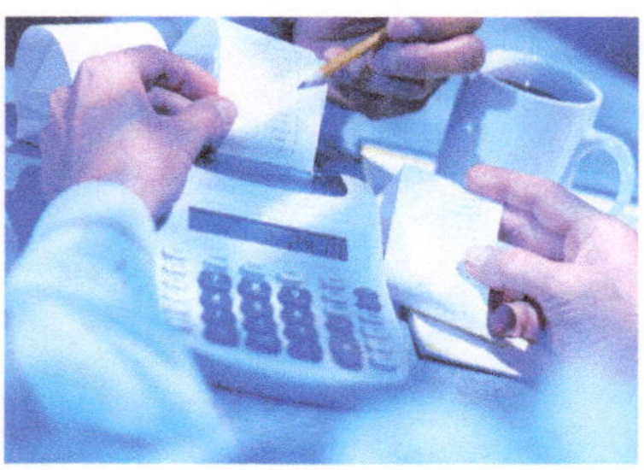

The front office cashier receives payments for a guest's stay in the hotel. This is the point where all the charge vouchers (bills) generated by the guest are received, to be included in the overall bill. Close liaison between the lobby staff and cashier is imperative. The Bell Captain must inform the cashier about the intended check out of a guest so that the guest's bills are updated and kept ready for presentation. Also, the cashier is informed of a new arrival by the Reception by opening and forwarding a new folio in the guest's name giving room number and time of check in, with defined billing instructions which the cashier places in the bill tray against the appropriate room.

The Night Auditor audits all guest bills received by the front office cashier and prepares and proves for the calendar day. This is the credit section that receives bills from front office that has extended credit as per previous arrangement between the hotel and the guest. This department follows up with the individual or company for the payment of the bills.

The Room Service is kept closely intimated on arrivals and departures of guests. It is this department that provides food and beverage services to the room and must be informed as to the occupant in order to raise bills accordingly.

The front office informs room service through the Amenities Voucher and a List of the VIPs' expected to arrive in the hotel so that special service is extended. Also the room service provides a complimentary basket of fruit, liquor, cakes and pastries or whatever gesture the establishment wishes to extend to a VIP as per the policy.

Immediately after the arrival of the guest the reception gives the duplicate of arrival slip to the billing section. The billing section then opens the bill, stating room number, guest' name, date of arrival and room rate. The number of the arrival slip is written on the bill, too. It becomes the bill-number. The bills are not pre-numbered.

When typing the heading of the bill it is possible to write out at the same time, by means of carbon paper, the information slip for the room rack, information rack and phone operator. In this case a reception assistant usually opens the bill.

Posting of Voucher

All vouchers arriving at the front office are to be posted immediately. Originals of voucher usually are stored room-wise to have them ready when the guest asks for them. The duplicates are given back to the department (restaurant cashier) where they come from. This can be done by a computer-based system also.

Guest Bill

(Hotel Letter head)

Manual GRC ______________ Bill No. ____________

Room No.	Name	Room Rate	Pax	Room Type	Days	STD (Executive 5)	Company/TA/TO

Name and Address	Arrival Date	Departure Date
______________________ ______________________ ______________________	01/10/2011 02:05	02/10/2011 21:25

Date	Description	Charge	Credit	Balance
	Tariff	Rs. 17,200.00		17,200.00
	Luxury Tax	1,720.00		18,920.00
	Laundry (5380)	180.00		19,000.00
	Total			**19,000.00**
	Advance			5,000.00
	Advance refund			00.00
	Net			**14,000.00**

Please Return Your Keys on Departure

I agree that I am responsible for the full payment of this bill in the event of not paid by the company/organization or person indicated.

Billing Instruction: DIRECT

Cashier – XXXXXX

Cashere's Signature Guest Signature

______________ ______________

-------Thank you for Honoring us by your visit-----

Fig. 10.1. Specimen Guest Bill

Presenting the bill to the customer

When the customer leaves and asks for his bill, the bill is presented to him. Any bill should be ready to be shown at any time. (Ref Fig. 10.1). The cashier has to look through the bill, whether or not breakfast and depending on the time of departure, lunch and dinner are charged. The cashier has to ask the customer if he had some further charges not figuring on the bill. When the customer specifies any such charge, the cashier has to phone to the concern department and ask for the amount. When charging, a note slip or provisional voucher is to be an inserted in the voucher-printer of posting machine. This slip is then stuck to the voucher as soon as it arrives at the reception.

Automating billing

Automatic billing means, 'optimizing your business. It means becoming more efficient and productive, using the time gained in the service of your guests.

The automation of the billing process is one component of the hotel business that can free administration time in order to invest it in strategic planning, customer service etc.

Room Rates/Tariff

The hotel management assigns to each room category a rack rate. In accordance, front office employees are expected to sell rooms at rack unless a guest qualifies for an alternative room rate e.g. corporate or commercial rate, group rate, promotional rate, incentive rate, family rate, day rate, package plan rate, complementary rate.

While pricing rooms, the hotel shall keep in mind that rate should be between a minimum (determined by cost structure) and a maximum (determined by competition structure) boundary as depicted below:

Minimum (**Hurdle Rate**) < Room Rate < Maximum (**Rack Rate**)

Cost Structure < Room Rate < **Competition Structure**

While establishing room rates, management shall be careful about its operating costs, inflationary factors, and competition. Generally, there are three popular approaches to pricing rooms:

1. Cost Approach
2. Market Condition Approach
3. Rule-of-thumb Approach
4. Hubbard formula Approach.

1. Cost Approach

The starting point of this approach is to find out the per room occupied daily, direct expenses and indirect expenses.

Example

Q.1. Manjri-Mussoorie Hotel has estimated the following Indirect Expenses (i.e. Undistributed Expenses and Fixed Charges) for the upcoming Year:

Expense Type	Amount	Allocation to Rooms Division	Rooms
Administrative & General Expenses	₹ 50,00,000	30 %	₹ 15,00, 000
Utility Expenses	₹ 26,00,000	70%	₹ 18,20,000
Debt Expenses	₹ 30,00,000	70%	₹ 21,00,000
Depreciation Expenses	₹ 35,00,000	60%	₹ 21,00,000
Rent Expenses	₹ 10,00,000	70%	₹ 7,00,000
Marketing Expenses	₹ 6,50,000	80%	₹ 5,20,000
Maintenance Expenses	₹ 14,00,000	70%	₹ 9,80,000
Insurance Expenses	₹ 10,00,000	N/A	₹ 7,00,000
Total	₹ 18,15,0000	N/A	₹ 1,04,20,000

Furthermore, the Manjri-Mussoorie Hotel has 150 Rooms (90 of them are single and the remaining are double) and that the Forecasted Single Room Occupancy Rate is 80 % and the Double Room Occupancy Rate is 85 %.

(1) Calculate:

(a) Total Number of expected single rooms sold per Year

(b) Total Number of expected double rooms sold per Year

(c) Daily per room indirect expenses.

Moreover, suppose that Manjri Mussoorie Hotel estimated the following daily per room Operating Expenses (i.e. Direct Expenses):

- Frills Expenses (Single) : ₹ 75.00
- Frills Expenses (Double) : ₹ 82.50
- Staff Expenses (Single) : ₹ 80.00
- Staff Expenses (Double) : ₹ 90.00
- Laundry Expenses (Single) : ₹ 65.00
- Laundry Expenses (Double) : ₹ 72.50

(2) Calculate:

(a) Total Single Daily per room Direct Expense

(b) Total Double Daily per Room Direct Expense

(c) Total Daily Single Room Expense

(d) Total Daily Double Room Expense.

Solution: (1)

(a) Total Number of Expected Single Rooms Sold per Year

$= 90 \times 0.80 \times 365 =$ **26,280 Rooms.**

(b) Total Number of Expected Double Rooms Sold per Year

$= 60 \times 0.85 \times 365 =$ **18,615 Rooms**

(c) Daily per Room Indirect Expenses

= ₹ 1,0420,000 / (26,280 + 18,615) = ₹ **232.10.**

Solution: (2)

(a) Total Single Daily per room Direct Expense

= ₹ 75 + ₹ 80 + ₹ 65 = **₹ 220**

(b) Total Double Daily per Room Direct Expense

= ₹ 82.50 + ₹ 90 + ₹ 72.50 = **₹ 245**

(c) Total Daily Single Room Expense

= ₹ 232.1 + ₹ 220 = **₹ 452.10** (Hurdle Rate)

(d) Total Daily Double Room Expense

= ₹ 232.10 + ₹ 245 = **₹ 477.10** (Hurdle Rate)

Determining Rack Rate

The answer found above is the minimum price of Single and Double rooms as to have no loss or profit from the operations. This situation is refereed to as the Break-Even price.

In order to find the rack rate (i.e. the maximum price potential guests can be charged), the hotel shall apply some of the above-mentioned methods:

(a) **Multiplier Method**

Under this very method, hotels shall try to set a Multiplier, by which the Room Cost shall be multiplied, in order to come up with the hotel Room Rack Rate (for each room type):

Multiplier = 1 / (Desired Room Cost Percentage)

Desired Room Cost Percentage

= (Forecasted Total Room Cost) / (Forecasted Total Room Revenue)

Example

Suppose the Management of the Manjri-Mussoorie decided, prior to a certain price demand analysis, to have a Desired Room Single Cost Percentage of 75 % and a Desired Double Cost Percentage of 60 %.

Calculate:

(1) Single Multiplier

(2) Double Multiplier

(3) Single Rack Rate

(4) Double Rack Rate.

Solution.

Calculation of Multipliers & Double Room Rack

(1) Single Multiplier = 1 / 0.75 = **1.33**

(2) Double Multiplier = 1 / 0.60 = **1.67**

(3) Single Rack Rate = ₹ 452.10 × 1.33 = **₹ 601.29**

(4) Double Rack Rate = ₹ 477.10 × 1.67 = **₹ 796.76**

(b) **Mark-up Method**

Under this method, an addition (or add-on) to the cost of a product will be applied to come up with the Single and Double Rack Rates.

Suppose Manjri-Mussoorie Hotel decided to have a 25 % mark-up on room costs for both single and double Rooms.

Single Rack Rate = ₹ 452.10 × (1 + 0.25) = ₹ 452.10 × 1.25 = ₹ **565.13**

Double Rack Rate = ₹ 477.1 × 1.25 = ₹ **596.38**

Later, the hotel might adjust this figure to a whole number and communicate it as its List Price (for guest and accounting convenience)

The most important handicap of the Cost Approach pricing is that it does not take into consideration how much customers are actually willing to pay for the hotel services, and how other hotels are actually charging for their hotels.

2. Market condition approach

Under this approach, management shall look at comparable hotels in the geographical market, see what they are charging for the same product, and "charge only what the market will accept".

Some drawbacks of this approach are that it does not take into consideration the value of the property, and what a strong sales effort may accomplish. Last but not least, there is always subjectivity in coming up with sets of criteria against which hotel rooms can be compared and measured for similarity.

1. This approach is the commonsense approach. Management looks at comparable hotels in the geographical market and sees what they are charging for the same product.
2. How do our rates compare to those of our competition?
3. Are our rates much lower or higher than those of the competition?
4. How are our rates affecting our revenue and our share of the business?
5. What is our occupancy percentage?
6. What is the occupancy % of the competitive set?
7. Will our total revenue improve if we increase (decrease) our rates?
8. Have any trends emerged during the past six months?

3. Rule of thumb approach

In this very approach, the rate of a room shall be **₹ 1 for each ₹ 1,000** of construction and furnishing cost per room, assuming a **70%** occupancy rate. The Rule-of-Thumb approach sets the rate of a room at ₹1 for each ₹1,000 of construction and furnishings cost per room, assuming 70 % occupancy.

Example

To illustrate, suppose a **150**-room hotel has costed **₹ 9,50,00,000** of Construction and Furnishing Costs. Therfeore, the cost per room is **₹ 6,33,333.33** which would mean that the price per room shall be **₹ 633.33**.

This approach, however, fails to take into consideration the inflation term, the contribution of other facilities and services towards the hotel's desired profitablity, and assumes a ceratin level of occupancy rate.

4. Hubbart formula approach

This approach considers operating costs, desired profits, and expected number of rooms sold (i.e. demand). The procedure of calculating a room rate is as follows:

(a) Calculate the hotel's desired profit by multiplying the desired rate of return (ROI) by the owner's investment.

(b) Calculate pre-tax profits by dividing the desired profit by one minus hotel's tax rate.

(c) Calculate fixed charges and management fees. This calculation includes estimating depreciation, interest expense, preperty taxes, insurance, amortization, building mortgage, land, rent, and management fees.

(d) Calculate undistributed operating expenses. This includes estimating administrative and general expenses, data processing expenses, human resourecs expenses, transportation expenses, marketing expenses, property operation and maintenance expenses, and energy costs.

(e) Estimate non-room operating department income or loss, that is, F&B department income or loss, telephone department income or loss ...

(f) Calculate the required room department income which is the sum of pre-tax profits, fixed charges and management fees, undistributed operating expenses, and other operating department losses less other department incomes.

(g) Determine the rooms department revenue which is the required room department income, plus other room department direct expenses of payroll and related expenses, plus other direct operating expenses.

(h) Calculate the average room rate by dividing rooms department revenue by the expected number of rooms to be sold.

Doubles sold daily

= Double occupancy rate × total number of rooms × occupancy %

Singles sold daily

= Rooms sold daily – number of double rooms sold daily

Singles sold daily × x + doubles sold daily × (x + y)

= (Average room rate) × (total number of rooms sold daily)

Where:

x = price of singles;

y = price differential between singles and doubles;

x + y = price of doubles.

Example

Assume that average construction cost of a room is ₹ 800,0000.00. Using this approach comes average selling price of ₹ 80,000 per room. Set up different rates for different room types, but ARR would be ₹ 8,000.00.

Solution.

Hubbart Formula approach considers operating costs, desired profits and expected number of rooms sold. In other words, this approach starts with desired profit, adds income taxes, and then adds fixed charges and management fee, followed by operating overhead expenses and direct operating expenses. It is consider a Bottom-up approach.

- Hubbart formula (basic) : 200 Room Hotel
- Desired net income yearly : ₹ 1,52500,000.00
- Plus depreciation, taxes : ₹ 6,00,00,000.00
- Plus operating expenses : ₹ 1,24,000,000.00
- Total required operated income : ₹ 3,36,500,000.00
- Less other department incomes : ₹ 2,00,00,000.00
- Total Rooms Division income : ₹ 31,65,00,000.00
- Rooms direct expenses + ₹ 5,47,50,000.00 (base on estimated
- Total ₹ 37,12,50,0000.00 75% occupancy of 200 rooms.
- Number of rooms sold in a year 54,750 1 year : 54,750)
- Required average room rate : ₹ 6781.00

  Available Rooms = Total rooms – out of order rooms.

$$\text{Occupancy \%} = \frac{\text{Number of occupied rooms}}{\text{Number of rooms available for sale}} \times 100$$

Depends on management decisions, most of the hotels maintain fixed number of available rooms without deducting out of order rooms.

2. Discounting

In all computations done so far, the Room Price that we have found is what is called the Room Rack Rate (i.e. The Maximum Rate a hotel can charge a guest). Yet, most often, only Walk-ins (i.e. guests without a reservation) are charged a Rack Rate, which would mean that a big proportion of guests actually pay a Discount on the Rack Rate.

Discounting is a method used by management to make their products and services attractive to Customers. This method may differ according to seasonality, type of customer, market segment, and type of product...

There is an important relation between Occupancy and Discount Percentage:

Equivalent Occupancy = (Current Occupancy) × ((Rack Rate – Marginal Cost) / (Rack Rate × (1 – Discount Percentage) – Marginal Cost))

Example

To illustrate, suppose that an occupied single room has a daily variable cost of **₹ 1000** and that management are right now selling at Single Rack Rate **₹ 5000** and managing to have Single Occupancy of **70 %**. Suppose, furthermore that management decided to discuss the effect of a 10 % discount on Single Rack Rate on the eventual demand. Hence, whether to discount or not!

Solution.

In order not to be economically affected by the discount, the minimum Occupancy at that discounted price (i.e. at **₹ 4500**), shall be:

Equivalent Occupancy = 70 % × ((₹ 5000 – ₹ 1000) / (₹ 5000 × (1 – 10 %) – ₹ 1000)) = 70 % × (40 / 35) = **80 %**

Management, shall conduct a feasibility study on the effect of that pre-determined discount on demand and if the effect proves to yield an occupancy which is more than **80 %**, discounting can be applied. If, not than the discounting idea shall be discarded.

3. Other Pricing Techniques

(1) **Market-skimming Pricing:** Setting a high price for a new product to skim maximum revenues layer by layer from the segments that are willing to pay the high price.

(2) **Market-penetration Pricing:** Setting a low price for a new product in order to attract a large number of customers and a large market share.

(3) **Optional Product Pricing:** Pricing optional or accessory products that are being sold along with a main product.

(4) **Captive Product Pricing:** Setting a price for products that must be used along with a main product (ex. Frills no more free of charge but charged a price to customers)

(5) **Product Bundle Pricing:** Combining several products and offering the bundle at a reduced price (i.e. packaging & discounting).

Forecasting

Forecasting room availability is forecasting the number of rooms available for sale on any future date. This type of forecasting helps manage the reservation process, guides the front office staff for an effective rooms management, and can be used as an occupancy forecast, which is, further, useful in attempting to schedule the necessary number of employees for an expected volume of business.

In order to forecast room availability, the following data are needed:

(a) Number of expected room arrivals

(b) Number of expected room walk-ins

(c) Number of expected room stayovers

(d) Number of expected room no-shows

(e) Number of expected room cancellation

(f) Number of expected room understays

(g) Number of expected room checkouts

(h) Number of expected room overstays

Formula for calculating number of rooms accountable for sale.

- **Total Number of Guest Rooms**

– Number of Out of Order Rooms

– Number of Stopovers Rooms

– Number of Reserved Rooms
+ Number of No-show Rooms
+ Number of Cancellation Rooms
+ Number of Check-Out Rooms
+ Number of Understay Rooms
+ Number of Overstay Rooms
= **Number of Rooms Available for Sale**

QUESTIONS AND DISCUSSIONS

Practical Exercises

Q.1. Negies Palace Hotel has 204 rooms: 45 are triple, 60 are double and the remaining is single. On the night of March 7th, the night auditor counted 195 rooms occupied, 43 are triple, 58 are double, and the remaining are single. Moreover, the housekeeping department communicated only 4 rooms (all single) out of order for the night of March 7th.

(a) What is Negies Palace Hotel's Occupancy Rate for the night of May 07th?

(b) What is Negies Palace Hotel's Single, Double, and Triple Occupancy rates for the night of May 07th ?

Q.2. Taxila Hotel has 120 rooms: 53 of them are single and 67 are double. On the night of 07/10/20, Taxila Hotel's Night Auditor counted a total of 85 rooms occupied, 42 of which were occupied by more than one guest. Moreover, on the same night 127 guests were registered. In addition, 2 rooms were on a complimentary basis. From the Housekeeping Room Status Report (for the night of 07/10/20), there were a total of 4 rooms Out of Order, 3 of which were Single. Lastly, the Actual Room Revenue for the same night was at the order of ₹ 6,96,000 and Actual Hotel Revenue was ₹ 10,00,000.

Calculate:

(a) The Average Guest Per Room Sold

(b) The Average Daily Rate

(c) The Revenue per Available Customer (RevPAC)

(d) The RevPAR

(e) The Average Rate per Guest

Q.3. Given the following data, calculate the percentage of overstays:

(a) Number of room no-shows: 30

(b) Number of room walk-ins: 60

(c) Number of overstays rooms: 40

(d) Number of understay rooms: 20

(e) Number of room reservations: 300

(f) Number of room arrivals: 340

(g) Number of expected checkouts: 380

Q.4. Given the following data, calculate the rooms available for sales:

(a) Number of room no-shows : 30

(b) Number of room walk-ins : 60

(c) Number of overstay rooms : 40
(d) Number of understay rooms : 20
(e) Number of stay over room : 300
(f) Number of room arrivals : 40
(g) Number of expected checkouts : 80

Short Answer Type

Q.5. Write notes on:
(a) Automatic billing
(b) Voucher
(c) Guest Bill.

Descriptive Type

Q.6. Discuss front office accounting fundamentals.

Q.7. Create and maintain accounts.

Q.8. Track transactions.

Q.9. Discuss the importance and different types of internal controls

Q.10. Define the terms source documents, voucher, department journal, folio, posting, city ledger, cash sheet, petty cash, float, and point-of-sale as they apply to hotel billing procedures.

Q.11. State the functions of a hotel front-office accounting system.

Q.12. Describe the typical hotel accounting cycle used to bill guest for charges.

Q.13. Give examples of various charges that appear on a guest folio.

Q.14. Describe the procedure used by the desk clerk to assure that guest late charges are billed.

Q.15. Describe the duties of the hotel cashier to complete the guest folio and collect for charges.

Q.16. Describe the cashier's responsibility to inform other departments when the guest has departed.

Q.17. Define the terms room revenue, corporate traveler, no-show, due-out, turn-away, walk-in, group booking, stay-over, full-house management, run of the house, occupancy rate, blocked rooms, yield management, and guaranteed payment as they apply to room availability and rates.

Q.18. State the formula used to find percent of occupancy.

Q.19. Describe the factors that influence the percent of occupancy for a hotel operation.

Q.20. Name the forms and charts that aid front desk personnel in full-house management.

Q.21. Discuss the philosophy of yield management as it relates to rooms utilization.

Q.22. Describe the procedure used to determine the expected number of no-shows, cancellations, and stay-overs, and discuss their impact on the number of reservations that may be accepted.

Q.23. Discuss hotel policies concerning guest negotiating room rates.

Q.24. Describe the factors that are considered when establishing the rack rate for specific rooms within a hotel.

Q.25. Give examples of special rates and discuss their application in hotel operations.

Q.26. Explain the automatic billing procedure.

Assignment / Activity Type

Q.27. Demonstrate a typical guest account from check-in to settlement.

11

Credit Limits for Customers

CHAPTER OBJECTIVES

After studying this lesson you should be able :

- To explain the term credit limit
- To apply the credit limit in the hotel,
- To understand the terms and conditions of application of credit limits,
- To know the credit limits of various organisations, travel agents, airlines, companies, corporate houses individuals etc.

Different hotels have different policies to fixed credit limit to customer /guest availing hotel services and facilities. The higher management decides these limits and the credit limit varies from establishment-to-establishment and person-to-person depending on number o f factors. Mostly these limits are fixed for the following category of customers:

1. Travel agents
2. Airlines
3. Companies
4. Individuals
5. Guest ledger
6. Banquets
7. Food and Beverages.

Some these credit limits as followed in most of the hotel are as follows:

Travel Agents & Airlines

1. No credit should be allowed to any individual until unless they are holding authorization letter from their respective travel agents (IATA approved) or airlines unless cleared by general Manager.
2. For certain travel agent namely, TCI, SITA etc, no credit limit can be fixed but an effective follow up system has to be followed so that the maximum possible payment is received in 75days period.
3. All other medium sized travel agents such as Holidaymakers, KAI, ACM and T.I.B., etc has a certain limit fixed jointly by Sales a

Manager, Chartered Accountant/ General Manager/ Front Office Manager. The maximum credit of 45 days can be given.

4. Other travel agents credit limit of 30 days to be given.
5. According to the time factors of payments commission of 10% can be given. If the agents are not making payment with in the time frame following steps could be considered:
   (i) Reduction of Commission
   (ii) Higher room rate
   (iii) Bank guarantee
   (iv) Deposit
   (v) Cash basis, etc.
6. New agencies should not be given credit facilities; in case it has been given a bank guarantee is required.
7. Any credit facility to a travel agent should have the joint approval of the general manager, Chief Accountant, Sales Manager, and the Front Office Manager. A bank guarantee or deposit to be taken. The meeting of this committee should be called once in a month.
8. Sales Manager or Front Office manager when introducing a Travel Agent should clarify the payment terms in the letter with an acknowledgement from the agent.
9. In case of Airlines (lay-over passenger) proper authorization is required. The authorization number should be mentioned on the bills to avoid delay and any error.
10. Airlines and travel agent staff are not allowed any credit limit until and unless they are holding a credit Card.

Foreign Travel Agents have no benefit of Credit limit. All business is to be made on Advance payments.

Companies and Corporate Houses

1. For every booking there should be an authority letter from the company.
2. The billing instruction to be clear and record to be maintained by reservation in alphabetical registers.
3. No more than 30 days credit should be allowed in nay case.
4. New companies should be introduced to credit facility only on production of Bank Guarantee. Amount to be decided depending upon the number of Room Night confirmed in a year. The General Manager, Chief Accountant and Sales Manager and Front Office Manger, should approve this jointly.

Individual

1. No personal cheque will be accepted from individuals.
2. Individual persons outstation cheques not to be accepted
3. Only the credit card holders should be allowed credit in individual capacity and a limit of Rs. 50.000/- to be fixed on every card.

4. Credit card holder payment to be made with in 15 days.
5. Credit card should not be used for Banquet parties.
6. Individual persons using room will complete necessary credit facility details to have credit facility.
7. Walk-in scanty baggage guest have to pay a 3 days advance payment at the time of check in. The may be provided all other facilities such as food and beverages, **telephone, telex fax, etc on cash payment basis.**

Guest Ledger

1. Long staying guest on direct payment to make payment every 15 days or ₹ 15,00 whichever is earlier.
2. Guest on company account / embassy, the bills to be closed every 15 days with the Guest signature and transfer to City Ledger.
3. Careful observation of these account to be made every day to avoid any delay / misuse of the facilities such as Telephone/liquor. etc.

Banquets

1. All banquet parties should be on cash basis. Under no circumstances credit to be given.
2. Credit may be allowed on approval of Managing Director or General Manager or Chief Accountant or any Directors and Food and Beverage Manger, as applicable.
3. For partied above 300 pax an advance of ₹ 15, 000 at the time of booking.
4. For parties less than 200 pax an advance of ₹ 10, 000 at the time of booking.
5. For parties less than 100 pax an advance of ₹ 5, 000 at the time of booking.
6. In all parties 85% of the total amount including advance to be taken before the parties begins.

Food and Beverages

1. No credit is provided on restaurant bills.
2. Credit is allowed only with on the approval of Food and Beverage Manger or Sales manager. Such bills to be countersigned by restaurant managers with specific instructions.
3. For credit card holders such as hotels a restricted limit (say ₹ 3000) is applicable.

Last minutes billing instructions should be avoided as far a possible.

Guest signature is required on all credit bills.

QUESTIONS AND DISCUSSIONS

Short Answer Type

Q.1. Name some categories of customers for which credit limits are fixed.

Q.2. Write notes on:

(a) Credit card
(b) Travelers chouse
(c) Allowances
(d) Guest Ledger.

Q.3. Write a note regarding credit limits of the following category of customers:

(a) Travel agents and Airlines
(b) Companies and corporate houses
(c) Individuals
(d) Guest ledger
(e) Banquets
(f) Food and Beverages.

Descriptive Type

Q.4. Describe the duties of the hotel cashier when a guest presents an invalid check or credit card.

12

Settlement of Bill

CHAPTER OBJECTIVES

After studying this lesson you should be able :

- To describe the various methods of settlement of bills
- To under the procedure of payment by credit cards
- To explain the various credit cards
- To handle complaint, conc erning billing
- To know the rates of allowances given to various types of guests

The front office cashier should present the bill to the guest only because only he is or should be entitled and able to decide the various delicate questions arising when a customer settles his bill.

Payment in Cash

When a customer pays in cash, a receipt must be given to him. The posting machine immediately on the bill should print this receipt. Do not range the money in the cash drawer until the customer has checked the change. When there is no bank counter in the hotel, a special license must be obtained to accept foreign money.

CREDITS

Payment by Credit Cards

Credit card is a mixture of cash and credit. The customer who presents this card settles his bill immediately; from his point of view it is cash. The hotel sends the credit voucher to the credit cad company and receives the payment some weeks later. For the hotel a credit card is like endorsement of a bill. For this reason a stamped receipt 'Paid' is not given to the customer.

The cashier should always try to obtain cash payment only weeks after and charges approximately 5 to 8 % of the total sum of the bill as bank commission. Therefore a credit card should not be accepted for paid outs, unless the customer agreed to an overcharge on the paid outs covering the commission deducted by the credit card company.

Fig. 12.1. Specimen Credit Cards

When a customer presents a credit card that can be accepted in the hotel, the validity date must be checked. Expired cards are not to be honored. The company issues lists of lost or stolen cards from time to time. These lists must be consulted and the instructions must t be followed. The original of bill and original of the vouchers (card holder copy) are handed over to the guest.

The cashier's duties and responsibilities however should be clearly specified by the management. Some of the duties are:

1. The Chief Cashier is entitled to accept endorsement of bills for well-known customers (consult guest file) or if there is a written order of the endorsee.
2. The cashier can accept endorsement of bills up to an amount of Rs.........when the customer can provide references (take passport number, exact address, etc).
3. Endorsement of bills to foreign endorsees depends on rules and directions given by the government and additional directions given by the management (state those rules).
4. The cashier is not allowed to accept any personal cheques, expect for well-known customers (guest file) and by exception order given by the management.
5. The cashier is entitles to accept traveler cheques.
6. Credit cards can only be honored, if there is contract with the company. Paid out only can be endorsed to a credit card if the customer agrees to a (10% overcharge. (State the cards that can be accepted)
7. Foreign exchange can be accepted according tot eh government rules and directions given by the management. (State these rules). The exchange rate, limits and country of origin acceptable must be specified, etc.

Endorsement of Bills

Bills can be endorsed to another person or company, when there is either a written confirmation of the endorsee that he will take over the charges of the customer or it is well known client and an appropriate mark is written on the guest file.

When a well-known customer has no money, the supervisor (chief account officer, billing officer, lobby manager etc.) is to be called. The customer's name and passport number, date and place of issue and the exact address are to be taken. It is up to the supervisor to decide whether a personal cheques can be accepted, the luggage of the customer be kept. The notice is given to the police or, in case of a foreign guest, to the embassy.

Personal Cheques

Personal cheques usually are not accepted in any hotel. Exceptions are only made for well-known customers, after the management has approved or the approval has been recorded on the guest card already. In case an unknown guest cannot pay, a personal cheque is often the best solution. The cheque may be good and if it bounces, legal steps are easier to undertake with only the signed bill and customers address disposable.

Payment by Cheques

Although the rules for accepting cheques may vary from country to country, there are some international regulations a cashier must know. Presented below are some items that are a must on cheques:

1. Bank of drawer, name and address.
2. Order 'Pay' (often against this cheques).
3. Name of the payee. If nothing is filled in, and the cheques is not crossed, it is payable to the bearer.
4. Amount in words and figures\Place and a date of issue.
5. Signature of drawer.
6. A cheque may be marked with parallel line across the face (known as crossed). This means that the banker, to whom the cheque is presented for payment is not allowed to pay out in cash to the bearer, but only to credit this amount to the payee. The name of a banker or a bank can be written between these lines. The cheque then can only be presented to this bank.

Handling of Complaints Concerning Billing

When a customer complaints about charges on the bill, listen to him attentively and politely. Inquire about his complaint. Check the vouchers and if the customer is right (the voucher has been enormously charges to his bill or the amount is too high), make deduction and apologize.

If the voucher is enormously charges to his bill and the deduction has been charged and charge it thee. In case this guest has left, the supervisor has to decide what to do. Wither this charge is sent to the customer or charged tot eh employee who made the mistake.

Allowance

Allowances are given to several guests or groups of guest. Usually they are extended on room rates only. Detailed directions have to be given by the management.

For example:

	Category of Guest	Allowance Extended on Percentage Basis	On Amount
1.	Head quarter (official)	......................%	Total
2.	Head quarter (private)	......................%	Total
3.	Manager of Sister Hotels (official)	......................%	Room
4.	Manager of Sister Hotels (private)	......................%	Total
5.	Manager of Sister Hotels (official)	......................%	Room
6.	Manager of Special Categories Sister Hotels .	......................%	Room
7.	Other Hotel Managers	......................%	Room
8.	Managers of Airlines	......................%	Total
9.	Managers of Travel agencies.	......................%	Total
10.	Diplomatic Services	......................%	Room
11.	Others	.... %	etc.

With the help of this schedule the cashier is entitles to extend allowances without contacting the management. Special allowances have to be confirmed in writing by the management.

QUESTIONS AND DISCUSSIONS

Objective Type

Q.1. Choose the correct answer from the following questions:

(a) In a small hotel the front office equipment(s) include:

(i) Cash register (ii) Guest account file and reservation book

(iii) Key rack (iv) All the above.

(b) An inventory table by the roomkeepers of the status of all guest rooms, describing each as occupied, vacant or on-change/checked out is called:

(i) The house's report (ii) The housekeeper's report / maid's report

(iii) The discrepancy report (iv) None of these.

(c) The report sent back to the housekeeping department, indicating the difference between the report and the room rack is called as:

(i) The housekeeper's report (ii) Maid's report

(iii) Discrepancy report (iv) None of these.

(d) A rate plan which includes the rate for room only:

(i) Modified American plan (ii) American plan

(iii) European plan (iv) None of these.

(e) A rate plan which includes the room rate plus breakfast and dinner, guests are free to make their own lunch on arrangement is known as:

(i) American plan (ii) European plan

(iii) Modified American plan (iv) None of these.

(f) An American plan includes the charge for the followings:

(i) The price of the room (ii) The breakfast

(iii) The lunch and dinner (iv) All of the above.

(g) The development of an accounting system is based on:

(i) To provide effective internal control

(ii) To enhance cash flow

(iii) To produce analytical reports of operation

(iv) All of the above.

(h) Money paid out by the desk on behalf of the guest for service reduce such as gratuities (tips), payment to inhouse shops, delivery charges for parcel etc. is called as:

(i) Billed (ii) Paid out

(iii) Payments (iv) None of the above

(i) The original copy of an order and statement of purchases in an operating department is called:

(i) A voucher (ii) A guest check

(iii) A bill (iv) None of the above.

(j) A cash sheet is used to process all cash transactions that worked include:

(i) Cash payment against folio account

(ii) All cash received by the hotel

(iii) All cash paid by the hotel

(iv) None of the above.

[**Ans.:** (1) (iv) (2) (ii) (3) (iii) (4) (iii)
(5) (iii) (6) (iv) (7) (iv) (8) (ii)
(9) (ii) (10) (i)]

Short Answer Type

Q.2. Write a note on Front Office Accounting.

Q.3. List the functions of checkout and settlement.

Descriptive Type

Q.4. Discuss fundamentals of front office accounting.

Q.5. How accounts are created and maintained?

Q.6. Discuss the importance and different types of internal controls.

Q.7. Explain the procedure of Checkout and Settlement.

Q.8. Explain what to do with unpaid balance on accounts and how to handle collections.

Q.9. Define the terms source documents, voucher, department journal, folio, posting, city ledger, cash sheet, petty cash, float, and point-of-sale as they apply to hotel billing procedures.

Q.10. State the functions of a hotel front-office accounting system.

Q.11. Describe the typical hotel accounting cycle used to bill guest for charges.

Q.12. Give examples of various charges, which appear on a guest folio.

Q.13. Describe the procedure used by the desk clerk to assure that guest late charges are billed.

Q.14. Describe the duties of the hotel cashier to complete the guest folio andcollect for charges.

Q.15. Describe the cashier's responsibility to inform other departments when the guest has departed.

Q.16. Describe the duties of the hotel cashier when a guest presents an invalid check or Credit card.

Q.17. Describe departure procedures and check-out options.

Q.18. Explain what to do with unpaid balance on accounts and how to handle collections.

Q.19. Describe what to do with front office records.

Assignments /Activity Type

Q.20. Demonstrate the techniques used by desk clerks to identify guest payment methods.

Q.21. Demonstrate processing of credit cards when guest is registering at a hotel.

Q.22. Demonstrate the registration process including the key security issue

Q.23. Demonstrate different types of front office selling techniques

Q.24. Demonstrate the preparation and processing of credit card voucher.

Q.25. Demonstrate the procedure for processing a guest's personal check.

Q.26. Demonstrate the settlement of an account.

Q.27. Demonstrate a typical guest account from check-in to settlement.

13

Night Reception Work

CHAPTER OBJECTIVES

After studying this lesson you should be able :

- To describe the night audit procedure
- To prepare the Night Room Report
- To calculate the various types of percentages relating to occupancy, room rate etc.

Usually the work of the hotel continues thought out twenty-four hours, 7-days a week. During the night shift, the day's procedures are summarized and consolidated statements are made. The procedure to be followed, is as under:

1. Bring out the reservations for the next day along with carrier rack and place at the Reception Desk.
2. Check the reservations of the present day of the guests who have not shown up. Do not destroy these reservations as the guest may be delayed due to unforeseen circumstances and may be willing to pay retention charges when he shows up the next day. The reservation correspondence file for the next day is also brought out and arranged in alphabetical order.
3. First the Reception rack is tallied with the information.
4. Cross-check (on telephone) information racks and the rack maintained by the telephone exchange to avoid any discrepancy. Cross check the reception racks with the Rom Service for the same purpose.
5. Check the mail held against the names of guest already staying in the house and those expected the next day. Also check cables, packets etc.
6. Make out the following statement:
   (a) Room Report
   (b) Night Clerks Report

(c) Key tallying is done every night between 2.00 a.m. and 3 a.m. All the keys on the Key rack are to be checked with the room rack. Key to any occupied rooms are there on the rack; check if the guest has left instructions about his whereabouts. The guest may have gone out of town retaining the room or may be having a late night. If there is no instructions then check the room. It could be either a missed departure or the guest may have left without setting his bill.

Night Room Report

After reconciling the "Room Rack" with the Housekeeping Room Report, the Front Office Reception compiles data on the "Occupancy" position of the hotel for the day in the form of a report for the purpose of management information. This compilation and analysis of occupancy data is referred to as "Night Room Report" and is invariably prepared by the night receptionist (Ref. Fig. 13.1).

HOTEL ....
NIGHT ROOM REPORT

First Floor				Second Floor				Third Floor				Fourth Floor				Auditor's Coulstment	
Room No.	Code	Guests	Rate	Room No.	Code	Guests	Rate	Room No.	Code	Guests	Rate	Room No.	Code	Guests	Rate		
102				202				302				402					
103				203				303				403					
104				204				304				404					
105				205				305				405					
								306				406					Code
				207				307				407					Travel Agent
				209				309									Airlines —
				210				310				410					
111				211				311				411					
112				212				312				412					
119				213				319				416					
120				220				320				420				Total	
										Groups						Reception	
									Name		Race					F. No. Guests Amount	
																1st	
																2nd	
																3rd	
																4th	
Total				Total				Total				Total					Grand Total

Fig. 13.1. Specimen Night Room Report

After reconciling the "Room Rack" with the Housekeeping Room Report, the Front Office Reception compiles data on the "Occupancy" position of the hotel for the day in the form of a report for the purpose of management information. This compilation and analysis of occupancy data is referred to as "Night Room Report" and is invariably prepared by the night receptionist.

Night Clerks Report

There is vital information to be calculated for the Night Clerks Report. Some of the percentages re given below:

1. **Percentage of Occupancy:**

$$= \frac{\text{Number of rooms occupied}}{\text{Number of rooms available for sale}} \times 100$$

2. **Percentage of Occupied To date:**

$$= \frac{\text{Number of rooms occupied to date}}{\text{Number of rooms available}} \times 100$$

3. **Percentage of double Occupancy:**

$$= \frac{\text{House count} - \text{Number of rooms occupied}}{\text{Number of rooms occupied today}} \times 100$$

4. **Percentage of double occupancy To date:**

$$= \frac{\text{House count to date} - \text{Number of rooms occupied to date}}{\text{Number of rooms occupied to date}} \times 100$$

5. **Percentage of Indian occupancy:**

$$= \frac{\text{Indians in the house}}{\text{House count}} \times 100$$

6. **Percentage of Indian occupancy to date:**

$$= \frac{\text{Indians in the house to date}}{\text{House count to date}} \times 100$$

7. **Average room per room:**

$$= \frac{\text{Total room revenue to day}}{\text{Number of rooms occupied today}}$$

8. **Average room per person:**

$$= \frac{\text{Total room revenue to day}}{\text{House count to date}}$$

9. **Multiple Occupancy Percentage:**

$$= \frac{\text{Number of rooms occupied}}{\text{Total number of rooms available for sale}} \times 100$$

10. **Single Occupancy Percentage:**

$$= \frac{\text{Number of single rooms occupied}}{\text{Total number of single rooms available for sale}} \times 100$$

11. Double Occupancy Percentage:

$$= \frac{\text{Number of double rooms occupied}}{\text{Total number of double rooms available for sale}} \times 100$$

12. Triple Occupancy Percentage:

$$= \frac{\text{Number of triple rooms occupied}}{\text{Total number of triple rooms available for sale}} \times 100$$

Formulas for calculation of Hotel's Single, Double, and Triple Occupancy rates

1. Average Guests Per Rooms Sold

$$= \frac{\text{Total number of guests}}{\text{Total number of rooms sold}}$$

2. Average Daily Rate

$$= \frac{\text{Actual room revenue}}{\text{Total number of rooms sold}}$$

3. Revenue Per Available Room (RevPAR)

$$= \frac{\text{Actual room revenue}}{\text{Number of available rooms}}$$

4. Revenue Per Available Customer (RevPAC)

$$= \frac{\text{Actual hotel revenue}}{\text{Number of guests}}$$

5. Average Rate per Guest (ARG)

$$= \frac{\text{Total room revenue}}{\text{Number of guests}}$$

6. No-shows % Formulas in Daily operations Ratio

$$= \frac{\text{Number of no-show rooms}}{\text{Number of rooms reserved}} \times 100$$

7. Cancellation %

$$= \frac{\text{Number of cancellation rooms}}{\text{Number of rooms reserved}} \times 100$$

8. Walk-ins %

$$= \frac{\text{Number of walk-in rooms}}{\text{Total number of rooms available}} \times 100$$

9. Overstays %

$$= \frac{\text{Number of overstay rooms}}{\text{Number of expected check-outs}} \times 100$$

10. Understays %

$$= \frac{\text{Number of understay rooms}}{\text{Number of expected check-outs}} \times 100$$

QUESTIONS AND DISCUSSIONS

Objective Type

Q.1. Choose the correct answer from the following questions:

(a) Corporate rates are offered to the guests who fall in the category of :

(i) Business people (ii) Walk-ins

(iii) Travel agents (iv) Transit guests.

(b) A card which guarantees credit worthiness of a guest and against which the hotel charges the bill is known as :

(i) Credit card/debit card (ii) Traveller's cheque

(iii) Personal cheque (iv) None of these.

(c) Double occupancy percentage :

(i) $\frac{\text{Total Room sales}}{\text{Number of Rooms sold}} \times 100$

(ii) $\frac{\text{Number of Guests} - \text{Number of Room sold}}{\text{Number of Room sold}} \times 100$

(iii) $\frac{\text{Total Room sales}}{\text{Number of Rooms Available}} \times 100$

(iv) None of the above.

(d) Single occupancy percentage :

(i) $\frac{\text{Total Room sold}}{\text{Number of Rooms Available}} \times 100$

(ii) $\frac{\text{Total Room sales}}{\text{Number of Rooms sold}} \times 100$

(iii) $\frac{\text{Number of Guests} - \text{Number of Room sold}}{\text{Number of Room sold}} \times 100$

(iv) None of the above.

(e) A 100 room hotel with a daily average 65% occupancy and Rs. 590/- room rates annually generates sales of about :

(i) ₹ 19, 37, 950 /- (ii) ₹ 13, 97, 950 /-

(iii) ₹ 13, 99, 750 /- (iv) ₹ 13, 99, 77, 500 /-

(f) A level of service known as all suites is initiated for guests who want to experience :
 (i) The luxury of separate sleeping and living areas
 (ii) The kitchen facilities
 (iii) Wet bar and other facilities
 (iv) All of the above.

(g) The control process whereby the financial activity of guest's account, which reflect charges and payments (debit and credit), and the departmental receipts and charges are balanced and mentioned, is called as :
 (i) Checking system
 (ii) Night audit
 (iii) Accounting
 (iv) Control.

(h) Housekeeping and the front office communicate with each other about :
 (i) Room status
 (ii) Potential house court
 (iii) Security concerns and requests for amenities and supplies
 (iv) All the above.

(i) The food and beverage department and the front office cooperate by :
 (i) Relaying messages
 (ii) Providing accurate information on vouchers
 (iii) Reporting predicted house events and processing requests for paid-outs
 (iv) All of the above.

(j) The banquet department requires the front office to –
 (i) Relay information to guest about scheduled events
 (ii) Process payment of guest charges for scheduled events
 (iii) Prepare the daily announcement board and marquee
 (iv) All of the above.

[**Ans.:** (a) (i)   (b) (i)   (c) (iii)   (d) (iv)
(e) (iii)   (f) (iv)   (g) (ii)   (h) (iv)
(i) (iv)   (j) (iv)]

Short Answer Type

Q.2. List the functions of the night audit.

Q.3. List the management functions.

Q.4. Calculate the formula for establishing room rates.

Q.5. Calculate and evaluate the formulas and ratios for forecasting room availability.

Descriptive Type

Q.6. Calculate and verify a night audit

Q.7. Describe the daily report and explain its significance

Q.8. State the purpose of a hotel night audit.

Q.9. Name the elements necessary for completing a night audit.

Q.10. Compare and contrast the manual and automatic posting of charges and their impact on night audit procedures.

Q.11. Summarize the procedure for budgeting for operations

Q.12. Evaluate front office statistics for operating efficiency.

Assignments / Activity Type

Q.13. Process a night audit and discuss its relevance.

Q.14. Perform a night audit for a hotel.

14

Front Office Reports & Statistics

CHAPTER OBJECTIVES

After studying this lesson you should be able :

- To collect information for preparation of report.
- To prepare sales report
- To present various report to the management.

There are a number of statistics necessary at and from the front office. Most of these are done in close cooperation between the reception and billing section. It should be the aim to determine the work of these statistics without diminishing the completeness and clarity of them. This can be achieved by summarizing the data as much a possible in one form.

Turnover

There is a recapitulation book to report the turnover to the management. On the double page are vertical columns for each department as well as columns for the occupancy rate. Everyday the night auditor, after having made out the daily statement will enter the figures in the appropriate column of this book. After every ten days and at the end of the month the columns are added, showing the cumulated turnover of very department per month.

Then the brought forward from the last month is written in the next horizontal line and added to the turnover of the current month, showing the turnover accumulated from the beginning of the year up to now.

In the next month, two lines the corresponding figures (turnover of the month and accumulated) of the past's year are written to give the possibility of an immediate comparison with the past year.

Occupancy Report

The occupancy report shows the status of each room whether was occupied and by whom. In a separate column of this report the number of adults and children are marked as well as the nationality.

The room rate is stated and added floor wise, so that the auditor can check the room rate charges.

Concerning the nationality is sufficient to mark whether the customer is Indian or foreigner. Only the government law requires this. For purpose of public relations and sales analysis however it would be better to mark the specific nationality.

Departure List

In the departure list all guests are expected to leave this day are listed. Instead of typing a separate list, this can be included in the occupancy report, by using a special column and a sign for departure.

Plans

It is very important for the restaurants to know which customers have special arrangements such as American Plan, European Plan, and Modified American Plan, etc. This again can be included in the Occupancy Repot by giving special sign in the appropriate column 'Plan' of this report.

VIPs

VIP customers are specified on the Occupancy Report. No special list is written. A remark "VIP' behind the name is enough.

Sales Report

The Sales Report is a summary of the occupancy report. It shows the different subtotals of the floors, totaled to receive the total figures of the hotel's occupancy and room sales.

Room Sales

The first part of the Sales Repot is a summary of the floor occupancy as well as the adjustments as half and full rates (for late departures), day rooms and no shows. The total sum of the room rates divided by the number of rooms occupied gives the average room rate. The figure of this rate shows whether higher prices or lower priced rooms are preferred.

Occupancy

The second part of the Sales Repot shows how many clients, adults, and children, Indian and foreigners, are in the hotel, as well as the number of arrivals and departures, the fluctuation of guests.

According to the international standards, the room occupancy is considered to be more important than the bed occupancy. For this statistic only the available rooms are taken into consideration. For example, supposed a hotel has a total of 210 rooms, but 10 rooms are under renovation and 5 are blocked for internal use, so that only 195 rooms are available. The 195 rooms are then 100%, so that 156 occupied rooms' area equal to 80% occupancy, and not to 74% occupancy as it would be when compared to 210 rooms.

Presumed Occupancy

The presumed occupancy in the third part of the Sales Report only shows the number of expected residents according to the proofs available (reservation forecast).

Accumulated Occupancy

The statements of the Sales Report are entered in the accumulated occupancy book. This book then shows the occupancy of one month per day and accumulated. The necessary entries are:

1. Number of arrivals (adults and children).
2. Number of rooms blocked.
3. Number of rooms available.
4. Number and percentage of rooms occupied.
5. Average room rent.
6. All the above-mentioned items accumulated for the month. At the end of the month the brought forward from try preceding month is added. The comparative figures of the past year can be written underneath.

Presentation to the Management

It depends on the hotel's policy and the manager's wish to whether these statistics are shown to him regularly every day, every ten days or only monthly. It is the duty of the night auditor and the night receptionist to keep the turnover recapitulation and the accumulated occupancy report; both books should remain at the front office.

QUESTIONS AND DISCUSSIONS

Short Answer Type

Q.1. Explain the contents of a sales report.

Q.2. Write notes on:

(a) Occupancy report

(b) Turn over

(c) Room sales.

Descriptive Type

Q.3. Describe the procedure a desk clerk uses to determine the number of over bookings.

Q.4. Discuss the purpose and contents of the hotel housekeeping report and its use by the desk clerk.

Q.5. Describe the use of arrivals report, high-balance report, in-house guest list, and due-out report.

15

Salesmanship and Selling Techniques

CHAPTER OBJECTIVES

After studying this lesson you should be able :

- To understand the importance of salesman ship
- To acquire selling skills and techniques,
- To know the techniques of dealing with business tourists.

The difference between a successful hotel and an unsuccessful one is the ability of the staff to get a guest to spend an extra rupee and get the value for it. Very often a guest may enter a hotel without an exact idea of how he is going to utilize his free time. A gentle suggestion by an employee at the right time can stimulate a guest to utilize a service and pay for it. The front office staffs have a key role to play in hotel selling.

This is one of the most important factors for salesmanship. Here is a checklist of things that front office personnel should be knowledgeable about:

Location, view it commands, size, type, room rate, decor, guest facilities in the room such as hot/ cold water, channel music, telephone, refrigerator, television, weather controls, etc.

Number of outlets, locations, types of cuisine, entertainment, timings, buffet or a' la carte, menu, table reservation procedures. Service offered by travel agency, bank, post and telegraph office, health club, swimming pool, barber shop, pastry shop, shoe-shine, beauty saloon, drugstore and shopping. Telephones, party arrangements, baby sitter services, valet and laundry service, reservations for other hotels of the chain, telex, typist facility, doctor service. City tour facilities, church timings, theatre timings, maps and locations of shopping centers, historical, business and cultural places of interest, railway timings, airline schedule, inter-state bus terminals, nearest location of a 24-hour chemist shop and nearest hospital.

There are many more items of information that front office staff are equipped with to make them living encyclopedias. The important point to remember is that only with knowledge of the product can one actually sell it.

Front office staff must be aware that the guest attaches value to the service sold and will be prepared to spend for it. For example, if a room has a maximum, moderate and minimum rate attached to it, the maximum must be quoted but the value of this rate must be sold. The room may be overlooking the swimming pool, or be away from the noisy elevator foyer, or have soft decor to please a guest on a hot day. Whatever it be, each proposition must be given a value.

After the room is allotted the front office assistant may recommend a sauna bath and massage at the health club especially after the guest has returned from a long journey. The assistant may volunteer to reserve his table at one of the restaurants and bars.

The good front office assistant must always give the guest a choice so that he feels that the final decision was his. While offering a room two locations should be given. When recommending a restaurant two are offered to choose from (provided the establishment has more than one dining place). As individuals have varying needs, a guest may stay in a hotel for comfort, address value, entertainment, convenience of location, standards of facilities offered, etc. It is important to identify the needs of each guest and try to appeal to those needs. Another important aspect of a guest is that he has left his home and would like a home away from home. It is a question of emotional adjustments to unfamiliar surroundings. An employee should try and make him feel at home and anticipate his needs for home comforts through personalized service. By appealing to a guests' needs one can stimulate sales.

This trait could be the cornerstone to successful salesmanship in the hospitability industry—it is essential to be genuine in all communications with guests. The more genuine the front office staffs are in their approach, the greater is the desire to be helpful. A guest is sensitive and can see through a "put on" act as against sincerity in words and deeds. Unless an employee enjoys being hospitable, genuine concern becomes act. A simple way of bringing out this genuine concern is to display empathy. Empathy is energized by asking oneself, "What would I expect of the hotel if I were a guest".

How one speaks is important to all sales efforts. Brusque language is bound to put guests on the defensive and a sale can never be energized. Here are some typical phrases to use:

"May I help you"?

"May I suggest (or recommend).........."

"I beg your pardon"

"May I request you to.........."

"One moment please..........."

"Would you kindly............."

It is highly recommended that one should avoid the use of slang or abbreviation. Always refer to male guests as gentlemen and female guests as ladies or young ladies. Normally the establishment would select those candidates for the post of front office assistant who have a clear, mellow and proper mode of speech.

To make a sale, there are three ingredients needed:

1. A man
2. A need, and
3. A product.

The 'need' transforms the man into a customer to whom we call sell. According to the need, the wish, we can classify the customers into two groups:

1. The businessman, and
2. The tourists.

When analyzing the reasons why they come and what are looking for, we easily can make out what wee can and what we should offer to them. There is no reason offering a conference room to a tourist, but there are reasons to recommend the swimming pool to a businessman.

Dealing with Businessmen

He comes for business. We have to find out:

Dealing with Business Customer

The Businessman	**The Hotel**
1. What does he want?	1. What can we offer?
(a) Accommodation	(a) Rooms
(b) Need business friend's	(b) Suites
(c) Invite business friends	(c) Conference room
(d) Information	(d) Restaurants
(e) Communication	(e) Bars
	(f) Radio or television in the room
	(g) Telex
	(h) Free News paper
	(i) Quite accommodation
	(j) Bar
	(k) Swimming pool
	(l) Health Club, etc

Dealing with Tourists/Customers

The Tourist	**The Hotel**
1. What does he wants?	1. What can we offer?
(a) Accommodation	Room
(b) Local food	Different restaurants
(c) International food Car	Different restaurants Folders, Information
(d) Sightseeing	Travel counter
(e) Tours	Travel counter
(f) Shopping	Shopping arcade, list of references where to buy, what attractions in the hotel, performances, what's on in town, nightclubs etc.
(g) Sport, relax	Swimming pool, tennis, mini golf, health club.

The fact, which we roughly know what the customer wants, enables us to offer a whole range of service to meet his requirements. Although, the main products to be sold by the front office are rooms, the surroundings are very important. The customer, whom we would convince that the hotel meets all requirements, will take a room in it.

Selling techniques

When selling observe some basic rules:

1. Do not quote minimum rates, unless the customer asks for it.
2. Start offering higher priced accommodation. It is always possible to go down, but it is hard to go up once the customer has agreed. When starting low, the possibility of selling a suite often is spoiled. However, do not push the customer to take the more expensive room.
3. Give choice of two rooms to the customer, clearly indicating the advantages, size and location of each room. Offer more only when you see, the customer hesitates and cannot make up his mind. When you start offering 5 or more rooms, the customer gets confused, he cannot keep in mind all details you mentioned.
4. Describe the room, size, location, and furniture. Avoid diminishing comparisons such as:

   "Room 111 is smaller than 222".

   Say instead: "Room 222 is larger than 111".
5. A good knowledge of the rooms is necessary and appropriate marks on the room rack are great help. When describing a room common phrases may be used, such as

   "Specious room with a comfortable setting arrangement, etc"
6. Sell the room, not the rate. Emphasize the comfort of the room, not that it is a very cheap one.
7. Do not criticize the competitor. It does not prove that your business policy is unfair.
8. Do not ask the customer what prize range he prefers. He does know your tariff, so he only can guess, but not answer.
9. Show the customer up see the room when he cannot make up his mind if possible, go up yourself.
10. Your personal attitudes have to back, and can back or spoil all the other selling efforts you make.
11. Be patient. Contrary to shop, the customer is going to buy something he has not yet seen. That is why he hesitates, why he is asking questions like:

    'What do I get for the money I am going to pay?'
12. Be quite. The customer has traveled a good part of the day; he is in strange new surrounding which can make him anxious. Your quite voice can calm him.
13. Be ready to service, but avoid a servile behavior. Servility, not service makes the slave.

14. Be courteous. Courtesy is like an air cushion. There is nothing in it, but it can soften the shocks of life.

Salesmanship is not only required when a customer checks in unexpectedly. In fact, selling starts with his first contact with the hotel through the reservation. Selling continues during the whole stay of the guest at the hotel, and it often continues even a log time after his stay (mailing of folders etc). Salesmanship is service, it is successful when the customer comes back and praises and recommends the hotel to his friends.

QUESTIONS AND DISCUSSIONS

Descriptive Type

Q.1. Explain the importance of front desk selling.

Q.2. Explain the importance of maximizing profits in establishing room rates, forecasting room availability, budgeting, and using revenue management techniques.

Assignment / Activity Type

Q.3. Visit a hotel and discuss with guest regarding salesmanship and prepare a brief note on the dialogue you have with him.

16

Staffing

CHAPTER OBJECTIVES

After studying this lesson you should be able :

- To describe the traits of front office staff
- To explain the responsebilities of a Front Office Manager, Night Auditor, Receptionists etc.
- To face the interview and examination questions.

The front office personnel should be articulate, courteous, have a well-controlled temper, pleasant manners, sense of humor, positive attitude towards personal appearance, politeness, tact full and smiling face. Apart from some of the personal qualities mentioned above they should also be able competently handle a number of following tasks:s

1. Receive and greet guests
2. Give and receive information
3. Receive reservations and maintain reservation records
4. Maintain an inventory of rooms
5. Register guests and assign them rooms as per their needs
6. Handle mail, message and keys
7. Sell the room
8. Sell all other facilities available in the hotel
9. Interact with other departments and communicate with guest
10. Deal with guest compliant and emergencies.

The front office requires qualified and experienced personnel. A perfect receptionist should be outgoing and sociable when dealing with the guests and customers. At the same time he should be withdrawn and reserved when working at the office.

THE FRONT OFFICE STAFF SHOULD HAVE FOLLOWING TRAITS

Personal ability

He should have both facet of the personality. An excessive emotion is inappropriate as is too high degree of stability, which easily turns into a cold and unfriendly attitude. A candidate who makes the interviewer feel that he is a perfect must certainly has the ability to be a receptionist.

Professional ability

There are different responsibilities to fulfill at the front office and the organization schedule varies from hotel to hotel. It is not possible to give a complete list of all professional abilities requires in the front office. However some basic knowledge is always demanded. Good knowledge of language spoken in the country. A receptionist should fluently speak a good English. Knowledge of other desired languages are dependant on the customers frequenting the hotel. Knowledge of good arithmetic ability is essential quality. A new entrant can be trained for the specific type of job.

Specialized traits

Some positions require specialized traits to perform specialized tasks. Therefore basic knowledge of those areas is essential. For example, a cashier must know how to handle personal and traveler checks and credit cards. Similarly an auditor must know the principles of accounting. A room assistant is expected to know how to receive, process and accept reservations and how to room guest, etc.

Product knowledge

The room assistant must know the product (room) he is selling. When he starts his job, he has to go through the rooms in order to know where they are located, what kind of furniture there is in the room, and what color combination is there into room. The accommodation manager in association with the executive housekeeper has to go from time to time through all rooms, checking the conditions of each of them.

FRONT OFFICE MANAGER

Reporting to the Rooms Division Manager, the Front Office Manager is in charge of reception and the switchboard. He is responsible for welcoming guests and handling any complaints. In doing so, he or she:

1. Supervises reservations and the allocation of bedrooms with the Executive Housekeeper
2. Monitors the customer accounts and till accounts
3. Applies and ensures the application of the sales strategy to maximize occupancy and average room price
4. Co-ordinates the reception team, organizing its work and schedules

Responsibilities

1. To monitor the quality of welcome extended to guests
2. To recruit, train and motivate the members of the his or her team
3. To ensure that all hotel standards and procedures are applied
4. To manage daily billing and payments

Skills and Traits

1. Use of windows
2. The ability to train and motivate a team
3. The ability to be available to work nights, weekends or public holidays
4. Sales ability
5. Hospitality
6. Adaptability: coping with the diversity of customers and their needs
7. Self-sufficiency
8. Self-control: handling complaints
9. Good relationship skills
10. Team leadership
11. Good memory: remembering guests
12. Taking the initiative
13. Discretion.

Qualifications & Experience

1. Good general education preferably in hotel or tourism studies
2. Experience of reception
3. Fluency in a second language is an advantage
4. Good general level of education
5. Significant experience of latest reservations system.

RESERVATIONS MANAGER

He is responsible to organize the reservations system and take responsibility for the quality of the service it provides, whilst maximizing occupancy rates and average revenue per room.

Responsibilities

1. To ensure that all telephone, fax and Internet enquiries received from customers are handled to a high quality standard
2. To ensure that customers are offered high quality services and a high quality service
3. To ensure the continuation of the resources supplied for his or her use
4. To ensure that the brand standards are applied.

Skills & Traits

1. Using the Windows and Tars on-line environment
2. Self-control
3. Thoroughness
4. Organization
5. Readiness to take the initiative.

Qualifications & Experience

1. Good general education preferably in Hotel or Tourism studies
2. Experience in a hotel environment
3. Good general level of education
4. Fluency in a second language is an advantage
5. Significant experience of latest reservations systems.

NIGHT AUDITOR

He is to approve invoices, write the day's statistical and accounting report for the management team and prepare the documents required by the morning team.

Responsibilities

1. To take responsibility for the hotel after the daytime management team has left
2. To manage the till and bill payments as well as closing the day's Front Office transactions
3. To ensure the safety of guests: he or she takes all urgent decisions (walks, fire procedures, etc.)
4. To ensure that guests receive high quality service

Skills & Traits

1. Night working
2. Understanding how to manage priorities
3. Use of the Windows environment
4. Sales ability
5. Hospitality
6. Adaptability: coping with the diversity of customers and their needs
7. Self-sufficiency: usually working alone
8. Self-control: handling complaints
9. Good relationship skills

Qualifications & Experience

1. Good general education preferably in hotel or tourism studies with finance and accounting background
2. Beginner or with basic experience in a customer contact job
3. Fluency in a second language is an advantage

HOTEL RECEPTIONIST

Hotel receptionists are responsible for making guests feel welcome, dealing with room bookings and efficiently checking guests in and out of the hotel. They are trained to deal professionally with reservation enquiries, face to face and by phone, fax or email general booking questions and any complaints. Customer contact can be face to face and by phone, fax or email. They deal with general reservation enquiries, as well as answering guests' questions and dealing with complaints.

A hotel receptionist job involves a good deal of administration so would suit a candidate who is well organized and who has an administrative flair. Hotel receptionists need to be good administrators, but most importantly they have to be ambassadors for the hotel. A hotel receptionist should maintain a calm, courteous and professional demeanor at all times.

Functions and Duties

Typical duties are likely to include:

1. Welcoming guests as they arrive
2. Allocating rooms to guests
3. Giving guests their keys
4. Taking and passing on messages
5. Handling foreign exchange
6. Preparing guests' bills and taking payments
7. Helping guests with any special requests - such as storing valuables in the hotel safe or luggage area, ordering taxis or booking theatre tickets.

In a large hotel, the reception desk will usually have a computer to handle reservations, showing up-to-date information on the number and type of rooms available. Receptionists are responsible for inputting new information as guests make bookings or cancellations. He/she is responsible for the stays of guests in the hotel. He or she maintains the guest folder from arrival to payment on departure.

Most hotel receptionists will use a telephone switchboard to receive external calls and to take internal calls from hotel rooms and from different parts of the hotel.

There is also a sales aspect to the role of a hotel receptionist. They may encourage a guest to upgrade to a better room, to stay longer, to eat in the restaurant, or to return to the hotel, or another in the group, in the future, for a special occasion or event.

In an emergency receptionist may help guests evacuate the building and call the emergency services.

Every part of the hotel has to work well together, and receptionists liaise closely with the porters, with housekeeping and with security and maintenance staff.

In larger hotels, there is often a team of receptionists, each with specific duties. In a small hotel, they might carry out additional, non-reception tasks, such as serving drinks in the bar, helping the housekeeping staff or arranging flowers.

Responsibilities

1. Welcoming, friendly and helpful
2. Efficient and professional
3. Excellent communicators

4. Good at administrative tasks
5. Calm and efficient in all situations
6. Good with IT and confident learning to operate a switchboard
7. Well organized and able to handle several tasks at once
8. Able to pay attention to detail
9. A real 'people person', with tact and sensitivity
10. Able to think quickly and come up with solutions
11. Smart in appearance
12. Knowledgeable about the hotel and able to sell its services
13. Able to speak foreign languages, in some jobs.

Hours and environment

Hotels are open all hours, and someone is always needed to cater for the needs of the guests. Reception desks in larger hotels often stay open all night, but in smaller hotels, a porter might handle nighttime duties.

Working hours can include days, evenings, nights, weekends and public holidays. Receptionists might work shifts or split shifts (working in the morning and coming back later in the day for an evening shift).

There are many opportunities to work part time and seasonally, during busy holiday periods.

Reception areas are usually near the hotel entrance. Receptionists usually work behind a counter or desk using a computer terminal and telephone or telephone switchboard.

A hotel receptionist salary will depend on the size, type and location of the hotel however the starting salary for a hotel receptionist job, Hours of work may vary and can include days, nights, shifts, weekends and public holidays. Part-time work may be available which is paid pro-rate or at an hourly rate. Salaries in deluxe hotels are very high. Meals and accommodation may be provided as part of the salary package. Employers often provide uniforms. Extra payments for working unsociable hours or overtime may be available.

Many receptionists use a computer to handle reservations and may also operate the telephone switchboard. They may employ sales skills to encourage guests to upgrade to a better room, eat in the restaurant or book another visit. In larger hotels there is often a team of receptionists, each allocated specific duties. In smaller hotels, they might carry out additional non-reception tasks, such as serving drinks.

Reception desks in larger hotels often stay open and are staffed all night. In smaller hotels, the porter might take on nighttime duties. Working hours can include days, nights, weekends and public holidays. Receptionists might work shifts or split shifts. Seasonal and part-time opportunities are widely available.

Skills ad Traits

1. Team working

2. Using the Windows environment
3. Sales ability
4. Hospitality
5. Adaptability: coping with the diversity of customers and their needs
6. Availability: working nights, weekends and public holidays
7. Self-control: handling complaints
8. Good relationship skills
9. A welcoming, friendly and helpful attitude
10. Excellent communication skills
11. Confidence operating a computer system and switchboard
12. Good organization skills and the ability to handle several tasks at once
13. A calm, efficient manner
14. Enjoy dealing with people
15. Ensure that guests receive high quality service
16. Promote loyalty amongst a broad range of customers
17. Ability to manage a till.

Qualifications

Although receptionists do not need specific qualifications on entry, many employers like to see some evidence of communication skills. They might ask for certificate/diploma/degree or equivalent qualifications, particularly in English and math. Previous experience in customer service or office work may be useful.

1. Good general education/diploma or degree, preferably in Hotel or Tourism studies
2. Further education (degree in languages or service industry studies, or similar)
3. Previous experience in Reception
4. Must be fluent in English and a good level of French
5. Experience of latest reservations systems.

The Diploma in hospitality may be relevant for this area of work. There are also many different qualifications, which can be useful preparation for this kind of work.

These can be studied full or part time at a college prior to entry or once in the job. From studying these qualifications it is possible to accumulate credits on the new hospitality qualifications framework, which may enable better career mobility in the future.

Training

Training is usually a combination of structured training with working alongside experienced colleagues. Many larger hotels and chains offer in-house training schemes, which may also encourage receptionists to work towards qualifications as part of their development.

Hotel receptionists provide the first impression guests have of a hotel. A hotel receptionist job includes greeting guests and checking them in and out of the hotel, however a hotel receptionist job may also involve a large amount of administration work including taking reservations, allocating rooms, record keeping, passing on messages, compiling bills to name just a few.

A hotel receptionist job will have a great deal of contact with guests organizing special requirements, dealing with requests for taxis, theatre tickets, information about the local area and taking valuables for safe keeping.

Hotel Receptionists will be required to use a reservations computer system in all but the smallest hotels, although a hotel receptionist will often also use word processors as well as fax machines and switchboards.

In large hotels receptionists may work as part of a specialist team dealing with certain aspects of reception work, however in smaller hotels the hotel receptionist may handle a very large range of tasks.

Hotel Receptionists must also liaise constantly with the housekeeping department to know which rooms are occupied.

The hospitality, leisure, travel and tourism sector is growing. There are thought to be more than 17,000 hotel receptionists and there are plenty of opportunities, though competition for the best jobs with prestigious hotels can be high.

There are more than. ....hotels and guesthouses situated in all parts of the country-including cities, near the coast, in the countryside and in small towns.

Jobs are published in trade magazines, such as Caterer and Hotelkeeper, and their official job site. Vacancies may also be advertised in Jobcentre Plus offices, in the local press and by specialist hotel recruitment agencies and websites.

Prospects do vary depending on the size of hotels. Larger hotels and chains may offer more promotional opportunities. With experience and the right skills, receptionists could be promoted to jobs such as shift leader or supervisor, then on to front office manager or head receptionist. For this they may need to undertake further qualifications, for instance:

Receptionists could also move to different areas of hotel work, such as events management or banqueting services, sales, human resources or accounts management. Employers will often encourage staff to work in different departments to help broaden their skills. This may increase prospects for people wishing to progress into general management.

The skills acquired are equally valuable outside the hospitality industry, particularly in customer service and administrative roles.

Job Interview

The hotel industry is currently one of the most promising and lucrative sectors in an economy. It is rapidly developing and adapting to the requirements of our modern lifestyle. Nowadays there is wide range of employment opportunities in this field. If you wish to secure a decent receptionist job then you must prepare yourself to answer some questions. There are some of the frequently asked interview questions, which are listed as under:

Q.1. Can you please tell us about the roles and responsibilities of a hotel receptionist?

Ans. Guidance:

The business related responsibilities that a receptionist has to perform include to greet visitors, answering visitor inquiries about a hotel and its services, directing visitors to their destinations, sorting and handing out mail, answering incoming calls on multi-line telephones, filing, records keeping, keyboarding and performing a variety of other office tasks, such as faxing or emailing.

Q.2. Please elaborate about occupation specific tasks that you have performed in your previous organization?

Ans. Guidance:

In my previous Hotel I used to perform various important tasks. The occupation specific tasks that I performed include welcoming guests, receiving guests, dealing with room bookings, cancellations and handling general requests made by guests during their stay. I also handled telephone inquiries, managed customer relations and provided exemplary services.

Q.3. If there is any unsatisfied and irate customer. How do you handle him or her?

Ans. Guidance:

Unsatisfied customers are part and parcel of running a hotel. It is very important for any hotel to satisfy their customer. Well, I generally handle unhappy customers by listening them. The main thing an unsatisfied customer wants is to be heard. So I let them speak first and thereafter I try to solve their problem.

Q.4. There are so many hotels. Why you particularly applied in this hotel?

Ans. Guidance:

It is the most common and often asked interview question. One has to tell reasons as to why he or she fits into this position. Think of all the good qualities in your personality that makes you suitable for the job. Remember, you have to tell how your studies, skills, experience and personal qualities will contribute to the work of the hotel.

Q.5. Why are you leaving your previous job?

Ans. Guidance:

Remember, never abuse or disrespect your previous employer. You can politely answer this question by saying that there was no growth scope in my previous hotel that is why I left it. I am looking for a company with long-term growth opportunities.

QUESTIONS AND DISCUSSIONS

Short Answer Type

Q.1. Write notes on:

(a) The Receptionist

(b) Night Auditor.

Discriptive Type

Q.2. Explain some important traits of a front office staff.

Q.3. Describe the process for assessing hotel personnel hiring needs.

Q.4. Discuss the methods for recruiting hotel personnel.

Q.5. Describe the factors covered when conducting hotel personnel orientations.

Q.6. Explain the duties and responsibilities if a receptionist.

Assignment / Activity Type

Q.7. Write a question and answer session between an interview team and a candidate appearing first time for a position of receptionist in a hotel.

17

Telecommunication—Telephone Department

CHAPTER OBJECTIVES

After studying this lesson you should be able :

- To understand the significance of telephone operator,
- To describe the role of a telephone operator,
- To deal with various complaint and report
- To acquire skills of telephone handling
- To prepare the bills.

Telecommunication is another important feature of the front office in a hotel. Every hotel, irrespective of tits size and situations, has a telephone board/ exchange. In a small hotel it may have a switchboard placed at he reception counter, making the receptionist to take responsibilities of the switchboard operation in addition to his duties. In large hotels, a separate room is allotted to house telephone switchboard and operators. This room adjoins the reception because they both have to coordinate with each other for better services.

Generally three shifts are required for telephone department, as this is twenty-four hour a day work. To cover the traffic at peak hour's additional staff may be employed. A telephone operator can provide service to several hundred rooms because of automatic features like extension in guest rooms.

The different types of calls a guest may place during his stay in the hotel are:

1. Local calls
2. Domestic long distance calls
3. International calls
4. Calling card calls
5. Credit card calls
6. Conference calls
7. Person- to person calls
8. Toll free calls.

The hotel is obliged to charge for these services and thereby earn subsidiary revenue for the establishment.

Handling Telephones

Telephone operators are responsible to the telephone supervisor fro rendering superior telephone service. They can do this only by fulfilling the requirements of the hotel's guests satisfactorily satisfying the personal requirements of the guest calls by systematic exercise of cheerfulness, speed, accuracy, cooperation.

Accuracy

Careless and misunderstanding usually causes errors. They result in failure to give the service demanded, the aggravation of the guest, and wasted efforts on the part of the operator. All this can be avoided by the exercise of reasonable care, particularly in putting up connections, ringing, listening attentively, speaking and enunciating discreetly, allowing proper time for connection and paying close attention to signals.

Speed

Speed is one of the most important feature, but accuracy must be not be scarified at he cost of speed. An inaccurate connection no matter how quickly made, is not what the guest wants. Speed is a skilled performance of each operation without loss of time and with the least possible expenditure of energy. Particular attentions should be paid to the prompt answering of recalls and line signals. Consistency in the speed of service is also necessary, as one case of slow service more than off sets the good impression made by several cases of prompt service.

Co-operation

Co-operation among employees is essential to the successful performance of the hotel's business. Failure of other employees to do his /her part of work reacts seriously upon efforts of others.

The Operator and the guest

Operator must bear in mind that in al dealings with guest they represent the Management. Courtesy depends as much upon tone of voice and manner of speaking as upon what is actually said- courtesy makes work easy and pleasant fro fellow employees as well. Discourtesy though un-intentional, wastes time, causes irritation and dissatisfaction.

Be district, enunciate clearly, and deliberately make use of the guest's name if known to you. At any rate use expressions, such as

"Yes Sir",

"Thank You",

"No Madam",

"One moment please"

Complaints

When a guest is experiencing difficulty and complaints, connect him at once with the supervisor, saying,

"One moment please, I will connect you with the supervisor."

The operator's attitude in such a case must be that of concern. A guest resents indifference at any time. The Operator's personal number to be disconnected.

SECRECY OF TELEPHONIC CONVERSATION

The attention of the Operator is called to the fact that the rules and regulations make it an offence, punishable with dismissal from service to violate the secretary of telephonic communications. All employees are expressly forbidden to divulge any information regarding communications between users of the telephone. They are likewise cautioned against listening unnecessarily into connections.

Business Satellite Phone

Manner of Addressing Employees

All female employees will be addressed as

" Miss……" unless she is known be Mrs………, etc" and

all male employee as

'Mr................" unless Mrs. as the case may be.

The Operator and the Supervisor

In order that the operator may assume the proper attitude toward supervisor / assistant supervisor, it is necessary that she first understands clearly the supervisor's responsibilities. Consider the supervisor / assistant supervisor as her teacher in that spirit turn to him/her for training a d drilling in the operation rules. Do not hesitate to obtain from the supervisor any information regarding matters, which are not entirely clear. Show proper respect for the supervisor knowledge of operating, for his /her experience and for his/her judgment in all telephone matters. All operators should welcome criticism and instructions from the supervisor and not to resent these. Its only object is the betterment of the work: and an increase in the value of the operator tot eh hotel.

Service Observations

Service observations are necessarily made for the purpose of obtaining reliable data showing what kind of service is being given. As applied to the operator, these observations are not for the purpose of being unduly critical or making employment unpleasant. They are made to get an exact picture of the operator's work. If the work is not good, observations will enable he work need to be improved. Accordingly, an operator should welcome service observations, because they show the high grade pf work performed or because of the benefit available for a careful study of the unsatisfactory features of her work. Remember that whoever discusses the observations with you is doing so in a spirit of friendly assistance. Remember that showing warrants, criticism or reprimand, such action is solely for the purpose of emphasizing your welfare and towards those who are making the observations, have no feelings of animosity or fear. They are simply recording accurately and impartially what they observe. They are your friends at heart.

THE OPERATORS AND OTHER EMPLOYEES

Teamwork

Team work between operators, wherever located, whether seated side by side and dealing with each other personally, or whether indifferent locations is necessary for the proper handling of the traffic.

To secure uniformly prompt service, it is necessary that each operator answer, whatever possible, call within reach. Do not hesitate to pick up a call originating at the other console of section. It is also necessary to assist adjacent operator by passing and taking down calls, but only when requested to do so. A friendly and cooperative understanding between neighboring operators is necessary in order that they may quickly seize every opportunity to assist each other. In reaching to answer calls, or to put connections, be careful not interfere with the work of other.

Relief of Operator

Operator will not leave their positions at any time without obtaining the permission of the monitor or supervisor. Before leaving their position they will arrange their work so that the relieving operator can go without danger or delay or interruption. In general, it must be borne in mid that the guests have no knowledge of change or shortage of operator and the fat that a change is taking place cannot be accepted as an excuse for the poor service. Operator should not go out of the hotel without permission. Lang time relief is not allowed so operators should come back to the console immediately after their relief i.e. tea or lunch or dinner etc. When one operator on relief the working operator should be more careful, fast and accurate to avoid guess complain. The operator is expected to make the operating continuous by proceeding at once with her work. Any arranging of her dress or adjustment of the chair is to be attending to later, as the opportunity presents itself.

Operating routine-Memorizing House Directory

Operators are required to familiarize themselves with the house directory. Operators are required to memorize officials' extension numbers and locations and the names of officials.

Complaints

Guest desiring to complain of telephone service will be connected with the shift –in-charge/supervisor for fault complaints. In their absence inform maintenance. Electrician will help to attend the complaints, please follow it up. Don't keep guest's complain for a long time.

Log Book

A Logbook will be kept in which will appear records of all complaints and irregularities and experienced with the service. A weekly summary of these irregularities will be complied by the supervisor and forwarded to the Executive Manger.

Communicating Rules

In as much as the accuracy and speed of operating depends to a large extend up on the correct understanding of calls and orders transmitted verbally over the phone; it is essential that operators always speak distinctively and deliberately. It is better to take a little more time at first, then to proceed hurriedly with a call only to be obliged to repeat the operation because of some misunderstanding. Whenever repeating or passing telephone calls, the operator will emphasize the name with special distinctiveness, and communicate the letter and numbers in accordance with the Table 17.1 and 17.2.

Equipment Trouble

Telephone equipment trouble will be immediately reported to the Supervisor In charge who will have it corrected by the telephone department. The telephone supervisor in a special book provided for this purpose will enter a record of all equipment trouble.

Table. 17.1. Style of Pronunciation of Numbers

Serial No.	*Number*	*Technique of Pronunciation*	
1.	'0'	to be pronounces as	"OH" with a long "O"
2.	'1'	to be pronounces as	"WUN" with a long "N"
3.	'2'	to be pronounces as	"TOO" with a long T and long "OO"
4.	'3'	to be pronounces as and long "E"	"THR-REE" with a slightly rolling 'R
5.	'4'	to be pronounces as	"FO-WER" with a long "O"
6.	'5'	to be pronounces as	"FIVE" with a long 'I' and 'V'
7.	'6'	to be pronounces as	"SIKS" with a strong 'X'
8.	'7'	to be pronounces as	"SE-VEN" two syllabus
9.	'8'	to be pronounces as with a long A and strong	"ATE" 'T'
10.	'9'	to be pronounces as with a strong 'N' at the end	"NI-YEN"
11.	'10'	to be pronounced as sharp	'T' sound and strong 'E-N'

Table 17.2. Pronunciation of some selected Words

1.	'J'	to be pronounces as	"JAY"
2.	'R'	to be pronounces as	"AHR" with a strong 'R'
3.	'M'	to be pronounces as	"EM" with a short E and strong 'M'
4.	'W'	to be pronounces as	"Double U" with full value given to each syllabus

Fire Report

The operator upon receiving the alarm will immediately notify the Chief Engineer's Office and give location of fire. The initial of the person to whom fire is reported should be obtained. The operator will immediately notify the following:

1. General Manager
2. Lobby Manager
3. Security
4. Maintenance.

Time of location of the fire and the initials of the person to whom reports were given is to be recorded in the Log Book and the exact memorandum left for the supervisor.

NAME CODE

The operators may use the following name codes for surnames, initials and lettered room numbers given in Table 17.3.

Table. 17. 3. Name Code for Different Cities

Serial No.	Alphabet	Name of the City
1.	A.	AGRA
2.	B.	BOMBAY
3.	C.	CALCUTTA
4.	D.	DELHI
5.	E.	ENGLAND
6.	F.	FINLAND
7.	G.	GWALIOR
8.	H.	HOLLAND
9.	I.	INDIA
10.	J.	JAMES
11.	K.	KING
12.	L.	LONDON
13.	M.	MADRAS
14.	N.	NAGPUR
15.	O.	ORANGE
16.	P.	PUNJAB
17.	Q.	QUEEN
18.	R.	RAILWAY
19.	S.	SUGAR
20.	T.	TABLE
21.	U.	UMBRELLA
22.	V.	VICEROY
23.	W.	WILLIM
24.	X.	X-RAY
25.	Y.	YOUNG
26.	Z.	ZEBRA

Primary Steps in Answering Outgoing Call

On the first hand, we have a EPABX board and the guests can dial their outgoing number direct, but in some cases the guest will ask the operator to help him to get the number. Hence this procedure is laid down. When answering in-house telephone call the operator has to say:

"May I help you please"?

Be sure to speak with a rising cheerful inflection.

Busy Signal

If a busy signal is heard, say to the guest:

"I am sorry, 000000 No. is busy. May I call you again", and if the guest wishes to be called try the number again after the lapse of a couple minutes. If there is no answer, report to the guest.

"I am sorry 0000 number does not answer."

Before connecting to the required number, it is advisable to check with the connected party. If the dialed number is the correct one, repeating the dialed number.

Incoming Calls

All incoming calls will go through EPABX Switch board. In answering call say,

"Good Morning" - Cleridges" or to wish according the name of the day.

When the calling party asks for a certain person name, check the room number from the telephone information rack and ask the calling party name then announce the call to the guest. In case, there is no reply find out from the calling party if any message is to be left, then connect the party to the message desk for receiving the message and tell the calling party,

"I am connecting you to the message desk, you may pleas leave the message with them"

If any party wants to speak to guest in the house and only ask for room number, it is necessary that the operator gets the name of the guest who is wanted by the calling party and also the name of the calling party. Otherwise,

Until Noon .... Good Morning
12 Noon to 4 P.M .... Good Afternoon
04 P.M to Midnight .... God Evening.

If the number is busy and the calling party is willing to wait keep repeating back to him at frequent intervals, not later than 30 seconds, that the extension continues to be busy. If there has been an appreciable delay apologize for being kept him waiting. It costs nothing but earns a lot of goodwill.

If a line is busy,

If the called Room Number is busy, say

"I am sorry Mr......... is busy, will you wait please".

When the number is free, report,

"You may have Mr........., thank you for waiting."

Special service

When an outgoing room telephone is answered the guest states he may be reached in one of the restaurants located in the hotel, ask for the following information:

1. Number of Room
2. Guest's name and initials
3. Restaurant where he could be reached and till what time
4. Operator suggests to the guest that he leaves his table location with the captain, in order to receive his telephone calls promptly.
5. Repeat details to confirm if in nay doubt.

Request for the Time

If the operator gets a request for time, give the time shown on clock. Example of phrasing,

"Nine minutes after eight"

"A quarter to four"

"Twenty seven minuets to five", etc.

Morning Calls-receiving and handling

Morning calls or wake up calls are those left by guest who wishes to be called at the specific time the following day. These calls are recorded on a morning form. The room number and the name and the time call is required is to be double checked before releasing the line. The operator listens attentively and enters the call in the proper columns and says,

"Mr……… Room Number... ………six o'clock. We will call you."

The morning call operator carefully checks all the entries made on the Morning Call Sheet. When calling in the morning the operator has to be very careful in connecting the room to avoid making a connection to a wrong room. When the guest answers, the operator tells him,

"Good Morning, Mr……… It is six o'clock."

(She omit guest's name entirely, if uncertain of pronunciation or spelling).

When the guest receives the announcement without comment and hangs up, the operator rings back and announce the time again. She makes certain of an acknowledgement. When one is received, draw a diagonal line through the morning call listed on that number on the Call Sheet. If a guest requests that you call him back later on, say 7.15 a.m., repeat the time given. Enter the name, Room number and the time in proper column again.

Departure of a Guest

When notice is received from the Information assistant that a guest has departed, draw a line with reed pencil through the room number and name on the Board and write the time. Don't remove this slip till 11 o'clock in evening. If an outside call comes from Mr……… and the line is drawn through the name, inform the calling party that Mr……… was staying, but he has checked out today.

Announce Calls for all Guests

All calls incoming calls are to be announced

Before connecting, the operator must get the name of the calling party before ringing the room. Announce callers name to the guest and listen carefully to what report guest gives. If the guest says, he is not in, say,

"Thank you Sir,"

and report to the calling party and say,

"I am sorry Mr…….., does not answer."

Long Distance Calls

We charge for the local calls. The long distance calls are to be charged to the guest. A written notice is kept in every room requesting the guest to call the operator for a long distance call. When a customer wants to book a long distance call, take call the particulars including the name of the guest and the room number very carefully and make the entries in the lag. When the long distance call is through check up the charges and make charge voucher which is immediately sent to the front office cashier fro being posted at the guest folio. After the STD is complete check and confirm with guest if the call was successful.

Guidelines For Trunk Calls Booking

1. Always give the following information in the order shown below trunk bookings:
   (a) The Calling number and extension number from which the calling party will speak
   (b) The name f the called town
   (c) The called number
   (d) Name of the P. P., if required
   (e) Type of call – ordinary or urgent.
2. While booking P.P. Calls nominate an alternative particular person and or number if possible.
3. Note down trunk ticket number, quote this when making subsequent enquiries in respect of the call.
4. For making enquiries for the calls already booked, consult Trunk assistant Service. No?
5. When the Trunk Call matures, if the calling extension is busy, you must break in n the conversation to offer the call. But do so courteously.

Tips to Remember

1. An abrupt, listless, disinterested or discourteous tone will completely offset the technical efficient that you may command.
2. Avoid unnecessary conversational the switchboard.

Equipment Handling:

Any equipment you are holding needs to be carefully handled. Following guidelines may be observed:

1. A little care with your equipment will help you get the best out of it and fee pot trouble free. The first consideration is cleanliness.
2. Never spell water on your equipment. It will not only damage but is liable to give and electric shock,
3. Handle your hand set carefully. Place it in its proper position when not in use so that it's not liable to damage.

4. Handle your equipment carefully. Avid entire manipulation of keys as it wears out the keys. The entire equipment is electronic and has soft touch operations. Using jerky movements is liable to make the electronic equipment less efficient.
5. Don't scream or gossip in the exchange.
6. Do not use a pencil in place of your finger on the dial. This will damage the dial.
7. No arguments are allowed in the exchange.
8. Whenever you have direct number or junction, report the matter promptly to the telephone complaint service.
9. No operator is allowed to over hear conversation while sitting on board. Operator is not allowed to allow ant one else to cover the conversation except when ordered by the following Authorized Officials:
   (i) General Manager
   (ii) Director Operations
   (iii) Front Office Manager
   (iv) Telephone Supervisor.
10. Unauthorized persons entry into the Telephone Exchange is prohibited.
11. No one should make Trunk Calls or Local (paid or unpaid), call from the Exchange, including executives.
12. Position of booked call to be informed to each guest every ½ hour or one hour.
13. H/o and T/o should be completed and all equipment checked and is in working order.
14. All Lobby Managers to know and understand possible faults that can arise in the Front Office Cash, telephone Computer, to be able to correct possible faults, as computer has been known to have gone out of order at early morning hours and heavy guest bills have not been recovered.

EXTENSION AND ZERO FACILITY AREAS

Business Centre

For Headquarter Sales Office provision of separate extension number is required, as it is not possible to differentiate between business centre local calls and Holiday Inn sales office local calls.

Lobby Desk Phone

Private parties local calls to be charged and bill presented.

Restaurants

Zero facility to be given only on request and only from the telephone exchange. Reception and Front Office Cashier are not authorized to release "Zero Facility" of restaurants. Zero facility of restaurant to be closed immediately after use and log entries to be closed immediately after use and log entries to be made at exchange of each release of zero facility at restaurants including time of release number dialed and tome of closing and name of person releasing and closing). Same log need to be maintained at restaurant by Restaurant Manager/Captain.

Guest Rooms

1. Immediately on departure of guest from rooms, the front office Cashier to cut zero facility of the room.
2. Any call made after check out time (as per Bellboy Errand Card) and check in time of next guest (as per GRC) will be charged to the Front Office Cashier on duty at that time.
3. Telephone Supervisor to inform Housekeeping Department of all such calls made from rooms to find out Room Attendants responsible at time of duty.
4. Only reception is authorized to open zero facility of guest rooms, not ant other extension.
5. Lobby Manager/Floor Supervisor to periodically check zero facility in unoccupied rooms.
6. All administrative offices to inform exchange at lunch hour so that outside parties may be advised to call ½ an hour later or after or after lunch break. Every one should help to stop misuse of telephones calls by unauthorized persons during lunch and after office hours.
7. There is o staff to handle complaints of guest telephones in the morning. Staff is required for the same or otherwise maintenance to be advised of need to handle such complaints.

Emergency Numbers

These numbers to be written on the Board, for example,

1. Fire
2. Police
3. Ambulance
4. Airport Enquiry- Domestic
5. Airport Enquiry- International
6. Railways
7. Airlines Numbers
8. Hotels
9. Hotel Directors
10. Local Police Station.

House Service Extensions

Most guests will directly dial the number of the service desired, but in some cased the guest will directly call the operator. In such cases the operator may follow the following guidelines:

1. May give the house number of the particular department, after asking the guest whether he wants the umber of the department or does he want the operator to get the concerned department to get in touch with the guest.
2. Where the guest wants the department to be in touch with him the operator will:
   (i) Take the name of the guest
   (ii) Take the room number, and
   (iii) Pass on the above information to the correct department or Housekeeping.
3. Incase the operator is unaware of which department to call; he/she will give the message to Housekeeping who will then take desired action.

Generally it is not possible to connect inside calls from one extension to another by the exchange console. Only a specific number say, '48' has this facility in the exchange.

Handing over and Taking over the Check List

This list contains the following information:

1. Pending calls of any room Guests
2. Important Messages and special Instructions
3. Billing, if any
4. VIPs in House
5. Wake Calls
6. Racks position
7. All equipment in working order.

Billing

All billings are to be properly carried out. Follow the guidelines as given below:

1. Billing system and STD and local calls for guest's rooms and banquets are computerized
2. Front office cashier will take out the report and will disconnect "O" facilities at the time of check out of the guest's rooms and banquet hall also.
3. At the time of banquet billing banquet Captain will collect the report from the Front Office cashier.
4. Manual voucher has to be making for STD calls of any administrative Extension Number (i.e. Extensions starts with a number say "44").
5. Duration and amount to be taken from the Front Office Cashier.
6. For booked Trunk Calls- always-manual voucher has to be made.
7. STD-Cash/Guest's room calls from Lobby say extension "4498", the Lobby Manager will instruct the Operator. After the call has been matured Lobby Manger will take out the report from the Front Office cashier for payment and also will inform operator duration and amount to make the manual voucher.

QUESTIONS AND DISCUSSIONS

Short Answer Type

Q.1. Write notes on:

(a) Emergency Numbers

(b) Wake up Calls

(c) Xerox Facility

(d) Log Book

(e) Fire Report.

Q.2. State the minimum information recorded concerning telephone messages.

Descriptive Type

Q.3. Mention common name codes for surnames, initials and lettered room numbers used by operators in hotel.

Q.4. Explain the billing procedure carried out by telephone department.

Q.5. 'Any equipment you are holding needs to be carefully handled." Explain by giving examples.

Q.6. Define the terms paraphrasing, band-aiding, content level, feeling level, and perception checking as they apply to hotel front office communication skills.

Q.7. Describe the basic communication skills front desk personnel exhibit when serving guests.

Q.8. Use appropriate telephone communication skills as they apply to hotel operations.

Q.9. Describe the duties performed by hotel front desk representatives to handle guest complaints.

18

Front Office Tools & Equipment

CHAPTER OBJECTIVES

After studying this lesson you should be able :

- To get the knowledge of various equipment
- To suggest suitable tool and equipment for different types of hotels.

For smooth running of the front office and to full fill its tasks and responsibilities there is a need for several specialized tool and equipment to be installed in the front office. The requirement of these tools and equipment will vary according to the size and star category of the hotel. There are racks for books, racks for advance reservations, room racks to control occupancy, information racks where the names of the guests s are listed alphabetically, machines/computer to keep guest accounts, small calculating machines, pigeonholes for mail and keys, typewriter/computers and printers for pressing credit cards. A list of some the tools is given in Table 18.1.

Table. 18.1. Tools & Equipment in the Front Office

Serial No.	*Name & Description of Equipment*
1.	Front Office Counter: with drawers Cabinets, Top & Sides
2.	Reception, Cash & Information sigh boards Registration card holder–recessed with slots with facility for recessed monitors & sliding key board recessed message & key rack at the centre.
3.	Lobby Desk with drawer Cabinet on right side, top and sides.
4.	Chairs
5.	Bell Desk semi circular with drawers, cabinets.
6.	Computer linked by LAN with multi media facility.
7.	Room Rack (standard specification)
8.	Date & Time Stamping Machine (standard specification)
9.	Public Address System (standard specification)
10.	Credit Card Imprinter (standard specification)
11.	Printer
12.	Safe Deposit Box (standard specification)
13.	Paging Board with handle and bells attached
14.	File Server Intel
15.	Microsoft/Logitech Serial Mouse multi media kit
16.	Inkjet Printer
17.	Laser Printer with Jet Direct Card
18.	LCD Display
	Reservation Office:
19.	Table with drawer
20.	Chairs (Swivel type)
21.	Head set with mouth piece
22.	Wall mounted rack
23.	Space availability board with pegs
24.	Other items: As per requirement.

QUESTIONS AND DISCUSSIONS

Short Answer Type

Q.1. List different hotel front office forms and equipment.

Q.2. Identify different front office forms and equipment

Discriptive Type

Q.3. Name important equipments required in a front office.

Assignment/Activity Type

Q.4. Design an effective front desk.

SECTION – II

CONVERSATIONAL SKILLS

Some English, French, German (Deutsch) & Hindi Language

19

Conversation Between a Guest/Tourist and a Hospitality Executive : An Introduction

CHAPTER OBJECTIVES

After studying this lesson you should be able :

- To converse with the foreign tourists,
- To acquire a working knowledge of English, French, German and Hindi language for day to day working,
- To understand the custemers requirements.

The purpose of this chapter to serve as a simple guide to conversation for foreigners visiting India. Though English is understood by most people, the tourist is likely to come into contact with in the cities, yet it would be fun to speak to people in their own language. There is no better method of making friends.

The Hindi phrases in this chapter contain a sprinkling of English words, which are commonly used in everyday speech. However, their spellings in the Roman script differ from the English. Thus, the English word 'station' has been spelt as *'steshan'* in conformity with accepted principles for the transcription of spoken Hindi into Roman. Diacritical marks have been used to help the reader pronounce the Hindi words correctly.

The Section is divided into three phases:

Chapter I: It contains key to pronounciation for English, French, German and Hindi languages, a selection of conversational phrases in Hindi written in Roman characters and their equivalents in English, French and German;

Chapter II: It gives some key words, and

Chapter III: Deals about a vocabulary of basic words in everyday use.

Within its limited scope, if this lesson is of some help to the tourist its purpose will be regarded as amply served.

20

Conversational Skills

Exercise 20.1.

ENGLISH: KEY TO TRANSCRIPTION AND PRONUNCIATION

S.No.	*Alphabet*	*Pronunciation*			
1.	a̲	like	a	in	local
2.	a	like	a	in	father
3.	au	like	au	in	laundry
4.	ai	like	ai	in	bait
5.	e	like	e	in	they
6.	i̲	like	i	in	din
7.	i	like	ee	in	feet
8.	o	like	o	in	old
9.	u̲	like	u	in	put
10.	u	like	oo	in	soon
11.	bh	like	bh	in	nibholder
12.	ch	like	ch	in	teach
13.	dh	like	dh	in	madhouse
14.	d	like	d	in	drama
			or		
		th	in	there	
15.	gh	like	gh	in	ghost
16.	j	like	j	in	jet
17.	kh	like	ch	in	loch
18.	ṇ	sounded nasally likes n in song or *bon* in French			
19.	ph	like	ph	in	phut
20.	r	like	ṛ	in	drive
21.	th	like	th	in	health
22.	y	like	y	in	yes
23.	chh, dh, jh, rh and th have no equivalent sounds in English.				

Exercise 20.2.

FRENCH PRONOUNCIATION: TRANSCRIPTION ET PRONONCIATION DU HINDI

S.No.	*Alphabet*		*Pronunciation*		
1.	a̲		comme *e*	dans	revoir
2.	a		comme *a*	dans	ame
3.	au		comme *o*	dans	or
4.	ai		comme *ai*	dans	aimer
5.	e̲		comme *é*	dans	beauté
6.	i̲	(court)	comme *i*	dans	micmac
7.	i	(long)	comme *i*	dans	ile
8.	o	(ferme)	comme *o*	dans	apótre
9.	u	(court)	comme *oo*	dans	football
10.	ū	(long)	comme *ou*	dans	four
11.	ch		comme *tch*	dans	tchéque
12.	d	(mouillé)	comme *d*	dans	dame
13.	n̲	(nasalisé)	comme *n*	dans	bon
14.	ph		comme *ph*	dans	phrase
15.	y		comme *y*	dans	yoga
	bh, chh, dh, gh, jh, kh, r, rh et th		n'ont pas d'équivalents en francais.		

Exercise 20.3.

German Pronaunciation: SCHUSSEL ZUR AUSSPRACHEBEZEICHNUNG

S.No.	*Alphabet*		*Pronunciation*	
1.	a̱	wie *a*	in	Affe
2.	a	wie *a*	in	Jahrer
3.	au	wie *o*	in	Ordnung
4.	ai	wie *e*	in	ewig
5.	e	wie *ee*	in	leer
6.	i̱	wie *i*	in	Sinn
7.	i	wie *ie*	in	Miete
8.	o	wie *o*	in	hoch
9.	u̱	wie *u*	in	futter
10.	u	wie *u*	in	kur
11.	bh	wie *bh*	in	Halbheit
12.	ch	wie *tsch*	in	Patsche
13.	d	wie *d*	in	Drama
14.	dh	wie *d(e)h*	in	Badehose
15.	gh	wie *gh*	in	trdgheit
16.	j	wie *j*	in	Jazz
17.	kh	wie *ch*	in	Dach
18.	ṉ	wie *n*	in	Gesang
19.	ph	wie *v*	in	von
20.	y	wie *j*	in	ja
	th, c̈hh, jh, haben im Deutschen r, rh und ṭh keine entsprechenden Laute			

The Tribune

EXERCISE 20.4.

WELCOME: ON REACHING INDIA AT THE AIRPORT

ENGLISH	*FRANCAIS*
Guest:	
Where is the tourist office?	Ou est I' office due tourisme?
Hospitality Executive:	
India welcomes you.	L'lnde vous souhaite la bienvenue!
Hospitality Executive:	
Did you have a comfortable Journey?	Votre voyage s'est-il bien passé
Guest:	
Oh, yes, it was very good.	Oh, oui, c'était très bein.
Hospitality Executive:	
What is the port of our landing?	Quel est le port où nous debarquons?
Guest:	
Palam Airport	L'aérport de Palam
Hospitality Executive:	
Is the plane on time?	L'avion est-il à I'heure?
Guest:	
No, it is half an hour late.	Non, il a une demiheure de or retard.
Hospitality Executive:	
Yes, please.	Oui, s'il vous plait.
Guest:	
Good morning/afternoon/night/bye.	Bonjour/bonsoir/bonne/nuit/au revoir.
Hospitality Executive:	
Have the customs cleared baggage ?	Est-ce que vos bagages ont été dé douanés?
Guest:	
Where is the exit?	Où est la sortie?

German (DEUTSCH)	*ROMAN / HINDI*
Wo ist das Reiseburo?	Tūrist āfis kahan̄ hai? hai? टूरिस्ट ऑफिस कहां है?
Indien heisst Sie willkommen.	Bhārat āpkā swāgat kartā hai. भारत आपका स्वागत करता है।
Haben Sie eine angeneheme Reise gehabt?	Kyā āpkā safar ārām se guzrā ? क्या आपका सफर आराम से गुजरा।
Oh jä es war sehr schön.	Jee Hān ye bahut achhā gujrā . जी हाँ ये बहुत अच्छा है।
Wo werden wir landen?	Ham kis hawäi adde par utreṇge? हम किस हवाई अड्डे पर उतरेंगे।
Auf dem Palam-Flughafen.	Pälam hawāi adde par. पालम हवाई अड्डे पर।
Ist das Flugzug pünktlich?	Kyā jahāz thik samai par pahunchegā ? क्या जहाज ठीक समय पर पहुँचेगा।
Nein, es hat eline halbe Stunde erspätung.	Nahin, ādha ghantā let hai. नहीं आधा घण्टा लेट है।
Ja, bitte.	Ji hān. जी हाँ।
Guten Morgen/Tag/Abend/ Nacht/Auf Wiedersehen.	Namaste′. नमस्ते।
Hat der Zoll ihr Gepäck abgefertigt?	Kyā kastam ne āpkā sāmān dekh liyā? क्या कस्टम ने आपका सामान देख लिया।
Wo ist der Ausgang ?	Bāhar jāne kā rāsta kidhar hai? बाहर जाने का रास्ता किधर है।

ENGLISH	*FRANCAIS*
Hospitality Executive: Not this way.	Non, pas par ici.
Hospitality Executive: This is the entrance.	Voici l'entrele.
Hospitality Executive: Come here.	Venez ici.
Guest: Please call a taxi.	Appelez un taxi.
Guest: Bring my luggage and put in the taxi.	Apportez mes bagages et mettezles dans le taxi.
Guest: Make haste.	Dépéchez-vous.

German (DEUTSCH)	*ROMAN / HINDI*
Nicht hierher.	Is taraf nahin. इस तरफ नहीं।
Dies ist der Eingang.	Yeh andar āne kā rastā hai. यह अन्दर आने का रास्ता है।
Kommen Sie her.	Yahā āo. यहाँ आओ।
Rufen Sie ein Taxi.	Kripaya ek taxī bulāo. कृपया एक टैक्सी बुलाओ।
Bringen Sie mein Gepäck und laden Sie es in das Taxi.	Merā sāmān lākar texi men rakh do. मेरा सामान लेकर टैक्सी मैं रख दो।
Beeilen Sie sich.	Jaldi karo. जल्दी करो।

ENGLISH	*FRANCAIS*

EXERCISE 20.5.

CAB / TAXI SERVICE

Taxi	**Taxi**
Guest:	
How far is the hotel?	A quelle distance se trouve I'hotel?
Hospitality Executive:	
It is 9 kms (six miles).	A 9 kms.
Guest:	
Take me there.	Amenez-moi là.
Guest:	
What is the fare by the hour?	Quel est le tarif à I'heure?
Guest:	
What is the fare by the distance?	Quel est le tarif au Kilomètre?

EXERCISE 20.6.

SPEED & DIRECTIONS

Fast.	Vite.
Slowly	Doucement.
Hospitality Executive:	
Turn to the right.	Tornez à droite.
Hospitality Executive:	
Turn to the left	Tournez à gauche.
Hospitality Executive:	
Go straight.	Allez tout droit.
Hospitality Executive:	
Stop.	Arrêtez.
Guest:	
How much?	Combien?

German (DEUTSCH)	*ROMAN / HINDI*
Taxi	**Texi** **टैक्सी**
Wie weit ist es bis zum Hotel?	Hotal kitnī dūr hai ? होटल कितनी दूर है।
Es sind 9 km.	Nau kilometre (ya chhe mīl) hai. नौ किलो मीटर (या छः मील) है।
Bringen Sie mich dorthin.	Mujhe wahān le chalo. मुझे वहाँ ले चलो।
Wieviel beträgt der Fahrpreis pro Stunde?	Fi ghantā kyā kirāyā hai? फी घण्टा क्या किराया है।
Wieviel beträgt der Fahrpreis pro kilometer ?	Durī ke hisāb se kya kirāyā hai? दूरी के हिसाब से क्या किराया है।
Schnell.	Tez. तेज।
Langsam.	Dhīre. धीरे।
Nach rechts.	Dāhine muro. दाहिने मुड़ो।
Nach links.	Bāin muro. बांये मुड़ो।
Gerade aus.	Sīdhe chalo. सीधे चलो।
Halt !	Ruko! रखो!
Wieviel?	Kitne paise? कितने पैसे?

ENGLISH	*FRANCAIS*

EXERCISE 20.6.

HOTEL FACILITIES

Hotel	**Hotel**
Guest: What is the name of this hotel?	Quel est le nom de cet hôtel?
Guest: Show me the rooms.	Montrez-moi les chambres.
Guest: What kind of accommodation do you want ?	Quel genre de chambre voulez-vous?
Guest: We have single and double rooms, air-conditioned rooms and suites.	Nous avons des chambres à unlit, des chambres à deux lits, des lits, des chambres climatisées des appartements.
Guest: I want a single room.	Je désire une chambre à un lit.
Hospitality Executive: It is on the third floor.	C'est au troisième étage.

German (DEUTSCH)	*ROMAN / HINDI*
Im Hotel	**Hotal** होटल
Wie heisst dieses Hotel?	Is hotal kā kyā nām hai? इस होटल का क्या नाम है?
Zeigen Sie mir die Zimmer.	Mujhe kamre dikhāo. मुझे कमरे दिखाओ।
Wie möchten Sie untergebracht werdenous ?	Āpko kis tarah kī jagah chāhiye ? आपको किस तरह की जगह चाहिए?
Wir haben Einzel – und Doppel-zimmer, Zimmer mit. Klimaanlage und Appartments.	Hamāre pās singal aur dabal kamre hain aur iske alāwā ayerkandishan kamre aur sūit bhi hain. हमारे पास सिंगल और ड़बल कमरे हैं और इसके अलावा एयरकंडीशन्ड कमरे और स्वीट भी हैं।
Ich möchte ein Einzelzimmer.	Mujhe singal kamrā chāiye. मुझे सिंगल कमरा चाहिऐ।
Es ist im dritten Stockwerk.	Voh tīsrī manzil par hai. वह तीसरी मंजिल पर है।

ENGLISH	*FRANCAIS*
Guest: This room suits me.	Cette chambre me convient.
Guest: What is the rent?	Quel est le prix ?
Hospitality Executive: Rs. 4,000 per day with board.	4,000 roupies par jour, pension complete.
Guest: Call a porter.	Apeelez un porteur.
Guest: I have a suitcase, a bag and a trunk.	J'ai une valise, un sac et une malle.
Hospitality Executive: It is on the third floor.	C'est au troisieme étage.

Guest: Have you a swimming pool?	Y a-t-il une piscine?
Guest: Take out my luggage from the taxi and put it in the room.	Retirez mes bagages du taxi et portez-les dans la chamber.

German (DEUTSCH)	*ROMAN / HINDI*
Dieses Zimmer gefällt mir.	Mujhe yeh kamrā pasand hai. मुझे यह कमरा पसन्द है।
Wie sind die Preise?	Iska kirāyā kyā hai? इसका किराया क्या है?
₹ 40,000 pro Tag mit Essen.	Bhojan / khurāk samet chāllis hazār rupayā fi din. भोजन/खुराक समेत चालीस हजार रूपया फी दिन।
Rufen Sie einen Gepäckträger.	Portar ko bulāo. पोर्टर को बुलाओ।
Ich habe einen Handkoffer, eine Tasche und einen grossen Koffer.	Mere pās ek sūt – kes, ek beg aur ek trunck hai. मेरे पास एक सूट–केस, एक बेग और एक ट्रंक है।
Es ist im dritten Stockwerk.	Voh tīsrī manzil par hai. वह तीसरी मंजिल पर है।

Gibt es ein Schwimmbad? क्या यहाँ स्वीमिंग पुल है?	Kyā yahān suiming pūl hai?
Laden Sie mein Gepäck aus dem Taxi und bringen Sie es in mein Zimmer.	Texī se sāmān utāro aur mere kamre men rakkho. टैक्सी से सामान उतारो और मेरे कमरे में रखो।

ENGLISH	*FRANCAIS*
Guest:	
How far is the railway station?	A quelle distance se trouve la gare?
Hospitality Executive:	
It is only 8 kms (5 miles) from here.	C'est seulement à 8 km. d'ici.
Hospitality Executive:	
Yes, we have.	Oui.
Guest:	
What are the other amenities provided in your hotel?	Quelles sont les autres facilités- pourvues dans votre hôtel?
Hospitality Executive:	
There is an attached bath, running hot and cold water, a call bell, a telephone, a radio, a refrigerator in every room. Besides, there are laundry, shops and taxis within the hotel premises.	Il y a une salle de bain attenant à la chambre, I'eau courante chaude et froide, une sonnette, un téléphone, une radio, un refrigerateur dans chaque chambre. En outre, dans I' enceinte de I'hôtel se trouvent une blanchisserie, des boutiques et des taxis.
Bearer/Boy.	Garçon.
Guest:	
What time is breakfast/lunch/dinner?	A quelle heure est le petit déjeuner/le /déjeuner/le diner?
Guest:	
Lay the table.	Mettez la table.
Guest:	
Show me the menu card.	Montrez-moi le menu.
Guest:	

German (DEUTSCH)	*ROMAN / HINDI*
Wie weit ist es zum Bahnhof?	Yahān se railway steshan kitnī dūr hai? यहाँ से रेलवे स्टेशन कितनी दूर है?
Es sind nur 8 km von hier.	Yahān se sirf 5 mil (ya 8 kilometre) hai. यहाँ से सिर्फ पाँच मील (या 8 किलो मीटर) है।
Ja, wir haben eines.	Ji han, hai. जी हां, है।
Welche anderen Annehmlichkeiten gibt es in Ihrem Hotel?	Apke hotal men aur kyā suvidhāen / sahūliaten hain? आपके होटल में और क्या सुविधाएं/ सहूलियतें है?
Es gibt angeschlossene Badezimmer mit fliessend heissem und kaltem Wasser, eine Klingel, ein Telefon, ein Radio, einen Kühlschrank in jedem Zimmer. Weiter gibt es eine Wäscherei, Läden und Tatxis auf dem Hotelgelände.	Sāth men gusalkhānā, garm aur thandā pānī, aur har kamre men kāl bel, telefon, radio, refrijerator heiṇ. Iske alāwā hotel kī chārdiwārī ke aṇdar laundri, dukāno aur taxī kā intazām hai. साथ में गुसलखाना, गर्म और ठंडा पानी, और हर कमरे में कॉल बेल, टेलीफोन, रेड़ियो, रेफ्रीजरेटर हैं। इसके अलावा होटल की चार-दीवारी के अन्दर लांडरी, दुकानों और टैक्सी का इन्तजाम है।
Kellner !	Berā / boy ! बैरा/बॉय!
Wann gibt es Frühstück/ Mittagessen/Abendessen?	Nashtā / lanch / dinner kā kyā taim hai? नास्ता/लंच/डिनर का क्या टाईम है?
Decken Sie den Tisch.	Mez lagāo. मेज लगाओ।
Zeigen Sie mir die Speisekarte.	Mujhe mīnū kārd dikhāo. मुझे मेन्यू कार्ड दिखाओ।

ENGLISH	*FRANCAIS*
I am not hungry.	Je n' ai pas faim.
Guest:	
Bring me a glass of cold water.	Apportez-moi un verre d'eau froide.
Guest:	
Prepare my bed.	Préparez mon lit.
Guest:	
Open the windows.	Ouvrez la fenêtre.
Guest:	
Count these clothes and take laundry.	Comptez ces Vêtements et portezles au them to the blanchisseur.
Guest:	
You can go now.	Vous pouvez vous en aller maintenant.
Guest:	
Wake me up at 6o'clock.	Réveillez-moi à six heures.
Guest:	
Shut the door.	Fermez la porte.
Guest:	
Wait outside.	Attendez dehors.

German (DEUTSCH)	*ROMAN / HINDI*
Ich habe keinen Appetit.	Mujhe bhūk nahin hai. मुझे भूख नहीं है।
Bringen Sie mir ein Glas kaltes Wasser.	Mere liye ek gilas thandā panī lao. मेरे लिए एक गिलास ठण्डा पानी लाओ।
Bereiten Sie mein Bett.	Merā bistar bichhāo. मेरा बिस्तर बिछाओ।
Öffnen Sie das Fenster.	Khirkiyān kholo. खिड़कियां खोलो।
Zählen Sie diese Wäsche und tragen Sie sie zur Wäscherei.	In kapron ko gino aur landri men le jāo. इन कपड़ो को गिनो और लान्डरी में ले जाओ।
Sie können jetzt gehen.	Tum ab jā sakte ho jao. तुम अब जा सकते हो।
Wecken Sie mich um 6 Uhr.	Mujhe chhe baje jagā denā. मुझे छः बजे जगा देना।
Schliessen Sie die Türe.	Darwāzā band karo. दरवाजा बन्द करो।
Warten Sie draussen.	Bāhar thahro. बाहर ठहरो।

ENGLISH	*FRANCAIS*
Guest:	
Go at once.	Partez immédiatement.
Guest:	
Listen to me.	Ecoutez-moi.
Guest:	
Call a barber.	Faites venir un coiffeur.
Guest:	
Has the washerman come?	Le blanchisseur est-il venu?
Guest:	
Come back.	Revenez.
Guest:	
Take this note to the manager.	Portez ce message au directeur.
Guest:	
Who is that ?	Qui est là?
Hospitality Executive:	
Someone wants to see you.	Quelqu' un désire vous voir.

EXERCISE 20.8.

SIGHT SEEING

Guest:	
I want to go to the Qutub Minar.	Je veux aller au Qutub Minar.

German (DEUTSCH)	*ROMAN / HINDI*
Gehen Sie sofort.	Foran Chale jāo. फौरन चले जाओ।
Hören Sie mir zu.	Merī bat suno. मेरी बात सुनो।
Rufen Sie einen Friseur.	Nāi ko bulāo. नाई को बुलाओ।
Ist der Waschmann gekommen?	Kyā dhobī ā gayā? क्या धोबी आ गया?
Kommen Sie zurück.	Wāpas āo. वापस आओ।
Bringen Sie diese Notiz dem Direktor.	Yeh parchī / chitthī manejar ke pās le jāo. यह पर्ची/चिट्ठी मेनेजर के पास ले जाओ।
Wer ist das?	Kon hai? कौन है?
Jemand möchte Sie sprechen.	Koi āpse milnā chāhtā hai. कोई आपसे मिलना चाहता है।
Ich möchte zum Qutub Minar.	Main Qutub jānā chahtā hūn. मैं कुतुब जाना चाहता हूँ।

ENGLISH	*FRANCAIS*
Guest:	
Let him in.	Faites-le entrer.
Guest:	
Light the lamp.	Allumez la lampe.
Guest:	
Clean the room.	Nettoyez la chambre.
Guest:	
I shall be back by the evening.	Je serai de retour dans la soirée.

Mail

Guest:	
Is there a letter for me?	Y a-t-il des lettres pour moi?

EXERCISE 20.9.

RESTAURANT FACILITY : FOOD & BEVERAGES

Restaurant	**Restaurant**
Guest:	
Please take me to a good restaurant.	Emmeṅez – moi dans un bon restaurant.
Guest:	
Where is the dining hall?	Où est la salle à manger?
Hospitality Executive:	
Please come, I will show you.	Venez, s'il vous plait, je vais vous montrer.
Guest:	
What is readily available?	Que peut-on avoir tout de suite?
Guest:	
I want some soup/mutton/ omelette/boiled eggs/potato cutlet/chop/fish.	Je désire de la soupe (potage) du mouton/une omelette/des oeufs à la coque/des croquettes de pommes de tarre/une cotelette/du poisson.

German (DEUTSCH)	*ROMAN / HINDI*
Lassen Sie ihn herein.	Use andar āne do. उसे अन्दर आने दो।
Zünden Sie die Lampe an.	Lamp jalā do. लैम्प जला दो?
Reinigen Sie das Zimmer.	Kamrā sāf karo. कमरा साफ करो।
Ich werde abends zurück sein.	Main shäm tak lotungā. मैं शाम तक लौटूंगा।
Ist Post fü mich' gekommen?	Kya mere liye koi chitthi hai? क्या मेरे लिये कोई चिट्ठी है?
Im Restaurant	**Restorant** रेस्टौरैंट
Bitte bringen Sie mich zu einem guten Restaurant.	Mujhe ek achche restorant men le chalo. मुझे एक अच्छे रेस्टोरैंट में ले चलो
Wo ist der Speisesaal?	Dining hāll kahān hai? ड्राइनिंग हॉल कहँ है?
Bitte kommen Sie, ich werde es lhnen zeigen.	Kripyā / janāb mere sāth chaliye, main āpko dikhā det ā hun. कृपया/जनाब मेरे साथ चलिए, मैं आपको दिखा देता हूँ।
Was kann man gleich haben?	Apke pas is samaya kyā taiyār hai? आपके पास इस समय क्या तैयार है?
Ich möchte eine Suppe/ Hammelfleisch/Omelette/ gekochte Eier/Kartoffel-Kotelett/Kotelett/Fisch.	Mere liye sūp / matan / omlet / uble ande/ ālu katlet/chop/fish lāo. मेरे लिए सूप/मटन/ऑमलेट/ उबले अडे/आलू कटलेट/चौप/फिश लाओ।

ENGLISH	*FRANCAIS*
Guest:	
What are the special dishes of this place?	Quelles sont les spécialtiés de cette région?
Hospitality Executive:	
Shami kabab/seekh kabab/tan-doori chicken/shahi korma/ murgha-musallam/nargisi kofta curry.	Shami kabab/seekh kabab/tan-doori chicken/shahi korma/ murgha-musallam/nargisi kofta curry.
Guest:	
What else?	Quoi d'autre?
Pratha/poori/sabzi/tandoori roti/nan/idli/dosai.	Pr āthā / pūri / sabzi/ tan dūr ī rot ī / nān / idli / dosāī.
Guest:	
Which cold drink have you?	Qu'est-ce que vous avez comme boisson fraiche?
Lassi/lemon/soda/cola.	Du lassi/de la citronnade/du soda/du cola.
Guest:	
Do you have beer or gin?	Avez-vous de la bière ou du gin?
Hospitality Executive:	
It can be served only in rooms.	On ne peut vous les servir que dans les chambres.
Guest:	
I want a peg/bottle.	Je désire un peg/une bouteille.
Guest:	
Bring tea/coffee/milk/sugar/jam/ cream/butter /knife/ fork/spoon/ napkin/glass/cup/saucer.	Apportez du thè/du café/ du lait/du sucre/de la confiture/ de la crème/du beurre/un couteau/ une fourchette/une cuiller/une serviette/ un verre/une tasse/unesoucoupe.
Guest:	
The bill, please.	L'addition. s'il vous plait
Guest:	
There is an erro in it.	Il y a une erreur là.

German (DEUTSCH)	*ROMAN / HINDI*
Welche Spezialitäten gibt es in diesem Landesteil?	Is jagah ki kyā khās chiz khāne ki hai? इस जगह की क्या खास चीज खाने की है?
Shami kabab/seekh kabab/tandoori /Hühnchen/shahi korma/ murgh musallam/nargisi kofta curry.	Shami kabāb / seekh kabāb / tandūri chikan / shāhi kormā / murgh musallam / nargisī koftā karī. शामी कबाब/सीख कबाब/तंदूरी चिकन/शाही कौरमा/मुर्ग मुसल्लम/नरगिसी कोफता कड़ी।
Was sonst?	Aur kyā chīzen hain? और क्या चीजें हैं?
Pratha/poori/sabzi/tandoori roti/nan/idli/dosai.	Prāthā / pūri / sabzi/ tandūrī rotī / nān / idli / dosāī. पराठा/पूरी/सब्जी/तंदूरी राटी/नान/इडली/डोसा।
Was haben Sie an kalten Getränken? Lassi/Zitrone/Soda/Cola.	Cold drink kyā hai? कोल्ड ड्रिंक क्या है? Lassi/lemon/ sodā / kolā. लस्सी/लेमन/सोडा/कोला।
Haben Sie Bier oder Gin?	Kyā āpke pās biar yā jin hai? क्या आपके पास वियर या जिन है?
Ek kann nur auf dem Zimmer serviert werden.	Woh sirf kamre men dī jā sakti hai. वह सिर्फ कमरे में दी जा सकती है।
Ich möchte einen Schnaps/Flasche.	Mujhe ek peg/botal chāhiye. मुझे एक पैग/बोतल चाहिए।
Bringen Sie Tee/Kaffee/ Milch/Zucker/Marmelade/ Sahne/ But- ter/Messer/ Gabel/Löffel/Tasse/Untertasse.	Chāi / kāfi / dūdh / chīnī / jām / krīm / makkhan / chhurī / kantā / chammach/ nepkin/ gilās / pyālā / rakābi lāo. चाय/कॉफी/दूध/चीनी/जैम्स/क्रीम/मक्खन/छुरी/कांटा/चम्मच/नेपकिप/गिलास/प्याला/रकाबी लाओ।
Die Rechnung bitte.	Bill lāo. बिल लाओ।
Es ist ein Fehler darin.	Isme ek galtī hai. इसमें एक गलती है।

ENGLISH	*FRANCAIS*
EXERCISE 20.10.	
GUEST/VISITOR COMMUNICATION	
Visitor	**Visiteur**
Guest: Be seated, please.	Veuillez vous asseoir.
Guest: May I know your name?	Puis-je connaitre votre nom?
Guest: What is your address and telephone number ?	Donnez-moi votre adresse et votre numéro de téléphone?
Guest: What can I do for you?	Que puis-je faire pour vous?
Guest: I am going out now.	Je sors maintenant/je dois sortir maintenant.
Guest: Please, come tomorrow.	Venez demain.
EXERCISE 20.11.	
WEATHER IN THE CITY	
Weather	**Le temps**
Guest: The weather is very pleasant today.	II fait trè beau aujourd'hui.
Guest: It is hot/cold day.	II fait chaud/froid.
Guest: The sky is cloudy.	Le ciel est couvert.
Guest: It is raining!	II pleut !
Guest: It is stuffy, switch on the fan.	II fait lourd, mettez le ventilateur en marche.

German (DEUTSCH)	*ROMAN / HINDI*
Zu Besuch	**Mulākāti** मुलाकाती
Nehmen Sie Platz, bitte!	Baiṭhiye. बैठिए।
Darf ich nach Ihrem Namen fragen?	Āpkā shubh nām? आपका शुभ नाम?
Wie ist Ihre Adresse und Telephonnummer?	Āpkā patā aur telefon nmbar kyā hain? आपका पता और टेलीफोन नम्बर क्या है?
Was kann ich für Sie tun?	Āp kya chāhte hain? आप क्या चाहते हैं?
Ich gehe jetzt aus.	Main ab bāhār jā rahā hūn. मैं अब बाहर जा रहा हुँ।
Bitte Kommen Sie morgen.	Kal āiyegā. कल आइयेगा।
Das Wetter	**Mausam** मौसम
Das Wetter ist heute sehr schön.	Mausam āj bahut achchhā hai. मोसम आज बहुत अच्छा है।
Es ist ein heisser / kalter Tag.	Āj garmī / sardī hai. आज गर्मी/सर्दी है।
Der Himmel ist bewölkt.	Āsmān par bādal hain. आसमान पर बादल हैं।
Es regnet !	Bārish ho rahī hai ! बारिश हो रही है!
Es ist schwül bitte schalten Sie den Ventilator an.	Ghutan hai, pankhā kholo. घुटन है, पंखा खोलो।

ENGLISH	*FRANCAIS*

EXERCISE 20.12.

VISITS & OUTINGS

Visits and Outings	**Viseites et excursions**
Guest:	
Where is the tourist office?	Où est le bureau de tourisme?
Guest:	
What are the places worth visiting?	Quels sont les endroits qui valent la peine d'être visités?
Hospitality Executive:	
A tourist bus will take you to all the important places.	Un car de tourisme vous em-ménera dans tous les endroits importants.
Guest:	
I want a city guide map.	Je voudrais un plan de la ville.
Guest:	
I want a guide.	Je voudrais un guide.
Guest:	
Suggest me a good library.	Indiquez-moi une bonne bibliotheque.
Guest:	
Where does this bus go?	Où va ce car?
Hospitality Executive:	
Where do you want to go?	Où désirez-vous aller?
Guest:	
I want to go to the Qutb Minar.	Je veux aller au Qutb Minar.
Guest:	
Show me the way.	Montrez-moi le chemin.
Guest:	
Thank you.	Merci.
Guest:	
Please take me to Rajghat/ Shantivan/Vijay Ghat.	Emmenez-moi à Rajghāt / Shantīvan /Vijay Ghāt , s'il vous plait.

German (DEUTSCH)	*ROMAN / HINDI*
Besuche and Ausflüge	**Sair** सैर
Wo ist das Reisebüro?	Tūrist āfis kahān hai? टूरिस्ट ऑफिस कहाँ है?
Welche Sehenswürdigkeiten gibt es hier?	Yahān kaunsi jagah dekhne ki hain? यहाँ कौन सी जगह देखने की है?
Ein Touristenbus wird Sie zu allen wichtigen Plätzen bringen.	Tūrist bas āpko sab mashhūr jagah le jāyegi. टूरिस्ट बस आपको सब मशहूर जगह ले जाएगी।
Ich möchte einen Stadtplan.	Mujhe shahar kā nakshā chāiye. मुझे शहर का नक्शा चाहिए।
Ich möchte einen Führer.	Mujhe ek gāid chahiye. मुझे एक गाइड चाहिए।
Schlagen Sie mir eine gute Bibliothek vor.	Mujhe ek achchi lāibrarī batāo. मुझे एक अच्छी लाइब्रेरी बताओ।
Wohin fährt dieser Bus?	Yeh bas kahān jāyegi? यह बस कहाँ जाएगी?
Wohin wollen Sie gehen?	Ap kahān jāna chāhte hain? आप कहाँ जाना चाहते है?
Ich möchte zum Qutb Minar.	Main Qutb jānā chāhtā hūn. मैं कुतुब जाना चाहता हूँ।
Zeigen Sie mir den Weg.	Mujhe rāstā dikhāiye. मुझे रास्ता दिखाइए।
Danke.	Dhanyawād / Shukriyā. धन्यवाद/शुक्रिया।
Bitte bringen Sie mich zum Rajghat/Shantivan/Vijay Ghat मुझे राजघाट/शांतिवन/विजयघाट ले चलो।	Mujhe Rajghāt / Shantīvan /Vijay Ghāt le chalo.

ENGLISH	*FRANCAIS*

EXERCISE 20.13.

TRAVEL BY RAIL

English	Français
By Rail	**Par chemin-de-fer**
Guest:	
Where is the booking office?	Où est le guichet?
Guest:	
How far is Agra ?	A quelle distance se trouve Agra?
Hospitality Executive:	
It is only 195 kms (122 miles.)	C'est à 195 km seulement.
Guest:	
You can go by air, rail or road.	Vous pouvez aller par avion, par le train ou par la route.
Guest:	
What is the rail fare?	Quel est le prix du billet de chemin-de-fer?
Hospitality Executive:	
Class I fare is about Rs.1500	En premieleftre classe, c'est environ 1500 roupies.
Guest:	
When does the Taj Express leave the station ?	A quelle heure le Taj Express part-il?
Guest:	
I want a porter.	Je voudrais un porteur.
Guest:	
Which is the platform for the train to Agra?	Quel est le quai pour le train d' Agra?
Guest:	
Where is the enquiry office?	Où est le bureau de renseignements?
Guest:	
What time does the train arrive/depart?	A quelle heure arrive/part le train?
Guest:	
Is there a through train for Agra?	Y a-t-il un train direct pour Agra?

German (DEUTSCH)	ROMAN / HINDI
Mitder Eisenbahn	**Rail Se** रेल से
Wo ist der Fahrkartenschalter?	Tikat-ghar kahān hai? टिकट-घर कहाँ है?
Wie weit ist es von hier bis nach Agra?	Yahān se Āgrā kitni dūr hai? यहाँ से आगरा कितनी दूर है?
Es sind nur 195 km.	Sirf ek so bāis mil hai. सिर्फ एक सौ बाइस मील है।
Sie konnen mit dem Flugzeug,/ mitder Bahn oder mit dem Auto reisen.	Āp hawāi jahāz, rail yā motor se jā sakte hain. आप हवाई जहाज, रेल या मोटर से जा सकते है।
Wieviel beträgt der Eisenba-hnfahrpreis?	Rail kā kyā kirāyā hai? रेल का क्या किराया है?
Erster Klasse kostet es ungefähr	Pehle darje ka kiraya koi pandrāh sau rupaye hai. पहले दर्जे का किराया कोई पन्द्रह सौ रुपये है।
Wann fährt der Taj Express ab?	Tej Ekspress steshan se kab chhutati hai? ताज एक्सप्रेस स्टेशन से कब छूटती है?
Ich möchte einen Gepäckträger.	Mujhe ek portar chāhiye. मुझे एक पोर्टर चाहिए।
Auf welchem Bahnsteig fährt der Zug nach Agra ab?	Āgrā wali gāri kis pletform se chhūtegī ? आगरा वाली गाड़ी किस प्लेटफार्म से छूटेगी?
Wo ist das Auskunftsbüro?	Inquirī kā daftar kahān hai? इन्क्वायरी का दफतर कहाँ है?
Wann fährt der Zug ab, wann kommt der Zug an?	Tren āne /chhutne kā kyā tāim hai? ट्रेन आने/छूटने का क्या टाइम है?
Gbtes einen durchgehenden Zug nach Agra	Kyā Agrā ke liye thrū tren hai? क्या आगरा के लिए थ्रू ट्रेन है?

ENGLISH	*FRANCAIS*
Guest: Has the an attached dining car?	Est-ce que le train a un wagon-restaurant?
Guest: Reserve me a Clas I berth for Agra.	Réservez-moi une place pour Agra en premieleftre classe.
Hospitality Executive: Pay Rs. 100 as reservation charges.	Payez 100 roupies pour la réservation.
Hospitality Executive: The train is about to start.	Le train va partir.
Guest: What time does it reach Agra?	A quelle heure arrive-t-il à Agra?
Hospitality Executive: At six in the morning.	A six heures du matin.
Guest: What is the name of this station?	Quel est le nom de cette gare?

EXERCISE 20.14.

TRAVEL BY AIR

By Air	**Par avion**
Guest: Is the plane on time?	L'avion estil a I'heure?

German (DEUTSCH)	*ROMAN / HINDI*
Führt der Zug einen Speisewagen	Kya tren men dāining kār hai? क्या ट्रेन मे डाइनिंग कार है?
Reservieren Sie mir einen I. Klasse Platz nach Agra.	Āgrā jāne wāli gāri men pahle darje kā ek reserveshan chāhta hun. आगरा जाने वाली गाड़ी में पहले दर्जे का एक रिजर्वेशन चाहता हूँ।
Zhlen Sie Rs.100 für die Reservierning	Sau rupaye reserveshan ke liye. सौ रुपये रिजर्वेशन के लिए।
Der Zug fährt jetzt ab.	Gari chhutne wali hai. गाड़ी छूटने वाली है।
Wann wird er in Agra ankom-men?	Agra kis taim pahunchegi? आगरा किस टाइम पहुँचेगी?
Um sechs Uhr morgens.	Subah ke chhe baje. सुबह के छः बजे।
Wie heisst dieser Bahnhof?	Is steshan ka kya nam hai? इस स्टेशन का क्या नाम है?
Mit dem Flugzeug	**Hawāi Jahāz Se** हवाई जहाज से
Ist das Flugzug pünktlich?	Kyā jahāz thik samai par pahunchegā? क्या जहाज ठीक समय पर पहुँचेगा?

ENGLISH	*FRANCAIS*
Guest: Book me a seat for Mumbai.	Reservez-moi une place pour Mumbai.
Guest: Steward please.	Steward, s'il vous plait.
Guest: Do you have a paper bag?	Avez-vous un sac en papier?
Hospitality Executive: When do we land?	Quand allons- nous atterrir?
Guest: At 7 in the evening.	A 7 heures du soir.

EXERCISE 20.15.
SHOPPING

Shopping	**Emplettes**
Guest: Which is the main shopping centre here?	Quel est le principal quartier commercant?
Guest: Suggest me some dependable shop.	Indiquez-moi un magasin sérieux.
Guest: I shall go shopping tomorrow.	J'irai faire des achats demain.
Hospitality Executive: It is closed on Sundays.	C'est fermé le dimanche.
Guest: When do the shops open?	Quand ouvrent les magasins?
Guest: Can you come with me this evening?	Pouvez-vous m'accompagner ce soir?
Hospitality Executive: Sure !	Certainement/bein sûr.

German (DEUTSCH)	*ROMAN / HINDI*
Buchen Sie mir einen Platz nach Bombay.	Bombai ke liye ek sīt buk kar dījiye. बम्बई के लिए एक सीट बुक कर दीजिए।
Steward, bitte !	Steward ko bulāo. स्टुवर्ड का बुलाओ।
Haben Sie Papiertüten?	Kyā āpke pās pepar bag hai? क्या आपके पास पेपर बैग है?
Wann werden wir landen?	Ham kab utrenge? हम कब उतरेंगे?
Um 7 Uhr abends.	Shām ke sāt baje. शाम के सात बजे
Beim Einkaufen	**Kharīdadāri** खरीदारी
Welches ist das Hauptgesc- häftszentrum hier?	Yahān kā mashhūr bāzār kaunsā hai? यहाँ का मशहूर बाजार कौन-सा है?
Schlagen Sie mir einige zu- verlässige Läden vor.	Mujhe koī bharose/ aitbār layak dukān battāo. मुझे कोई भरोसे/एतबार लायक दुकान बताओ।
Ich werde morgen einkaufen gehen	Main kal kuchh kharidāri karne jānā chāhtā hūn. मैं कल कुछ खरीदारी करने जाना चाहता हूँ।
Sonntags ist geschlossen.	Itwār ko bāzār band rehtā hai. इतवार को बाजार बन्द रहता है।
Wann öffnen die läden?	Dukānen kis tāim khultī hain? दुकानें किस टाइम खुलती हैं?
Können Sie mich heute Ab-end begleiten?	Kyā āp mere sāth āj shām ko chal sakte hain? क्या आप मेरे साथ आज शाम को चल सकते हैं?
Selbstverstädnlich.	Avashya / Zarūr. अवश्य/जरूर।

ENGLISH	*FRANCAIS*
Guest:	
Take me to a jeweller.	Emmenez-moi chez un bijoutier.
Guest:	
I want to buy a ring.	Je voudrais une bague.
Guest:	
What is the price of this?	Combien coûte-t-elle?
Guest:	
This is very costly.	C'est tres cher.
Guest:	
Show me a less expensive one.	Montrez-m'en une moins chere.
Guest:	
Where can I get antiques and curios?	Oü puis-je trouver des antiquites et des bibelots?
Guest:	
I want to buy some presents for my wife and daughter.	Je voudrais acheter quelques Cardeaux pour ma femme et ma fille.
Hospitality Executive:	
There is a large variety to choose from–Banaras brocades, printed handloom fabrics, marble replicas of the Taj, Kashmir shawls, bidri and nirmal work, etc.	Il y a un grand choix de brocarts, de tissus imprimés, tisses à la main, de répliques miniatures en marbre du Taj Mahal, de chāles du Kashmir,d'articles de bidri et de nirmal etc.
Guest:	
I want to buy some gifts.	Je voudrais acheter des cadeaux.
Hospitality Executive:	
The state emporia sell excellent gift articles.	Les state emporia vendent d'excellents articles de cadeaux.

German (DEUTSCH)	*ROMAN / HINDI*
Führen Sie mich zu einem Juwelier.	Mujhe jauharī ki dukān par le chalo. मुझे जोहरी की दुकान पर ले चलो।
Ich möchte einen Ring kaufen.	Main ek angūthi kharidnā chāhtā hun. मैं एक अंगूठी खरीदना चाहता हूँ।
Wieviel kostet dieser?	Iskī – kyā kimat hai? इसकी क्या कीमत है?
Dieser ist sehr teuer.	Yeh bahut mehngi hai. यह बहुत मंहगी है।
Zeigen Sie mir einen billigeren.	Koi sasti dikhāo. कोई सस्ती दिखाओ।
Wo' finde ich Antiquitäten und Kuriositäten?	Purāni aur ajīb chīzain mujhe kahān milengī? पुरानी और अजीब चीजें मुझे कहाँ मिलेगी?
Ich möchte für meine Frau und Tochter einige Geschenke kaufen.	Main apnī patnī / bīwī aur larkī ke liye kuchh prezents kharidnā chāhtā hun. मैं अपनी पत्नी/बीवी और लड़की के लिए कुछ प्रेजेन्ट खरीदना चाहता हूँ।
Es gibt eine grosse Auswahl- Banaras Brokate, gedruckte Handwebereien. Marmornach-bildungen des Taj, Kaschimir Schals, Bidri und Nirmalaritikel usw.	Prezenst ke liye bahut chīzen hain. Banaras kā zarī kā kām, hāth ke chhape kapre, sangmarmar ke Taj ke namūne, Kashmiri shāl, bidrī aur Nirmal kā kām vegerar̄. प्रेजेन्ट के लिए बहुत चीजे हैं। बनारस का जरी का काम, हाथ के छपे कपड़े, संगमरमर के ताज के नमूने, कश्मीरी शाल, बिदरी और निर्मल का काम वगैरह।
Ich möchte einige Geschenke kaufen	Main kuchh prezents kharidnā chāhtā hun. मैं कुछ प्रेजेन्ट खरीदना चाहता हूँ।
Die staatlichen Emporien (Geschäfte) verkaufen ausgezei chnete Geschenkartikel.	Rājyon / Sūbon kī dukanon men āpko prezents ke liye bahut sunder chīzain milengī. राज्यों/सूबों की दुकानों में आपको प्रेजेन्ट के लिए बहुत सुन्दर चीजें मिलेंगी।

ENGLISH	*FRANCAIS*
Guest:	
Do all the indian states have emporia here?	Tous les états de I' Inde ont- ils un magasin officiel ici?
Most of them have.	La plupart en ont.
Guest:	
What do you call this in your language?	Comment appelez-vous cela dans votre langue?
Guest:	
Is it genuine?	Est-ce authentique?
Guest:	
I do not fancy this.	Je n'aime pas beaucoup cela.
Guest:	
How much per metre?	Combien le mètre?
Guest:	
Show me some samples.	Montrez-moi des échantillons.

EXERCISE 20.16.

ENTERTAINMENTS FACILITIES

Entertainments	**Divertissements**
Guest:	
What entertainments are available here?	Quels divertissements/spectacles ya-t-il ici?

German (DEUTSCH)	*ROMAN / HINDI*
Haben alle indischen Staaten Emporien hier?	Kyā yehān sabhī rājyon / sūbon kī dukāne hain? क्या यहाँ सभी राज्यों/सूबों की दुकानें है?
Die meisten.	Kaī rājyon / sūbon ki hain. कई राज्यों/सूबों की हैं।
Wie nennen Sie dies in Iherer Sprache?	Ap ise apnī bolī men kyā kehte hain? आप इसे अपनी बोली में क्या कहते हैं?
Ist es echt?	Kyā yeh aslī hai? क्या यह असली है?
Dies gefällt mir nicht.	Mujhe ye pasand nahīn hai. मुझे यह पसन्द नहीं है।
Wieviel kostet dies pro Meter?	Kyā metar hai? क्या मीटर है?
Zeigen Sie mir einige Muster.	Mujhe kuchh namūne dikhāo. मुझे कुछ नमूने दिखाओ।
Unterhaltung	**मनोविनोद**
Welche Art der Unterhaltung gibt es heir?	Yahān manoranjan ke kyā sādhan hain? यहाँ मनोरंजन के क्या साधन हैं?

ENGLISH	*FRANCAIS*
Hospitality Executive:	
You can see an exhibition, cinema, dance, drama, music concert, or son-et-lumiere.	Vous pouvez aller voir une ex-position, un film, un spectacle de danse classique, une piece de théâtre; ou vous pouvez assister à un concert ou aller voir le spectacle de son-et-lumieleftre.
Guest:	
What are the most famous Indian dances?	Quelles sont les danses Indiennes les plus céleleftbres?
Hospitality Executive:	
Bharata Natyam, Manipuri, Kathak, Kathakali.	Bharata Natyam, Manipuri, Kathak, Kathakali.
Guest:	
Can I get a copy of the programme?	Puis-je avoir un programme?
Guest:	
Where can I see an English film?	Où puis-je voir un film anglais?
Guest:	
The local newspapers give the programme.	Le journal local indique les programmes.
Hospitality Executive:	
Are you interested in cricket/ football/hockey match?	Êtesvous interesse par un match de cricket/de football/de hockey?
Guest:	
Okhla is an ideal place for fishing.	Okhla est un endroit idéal pour la pêche.
Hospitality Executive:	
Also, there is a good zoo here.	Il,y a également un zoo intéresant ici.

German (DEUTSCH)	*ROMAN / HINDI*
Sie können eine Ausstellung, eine Filmvorführung, eine Tanzveranstaltung, ein Schauspiel, ein Konzert oder Son-et Lumière besuchen.	Āp numāyesh, sanīma, nrityā drāmā, sangīt yā son-et-lumiere sho men jā sakte hain. आप नुमाइश, सिनेमा, नृत्य, ड्रामा, संगीत या सानेल्यूमर में जा सकते हैं।
Welches sind die bekanntesten indischen Tänze?	Bhārat / Hindustān ke kōn se prasidha/ mashhūr nāch hain ? भारत/हिन्दुस्तान के कौन से प्रसिद्ध/ मशहूर नाच हैं?
Bharata Natyam, Manipuri, Kathak, Kathakali.	Bhārāt Natyam, Manipurī, Kathak, Kathākalī. भारत नाट्यम, मणिपुरी, कथक, कथाकली।
Kann ich ein Programm haben?	Kyā mujhe program kī ek kapī mil saktī hai ? क्या मुझे प्रोग्राम की एक कापी मिल सकती है?
Wo kann ich einen englischen Film sehen?	Angrezī film kahān dekh saktā hūn? अंग्रेजी फिल्म कहाँ देख सकता हूँ?
Die Lokalzeitungen geben das Programm an.	Progrām lokal akhbāron men milēgā. प्रोग्राम लोकल अखबारों में मिलेगा।
Haben Sie interesse an einem Cricket/Fussball/Hockeyspiel?	Kyā āp kriket / futbāl / hāki maich dekhnā passand karenge? क्या आप क्रिकेट/फुटबाल/हाकी मैच देखना पसन्द करेंगे?
Okhla ist ein idealer Ort zum Fischen.	Okhlā machhlī ke shikār ke liye bahut achchhī jagah hai. ओखला मछली के शिकार के लिए बहुत अच्छी जगह है।
Heier gibt es auch einen guten zoo	Yahān ek achchhā zū bhī hai. यहाँ एक अच्छा जू भी है।

ENGLISH	*FRANCAIS*

EXERCISE 20.17.

POLICE ASSISTANCE

Guest:

Where is the nearest police station?	Où est le commissariat de police le police plus proche?

EXERCISE 20.18.

POSTAL SERVICES

Post office	**Bureāu de poste**

Guest:

Post this letter.	Mettez cette lettre à la boite.

German (DEUTSCH)	*ROMAN / HINDI*
Wo ist das nächste Polizeirevier?	Sabse nazdīk thanā kahān hai? सबसे नजदीक थाना कहाँ?

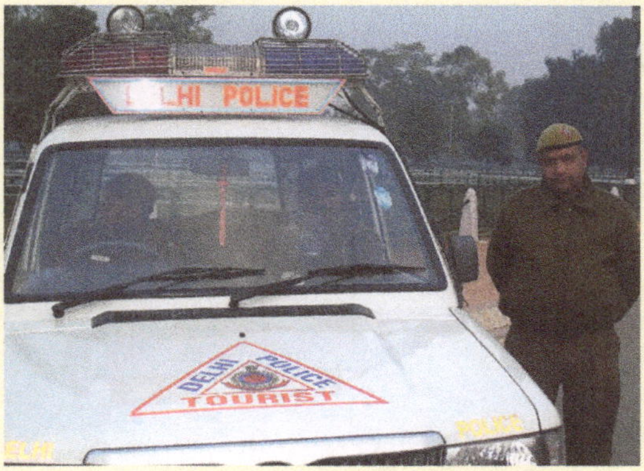

Auf dem Postant	**Dakkhānā** डाकघर
Geben Sie diesen Brief auf.	Yeh khat leter-baks men dalo. यह खत लेटर-बॉक्स में डालो।

ENGLISH	*FRANCAIS*
Guest: Where is the posts and tele- graphs office?	Où se trouve le bureau de poste et télégraphe?
Guest: Is it open today?	Est-ce-qu il est ouvert aujourd'-hui?
Hospitality Executive: No, it remains closed on Sundays.	Non, il est fermé le dimanche.
Guest: I want to send a cable to New York.	Je voudrais envoyer un télégramme à New York.
Guest: When is the next clearance?	Quand aura lieu la prochaine levée?
Guest: Bring me a 75 P. stamp.	Apportez-moi un timbre de 75 P.
Guest: What is your telephone number?	Quel est votre numéro de téléphone?
Guest: Ring me at this number to morrow.	Appelez-moi demain à ce numéro.

EXERCISE 20.19

TIME

Guest: What is the time?	Quelle heure est-il?
Hospitality Executive: It is eight o'clock.	Il est hit heures.
Guest: My watch is fast/slow.	Ma montre avance/retarde.
Guest: It is time to go.	Il est temps de partir.
Hospitality Executive: Tomorrow is a holiday.	Demain c'est férié.

German (DEUTSCH)	*ROMAN / HINDI*
Wo ist das Post- und Telegraphenamt?	Dāk aur tār ghar kahān hai? डाक और तार घर कहाँ है?
Ist es heute geöffnet?	Kyā woh āj khulā hai? क्या वह आज खुला है?
Nein, sonntags bleibt es geschlossen.	Nahīn, ītwār ke din woh band rahtā hai. नहीं, इतवार के दिन वह बन्द रहता है।
Ich mochte ein Telegramm nach New York schicken.	Main New York ko kebil bhejnā chahtā hun. मैं न्यूयार्क को केबिल भेजना चाहता हूँ।
Wann ist die nächste Leerung levée?	Dāk kab niklegī ? डाक कब निकलेगी?
Bringen Sie mir eine 75 P. Briefmarke.	Pachhatar paisē kā ek tikat lāo. पच्चहत्तर पैसे का एक टिकट लाओ।
Wie ist Ihre Telefonnummer?	Apkā telephone nambar? आपका टेलीफोन नम्बर?
Rufen Sie mich morgen zu	Mujhe is namber par kal telefon karnā.
Wieviel Uhr ist es?	kyā bajā hai? क्या बजा है?
Es ist acht Uhr.	Is samay āth baje hain. इस समय आठ बजे हैं।
Meine Uhr geht vor/nach.	Merī gharī tez/sust hai. मेरी घड़ी तेज/सुस्त है।
Es ist Zeit zum Gehen.	Ab chalne kā tāim ho gayā. अब चलने का टाइम हो गया।
Morgen ist ein Feiertag.	Kal chhuttī hai. कल छूट्टी है।

ENGLISH	*FRANCAIS*
Guest: What is the speciality of this place?	Quelle est la spécialité de cet endroit?
Guest: I waited for a long time for you.	Je vous ai attendu longtemps.
Guest: Get me a newspaper.	Apportez-moi un journal.

EXERCISE 20.20
BANK SERVICES

Guest: Where is the bank?	Où est la banque?
Guest: Get these things from the shop.	Allez chercher ces articles dans le magasin.
Guest: I do not want it.	Je n'en veux pas.
Guest: What does he want?	Que désire t-il?
Guest: All right.	Très bien.

EXERCISE 20.21.
DOCTOR SERVICES

Guest: Bring the doctor.	Faites venir le docteur.

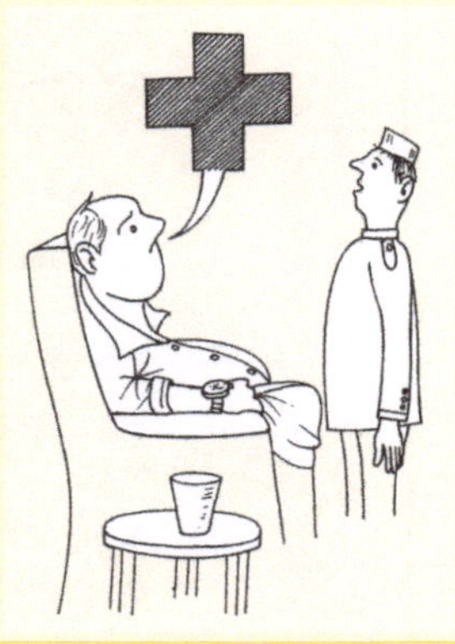

German (DEUTSCH)	*ROMAN / HINDI*
Welche Sehenswürdigkeiten hat dieser Ort?	Is jagah kā kyā tofah hai? इस जगह का क्या तोहफा है?
Ich wartete lange auf Sie.	Maine āpkā bahut der tak intzār ' kiyā. मैंने आपका बहुत देर तक इंतजार किया।
Bringen Sie mir eine Zeitung.	Akhbār lāo. अखबार लाओ।
Wo ist die Bank?	Bank kahān hai? बैंक कहाँ है?
Holen Sie diese Sachen vom Geschäft.	Yeh chizain dukān se le āo. ये चीजे दुकान से ले आओ।
Ich möchte es nicht.	Mujhe yeh pasand nahī. मुझे यह पसन्द नहीं।
Was will er?	Woh kyā chahta hai ? वह क्या चाहता है?
Gut.	Thīk hai. ठीक है।
Rufen Sie den Arzt.	Dāktar ko bulāo. डाक्टर को बुलाओ।

ENGLISH	*FRANCAIS*
Guest: Get me these medicines.	Apportez-moi ces médicaments.
Guest: Will you do me a favour?	Voulez-vous me rendre un service?

EXERCISE 20.22.

POLICE STATION

Guest: Where is the nearest police station?	Où est le commissariat de police le plus proche?
Guest: What is the meaning of this phrase?	Quel est le sens de cette phrase?

EXERCISE 20.23.

WILDLIFE FACILITIES

Guest: Is there a wildlife sanctuary nearby?	Y-a-t-il une réserve d'animaux sauvages dans les environs?

EXERCISE 20.24.

HILL STATION

Guest: Where is the nearest hill sation/ springs/waterfall?	Quelle est la station de montagne/la source chaude la chute d' eau la plus proche?

EXERCISE 20.25.

MISCELLANEOUS

Miscellaneous	**Divers**
Listen.	Ecoutez.
Hospitality Executive : I am very glad to see you.	Je suis tres heureux de vous voir.

German (DEUTSCH)	*ROMAN / HINDI*
Bringen Sie mir diese Med kamente.	Yeh dawāiyan le āo. ये दवाइयां ले आओ।
Können Sie mir einen Gefallen tun?	Kyā āp mujh per ek kirpa/ meharbani karenge? क्या आप मुझ पर एक कृपा/मेहरबानी करेंगे?
Wo ist das nächste Polizeirevier?	Sabse nazadīk thānā kahān hai? सबसे नहजदीक थाना कहाँ है?
Was bedeutet dieser Satz?	Is vākya /jumle kā kyā arth/ māni hai? इस वाक्य/जुमले का क्या अर्थ/माने है?
Gibt es einen Narightturs- chutzpark in der Nähe?	kyā karīb men koī janglī jānwar kī rakh haī? क्या करीब में कोई जंगली जानवर की रख है?
Welches ist die nächste Höhenortschaft/heisse Quelli/wasserfall	Sabse pās kā parhārī nagar/garam pānī kā jharnā/chashmā kon sā hai? सबसे पास का पहाड़ी नगर/गर्म पानी का झरना/चश्मा कौन सा है?
dieser Nummer an.	मुझे इस नम्बर पर कल टेलीफोन करना।
Verschiedenes	**Vibhinnya** **विभिन्न**
Hören Sie.	Suno. सुनो।
Ich freue mich sehr, Sie zu sehen.	Mujhe āpse milkar barī khushī hui. मुझे आपसे मिलकर बड़ी खुशी हुई।

Hospitality Executive:	
I am sorry.	Je suis désolé.
Guest:	
Excellent.	Excellent.
Guest:	
Wait for me.	Attendez-moi.
Guest:	
Do you smoke?	Est-ce que vous fumez?
Guest:	
Have you some ice?	Avez-vous de la glace?
Guest:	
Put it on the table.	Mettez-le/la sur la table.
Guest:	
Bring a chair.	Apportez une chaise.
Guest:	
Who is he?	Qui est-il?
Guest:	
He is lazy.	Il est paresseux.
Guest:	
Don't touch this.	N'y touchez pas.
Guest:	
Where are you putting up?	Où habitez-vous?
Guest:	
Switch on the light.	Allumez l'électricité.
Guest:	
I have a slight fever.	J'ai un peu de fièvre.
Hospitality Executive:	
Excuse me, I did not quite follow.	Excusez-moi, je n'ai pas très bien compris.
Hospitality Executive:	

Es tut mir leid.	Mujhe afsos hai. मुझे अफसोस है।
Ausgezeichnet.	Bahut achchhā. बहुत अच्छा।
Warten Sie auf mich.	Merā intzār karnā. मेरा इन्तजार करता।
Rauchen Sie?	Kyā āp sigrat pīte hain? क्या आप सिगरेट पीते हैं?
Haben Sie etwas Eis?	Kyā kuchh baraf hai? क्या कुछ बर्फ है?
Stellen Sie es auf den Tisch.	Mez par rakkho. मेज पर रखो।
Bringen Sie einen Stuhi.	Ek kursī lāo. एक कुर्सी लाओ।
Wer ist er?	woh kaun hai? वह कौन है?
Er ist faul.	Woh sust hai. वह सुस्त है।
Berühren Sie dies nicht.	Ise mat chhuo. इसे मत छुओ।
Wo wohmen Sie?	Āp kahān thehre hain? आप कहाँ ठहरे हैं?
Schalten Sie das Licht an.	Battī jalāo. बत्ती जलाओ।
Ich habe leichtes Fieber.	Mujhe thorā bukhār hai. मुझे थोड़ा बुखार है।
Entschuldigen Sie, ich konnte nicht ganz folgen.	Māf karnā, main samjhā nahi. माफ करना, मैं समझा नहीं।

Please speak slowly and distinctly.	Parlez lentement et distinctement s'il vous plait.
Guest:	
'What do you call this in Hindi?	Comment appelez-vous cela en Hindi?
Guest:	
I want a guide.	Je voudrais un guide.

Bitte sprechen Sie langsam und deutlich.

Meharbānī se dhīre aur sāf boliye.
मेहरबानी से धीरे और साफ बोलिए।

Wie nennen Sie dies in Hindi?

Āp Hindi men ise kya kahte hain?
आप हिन्दी में इसे क्या कहते हैं?

Ich möchte einen Führer.

Mujhe ek gāid chāhiye.
मुझे एक गाइड चाहिए।

21

Some Key Words / Quelques Mots-clés Einige Grundworte/ Kucch Khas Shabda English, French, German and Hindi

EXERCISE 21.1.

NUMBERS

	ENGLISH *Cardinal Number*	*FRANCAIS* *Nombres Cardinaux*	*DEUTSCH* *Grundzahien*	*ROMAN/HINDI* *Ginti* / गिनती
1.	One	un	eins	ek / एक
2.	Two	deux	zwei	do / दो
3.	Three	trois	drei	tīn / तीन
4.	Four	quatre	vier	chār / चार
5.	Five	cinq	fv̈nf	pānch / पाँच
6.	Six	six	sechs	chhe / छ:
7.	Seven	sept	sieben	sāt / सात
8.	Eight	huit	acht	āth / आठ
9.	Nine	neuf	neun	nau / नौ
10.	Ten	dix	zehn	das / दस
20.	Twenty	vingt	zwanzig	bīs / बीस
30.	Thirty	trente	dreissig	tīs / तीस
40.	Forty	quarante	vierzig	chālīs / चालीस
50.	Fifty	cinquante	fünfzig	pachās / पचास
60.	Sixty	soixante	sechzig	sāth / साठ
70.	Seventy	soixante-dix	siebzig	sattar / सत्तर
80.	Eighty	quatre-vingt	achtzig	assī / अस्सी
90.	Ninety	quatre-vingt-dix	neunzig	nabbe / नब्बे
100.	Hundred	cent	hundert	sau / सौ
	Thousand	mille	tausend	hazār / हज़ार
	Hundred thousand	cent mille	hunderttausend	lākh / लाख
	Ten million	dix millions	zehnmillionen	karor / करोड़

EXERCISE 21.2.

WEEK DAYS

ENGLISH The week	*FRANCAIS* Semaine	*DEUTSCH* Wochentage	*ROMAN/HINDI* Saptāh /hafte ke din सप्ताह/हफ्ते के दिन
Sunday	Dimanche	Sonntag	Itwār इतवार
Monday	Lundi	Montag	Somwār सोमवार
Tuesday	Mardi	Dienstag	Mangalwār मंगलवार
Wednesday	Mercredi	Mittwoch	Budhwār बुधवार
Thursday	jeudi	Donnerstag	Brahspatwār बृहस्पतिवार
Friday	Vendredi	Freitag	Shukrawār शुक्रवार
Saturday	Samedi	Samstag	Shaniwār शनिवार

EXERCISE 21.3.

TIME

ENGLISH Division of Time	*FRANCAIS* Division du temps	*DEUTSCH* Zeiteinteilung	*ROMAN/HINDI* Samaya kā vibhājan समय का विभाजन
Day	jour	Tag	din दिन
Night	nuit	Nacht	rāt रात
Evening	soir	Abend	shām शाम
Afternoon	apremidi	Nachmittag	tisrā pahar तीसरा पहर
Year	année	Jahr	Sāl साल
Month	mois	Monat	mahīnā महीना
Fornight	quinze jours	zwei Wochen	pākh पाख
Week	semaine	Woche	saptāh/haftā सप्ताह/हफ्ता

Today	aujourd' hui	heute	āj /आज
Tomorrow/yesterday	demain/hier	morgen/gestern	kal कल
Day before yesterday/ Day after tomorrow	avant-hier/ aprelefts-demain	vorgestern/übermorgen	parson परसों
At noon	à midi	am Mittag	dopehar ko दोपहरा को
Tonight	ce soir	heute Nacht	āj rāt आज रात
At midnight	à minuit	um Mitternacht	ādhirāt ko आधी रात को
Morning	matin	Morgen	prātahkāl /subah प्रात: काल/सुबह
Always	toujours	immer	hameshā /हमेशा
Never	jamais	niemals	kabhi nahīn कभी नहीं

EXERCISE 21.4.

MINUTES & HOURS

ENGLISH	*FRANCAIS*	*DEUTSCH*	*ROMAN/HINDI*
Second	seconde	Sekunde	sekind सैकेंड
Minute	minute	Minute	minat मिनट
Hour	heure	Stunde	ghantā घंटा
Ten past three	trois heures dix	zehn Minuten nach drel	tin bajkar das-minat तीन बजकर दस मिनट
Quarter past five	cinq heures et quart	viertel nach funf	sawā pānch सवा पांच
Quarter to six	six heures moins quart	viertel vor sechs	pone chhe पौने छ:

SEASONS

Seasons	**Saisons**	**Jahreszeiten**	**Reituyen** ऋतुए
Spring	printemps	Frühling	basant/ bahār बसन्त/बहार
Summer	été	Sommer	grishma/ garmī ग्रीष्म/गर्मी
Monsoon	mousson	Monsun	varshā / barsāt वर्षा/बरसात

Autumn	âutomne	Herbst	patjhar/khizan पतझड़/खिज़ाँ
Winter	hiver	Winter	shishir/jara शिशिर/जाड़ा

MONTHS

Months	**Mois**	**Monate**	**Mahinon ke nām** **महीनों के नाम**
January	Janvier	Januar	Janwarī जनवरी
February	Février	Februar	Farwarī फरवरी
March	Mars	März	Mārch मार्च
April	Avril	April	Aprail अप्रैल
May	Mai	Mai	Maī मई
June	Jūin	Juni	Jūn जून
July	Juillet	juli	Julāī जुलाई
August	Août	August	Agast अगस्त
September	Septembre	September	Sitambar सितम्बर
October	Octobre	Oktober	Aktūbar अक्तूबर
November	Novembre	November	Navambar नवम्बर
December	Décembre	Dezember	Disambar दिसम्बर

EXERCISE 21.5.

DICRECTIONS

ENGLISH	*FRANCAIS*	*DEUTSCH*	*ROMAN/HINDI*
Directions	Directions	Richtungen	Dishāyen दिशाएं
East	est	Ost	pūrab पूर्व
West	ouest	West	pashchim पश्चिम

North	nord	Nord	uttar उत्तर
South	sud	Süd	dakshin दक्षिण
Left	à gauche	links	bāin बायें
Right	à droite	rechts	dāin दायें
Straight	tout droit	gerade aus	sīdhe सीधे

EXERCISE 21.6.

PERSONAL PRONOUNS

ENGLISH *Some Personal Pronouns*	*FRANCAIS* *Quelques pronoms personnels*	*DEUTSCH* *Einige persönliche Fürwörter*	*ROMAN/HINDI* *Sarvanam* सर्वनाम
I	je	ich	main मैं
We	nous	wir	ham हम
You	vous/tu	Sie/du	āp / tum आप/तुम
He/she/it	il/elle	er/sie/es	woh वह
They	ils/elles	sie	vey वे
My	mon	mein	merā मेरा
Our	notre	unser	hamārā हमारा
His/her	son/sa	sein/ihr	uskā उसका
Your	votre/ton	ihr/dein	āpkā / tumhārā आपका/तुम्हारा
This	ceci	dies	yeh यह
That	cela	das	woh वह

EXERCISE 21.7.

COLOURS DISTINCTION

ENGLISH *Colours*	*FRANCAIS* *Couleurs*	*DEUTSCH* *Farbe*	*ROMAN/HINDI* *Rang* रंग
Colour	couleur	Farbe	rang रंग
White	blanc	weiss	safed सफेद
Black	noir	schwarz	kālā काला
Red	rouge	rot	lāl लाल
Blue	bleu	blau	nīlā / āsmānī नीला / आसमानी
Green	vert	grün	harā हरा
Yellow	jaune	gelb	pīlā पीला
Dark	foncé	dunkel	gehrā गहरा
Light	clair	hell	halkā हल्का
Grey	gris	grau	bhūrā भूरा
Violet	violet	violett	bainjanī बैंगनी
Orange	orange	orange	kesarī / nārangī केसरी / नारंगी

EXERCISE 21.8.

VEGETABLES IDENTIFICATION

ENGLISH *Vegetables*	*FRANCAIS* *Legumes*	*DEUTSCH* *Gemüse*	*ROMAN/HINDI* *Sabziyan* सब्जियां
Cabbage	chou	Kohl	band gobhī बन्द गोभी
Cauliflower	chou-fleur	Blumenkohl	phul gobhī फूल गोभी
Carrot	carotte	Karotte	gājar गाजर

Spinach	épinard	Spinat	pālak पालक
Tomato	tomate	Tomate	tamātar टमाटर
Potato	pomme de terre	Kartoffel	ālu आलू
Onion	oignon	Zwiebel	pyāz प्याज़

EXERCISE 21.9.

FOOD IDENTIFICATION

ENGLISH *Fruits*	*FRANCAIS* *Fruits*	*DEUTSCH* *Früchte*	*ROMAN/HINDI* *Phal* फल
Banana	banane	Banane	kelā केला
Mango	mangue	Mango	ām आम
Pineapple	ananas	Ananas	annānās अनन्नास
Lemon	citron	Zitrone	nīmbu नींबू
Orange	orange	Orange	santrā संतरा
Grapes	raisins	Traube	angūr अंगूर

ENGLISH
Please speak slowly and distinctly.

FRANCAIS
Parlez lentement et distinctement
s'il vous plait.

German (*DEUTSCH*)
Bitte sprechen Sie langsam und deutlich.

HINDI/ROMAN
Meharbāin se dhire aur sāf boliye.
मेहरबानी से धीरे और साफ बोलिए।

22

Multi Lingual Vocabulary/ Vocabulaire/ Wörterverzeichnis/ Shabdavali (शब्दावली)

EXERCISE 22.1

VOCABILARY

ENGLISH	*FRANCAIS*	*DEUTSCH*	*HINDI/ROMAN*
		A	
Address	adresse	Adresse	patā पता
Afternoon	apres-midi	Nachmittag	tīsrā pahar तीसरा पहर
Again	encore/à nouveau	wieder	phirse / dobārā फिर से/दुबारा
Animal	animal	Tier	Jānwar जानवर
Answer	réponse	Antwort	uttar / jawāb उत्तर/जवाब
Architecture	architecture	Architektur	sthāpatya kalā स्थापत्य कला
Arrival	arrivée	Ankunft	pahunchnā पहुँचना
(to) awake	réveiller	erwachen	jāganā जागना
		B	
Baby	bébé	Baby	bachchā बच्चा
Baggage	bagage	Gepäck	sāmān / asbāb सामान/असबाब
Barber	coiffeur	Friseur	nāī नाई

ENGLISH	*FRANCAIS*	*DEUTSCH*	*HINDI/ROMAN*
(to) bathe	se baigner	baden	isnān karnā / nahānā स्नान करना/नहाना
Bathroom	salle-de-bain	Badezimmer	gusalkhānā गुसलखाना
Beast	bête	wildes Tier	jānwar जानवर
Bed	lit	Bett	bistar बिस्तर
Big	grand	gross	barā बड़ा
Bike/bicycle	bicyclette	fahrrad	bāiskil बाइसिकल
Black	noir	schwarz	kālā काला
Book	livre	Buch	pustak / kitāb पुस्तक/किताब
Boy	garcson	Knabe	larkā लड़का
(to) bring	apporter	bringen	lānā लाना
Brother	frère	Bruder	bhāī भाई
Tourist bungalow	toruist bungalow	Touristen-Bungalow	turist banglā टूरिस्ट बंगला
Butter	beurre	Butter	makkhan मक्खन
		C	
(to) call	appeler	rufen	bulānā बुलाना
Camera	appareil photographique	Kamera	kemrā कैमरा
Cave	caverne/grotte	Höhle	guphā गुफा
Charges	frais/tarif	Kosten	kirāya / kharch किराया/खर्च
Cheese	fromage	Käse	panīr पनीर
Church	église	Kirche	girjāghar / charch गिरजाघर/चर्च
Cloth	tissu	Stoff	kaprā कपड़ा
(to) come	venir	kommen	ānā आना

ENGLISH	*FRANCAIS*	*DEUTSCH*	*HINDI/ROMAN*
Congratulations	félicitations	Glückwunsch	badhāī / mubārak बधाई/मुबारक
Cotton	coton	Baumwolle	rui / kapās रूई/कपास
Country	pays	Land	dēsh/mulk देश/मुल्क
Curios	objets rares	Kuriositäten	vichitra/ajīb chīzain विचित्र/अजीब चीज़ें
Curtain	rideau	Vorhang	pardā पर्दा
(to) cut	couper	schneiden	kātnā काटना
		D	
Dark	foncé/obscur/sombre	dunkel	andherā अन्धेरा
Date	date	Datum	tārikh तारीख
Democratic	démocratique	demokratisch	prajātantra jamhūriyat प्रजातंत्र/जमहूरियत
Difficult	difficile	schwierig	kathin/mushkil कठिन/मुश्किल
Dinner	diner	Abendessen	shām kā khānā शाम का खाना
Dish	plat	Platte	tashtarī/rakābī तश्तरी/रकाबी
(to) display	montrer/étaler	ausstellen	dikhānā दिखाना
Dog	chien	Hund	kuttā कुत्ता
Doll	poupée	Puppe	guriyā गुड़िया
Door	porte	Tür	darwāzā दरवाज़ा
Drama	le théâtre/drame	Drama	drāmā ड्रामा
Dress	costume	Kleid	poshāk/wardī पोशक/वर्दी
Driver	chauffeur	Fahrer	drāiver ड्राईवर
(to) dry	sécher	trocknen	sukhānā सुखाना

ENGLISH	*FRANCAIS*	*DEUTSCH*	*HINDI/ROMAN*
		E	
Earth	terre	Erde	prithvī/zamīn पृथ्वी/ज़मीन
East	est	Osten	pūrab पूर्व
Easy	facile	leicht	āsān आसान
Egg	oeuf	Ei	andā अंडा
Elephant	éléphant	Elefant	hāthi हाथी
English	anglais	englisch	angrezī अंग्रेजी
Entertainment	divertissement	Unterhaltung	manoranjan मनोरंजन
Entire	entier	ganz	pūrā/sābut पूरा/साबुत
Envelope	enveloppe	Umschlag	lifāfā लिफाफा
Evening	soir/soirée	Abend	sandhyā/shām संध्या/शाम
Every	chaque	jeder, jede, jedes	har ek हर एक
Excellent	excellent	ausgezeichnet	bahut uttam/achhā बहुत उत्तम/अच्छा
Exhibition	exposition	Ausstellung	pradarshīn / numāesh प्रदर्शनी/नुमाइश
Eye	oeil	Auge	āankh आंख
		F	
Face	figure/visage	Gesicht	mukh/chehrā मुख/चेहरा
Fair	foire	Messe	melā मेला
Famous	célelebre/fameux	berühmt	prasiddha/machhūr प्रसिद्ध/मशहूर
Fan	ventilateur	Ventilator	pankhā पंखा
Far	loin	fern, weit	dūr दूर
Fare	tarif	Fahrgeld	bhārā/kirāyā भाड़ा/किराया

ENGLISH	*FRANCAIS*	*DEUTSCH*	*HINDI/ROMAN*
Fast	rapide	schnell	tēz तेज़
Festival	fête	Fest	tewhār त्यौहार
(to) fetch	aller chercher	holen	lānā लाना
Few	peu	wenige	kuchh/thōrā कुछ / थोड़ा
Finger	doigt	Finger	unglī उंगली
Fire	feu	Feuer	āg आग
Fish	poisson	Fisch	machchhī / machhlī मच्छी / मछली
Flesh	chair	Fleisch	māns/gosht मांस / गोश्त
Food	nourriture	Essen	khānā खाना
Forest	forêt	Wald	van/jangal वन / जंगल
Fort	fort	Festung	durg/qillā दुर्ग / किला
Free	libre/gratuit	frei	muft मुफ्त
Fresh	frais	frisch	tāzā ताजा
Friend	ami	Freund	mitra/dost मित्र / दोस्त
Fruit	fruit	Frucht	phal फल
(to) fry	frire	braten	talnā तलना
Furniture	meubles	Möbel	farnīchar फर्नीचर
		G	
Garden	jardin	Garten	bāgh बाग
Gate	porte	Tor	phātak/darwāzā फाटक / दरवाज़ा
Gift	présent/cadeau	Geschenk	uphār/inām उपहार / इनाम
Glad	content/heureux	froh	harsh/khush हर्ष / खुश

ENGLISH	*FRANCAIS*	*DEUTSCH*	*HINDI/ROMAN*
Glove	gant	Handschuh	dastānā दस्ताना
(to) go	aller, partir	gehen	jānā जाना
Grave	tombe	Grab	kabar कबर
(to) grind	moudre	mahlen	pīsnā पीसना
Guest	hôte	Gast	mehmān मेहमान
		H	
Half	demi	halb	ādhā आधा
Hand	main	Hand	hāth हाथ
Hard	dur	hart	sakhth सख्त
Head	tête	Kopf	sar सिर
(to) hear	entendre	hören	sunanā सुनना
Heat	chaleur	Heizgerät	garmī गर्मी
Heater	radiateur	Ofen	hītar हीटर
Heavy	lourd	schwer	bhārī भारी
Here	ici	hier	yahān यहाँ
Hill station	station de montagne	Höhenortschaft	pahārī nagar/ hill steshan पहाड़ी नगर/हिल स्टेशन
Holiday	vacance, congé	Feiertag	chhuttī/sair छुट्टी/सैर
Honest	honnête	ehrilich	imandār ईमानदार
Horse	cheval	Pferd	ghorā घोड़ा
Hospital	hôpital	Krankenhaus	aspatāl अस्पताल
Hot	chaud	heiss	garam

ENGLISH	*FRANCAIS*	*DEUTSCH*	*HINDI/ROMAN*
			गर्म
Hot water	eau chaude	heisses Wasser	garam pānī गर्म पानी
House	maison	Haus	ghar/makān घर/मकान
How much ?	combien ?	wieviel ?	kitnā ? कितना ?
How far ?	à quelle distance ?	wie weit ?	kitnī dūr ? कितनी दूर ?
Hungry	faim	hungrig	bhūkhā भूखा
Hurry up !	dépêchez-vous!	Beeilen Sie sich !	jaldī karo ! जल्दी करो !
Husband	mari	Mann	pati/shohar पति/शौहर
		I	
Ice	glace	Eis	baraf बर्फ
Ill	malade	krank	bimār बीमार
India	Inde	Indien	Bhārat/Hindustān भारत/हिन्दुस्तान
Information	renseignement	information	sūchnā/khabar सूचना/खबर
Injury	blessure	Verletzung	chōt/zakhm चोट/जख्म
Ink	encre	Tinte	roshnāī/syahī रोशनाई/स्याही
Inside	à l'intérieur	drinnen/inwendig	andar/bhitar अन्दर/भीतर
Ivory	ivoire	Elfenbein	hathīdānt हाथीदांत
		J	
Jeweller	bijoutier	Juwelier	joharī जौहरी
Journey	voyage	Reise	yātrā/safar यात्रा/सफर
		K	
Kettle	bouilloire	Kessel	ketlī केतली
Key	clef	Schlüssel	chābī/kunjī चाबी/कुंजी

ENGLISH	FRANCAIS	DEUTSCH	HINDI/ROMAN
Kitchen	cuisine	küche	rasoighar/kichen रसोईघर/किचन
Knife	couteau	Messer	chākū/chhurī चाकू/छुरी
		L	
Lamp	lampe	Lampe	lamp लैम्प
Land	terre	Land	bhūmī/zamīn भूमि/ज़मीन
Large	grand	gross	barā बड़ा
Last	dernier	letzt/vorig	akhrī आखरी
Leg	jambe	Bein	tāng टांग
Letter	lettre	Brief	patra/chithī/khat पत्र/चिट्ठी/खत
Library	bibliotheque	Bibliothek	pustakālaya/laibratī पुस्तकालय/लाइब्रेरी
Linen	linge	Leinen	linin लिनन
Lion	lion	Löwe	singha/sher सिंह/शेर
Little	peu	wenig	kuchh/thorā कुछ/थोड़ा
Lunch	déjeuner	Mittagessen	lanch/dopahar kā khānā लंच/दोपहर का खाना
		M	
Man	homme	Mann	ādmi आदमी
Mango	mangue	Mango	ām आम
Many	beaucoup	viel	bahut बहुत
Marble	marbre	Marmor	sangamarmar संगमरमर
Market	marché	Markt	bāzār बाजार
Meal	repas	Mahlzeit	khānā खाना
Meat	viande	Fleisch	māns/gosht

ENGLISH	*FRANCAIS*	*DEUTSCH*	*HINDI/ROMAN*
			मांस / गोश्त
Medicine	médicament	Medizin	dawā दवा
Memorial	monument	Denkmal	smārak/yādgār स्मारक / यादगार
Message	message	Botschaft	sūchnā/khabar सूचना / खबर
Milk	lait	Milch	dūdh दूध
Mirror	glace/miroir	Spiegel	sh īshā शीशा
Money	argent	Geld	dhan/rupyā paisā धन / रुपया पैसा
Month	mois	Monat	mahinā महीना
Morning	matin	Morgen	subāh सुबह
Mosque	mosquée	Moschee	masjid मस्जिद
Mother	mètre	Mutter	mān मां
Mountain	montagne	Berg	pahār पहाड़
Mouth	bouche	Mund	munh मुंह
Museum	musée	Museum	ajāyābghar अजायबघर
Music	musique	Musik	sangīt संगीत
		N	
Name	nom	Name	nām नाम
Necktie	cravate	Kravatte	nektaī नैक्टाई
Never	jarmais	nie	kabhī nahī कभी नहीं
New	nouveau	neu	nayā/naī नया / नई
News	nouvelles	Nachrichten	samāchār/khabar समाचार / खबर
Newspaper	journal	Zeitung	samāchar patra/ akhbār

ENGLISH	*FRANCAIS*	*DEUTSCH*	*HINDI/ROMAN*
			समाचारपत्र / अखबार
Next	prochain/suivant	nächst/folgend	dūsrā दूसरा
Night	nuit	Nacht	rāt रात
No	non	nein	nahīn नहीं
Noise	bruit	Lärm	shor शोर
Noon	midi	Mittag	dopahar दोपहर
North	nord	Norden	uttar उत्तर
Nose	nez	Nase	nāk नाक
Nothing	rien	nichts	kuchh nahin कुछ नहीं
Now	maintenant	jetzt	ab/abhī अब / अभी
Now a days	de nos jours	heutzutage	ājkal आजकल
Nut	noix	Nuss	péch/ guthlī पेच / गुठली
		O	
Oil	huile	Öl	tēl तेल
Old	vieux	alt	purānā पुराना
Onion	oignon	Zwiebel	pyāz प्याज़
(to) open	ouvrir	öffnen	kholnā खोलना
Opposite	enface	gegenüber	sāmne सामने
Or	ou	order	yā या
Oyster	huitre	Auster	ostar अस्तर
(to) pack	emballer	packen	bandhanā बांधना
		P	
Pain	douleur	Schmerzen	dard

ENGLISH	*FRANCAIS*	*DEUTSCH*	*HINDI/ROMAN*
			दर्द
Paper	papier	Papier	kāghaz कागज़
(to) pardon	pardonner	verzeihen	kshamā karnā / māf karnā क्षमा करना / माफ करना
Passenger	passager	Passagier	yātrī/musāfir यात्री / मुसाफिर
Path	chemin	Weg	mārg/rāstā मार्ग / रास्ता
Pavilion	pavillon	Pavillion	paveliyan पवेलियन
Payment	paiement	Zahlung	bhugtān भुगतान
Pen	plume/stylo	Schreibfeder	kalam कलम
People	peuple/gens	Leute/Menschen/Volk	jan/log जन / लोग
Pepper	poivre	Pfeffer	kāli mirch काली मिर्च
Photograph	photographie	Photograph	fotogrāf फोटोग्राफ
Pickles	conserves (au vinaigre)	Pickles	achār अचार
Picture	image/tableau	Bild	chitra/taswīr चित्र / तस्वीर
Pillar	pilier	Sāule	khambā खम्बा
Pillow	oreiller	Kopfkissen	takiyā तकिया
Pipe	tuyau	Rohr	pāip पाइप
Place	endroit/lieu	Ort/Platz	sthān/jagah स्थान / जगह
Plan	plan	Plan	yojnā योजना
Please	s'il vous plait	bitte	kripā kar ke/ meharbānī se कृपा करके / मेहरबानी से
Police station	commissariat de police	Polizeiamt	thānā/ pulis chowkī थाना / पुलिस चौकी
Poor	pauvre	arm	garīb

ENGLISH	*FRANCAIS*	*DEUTSCH*	*HINDI/ROMAN*
			गरीब
Post office	bureau de poste	Postamt	dāk ghar/ dākhānā डाकघर/डाकखाना
Prayer	prière	Gebet	prārthnā/ibādāt प्रार्थना/इबादत
President	Président	Präsident	Rashrāpatī राष्ट्रपति
Price	prix	Preis	mūlya / kīmat मूल्य/कीमत
Prime Minister	Premier Ministre	Ministerpräsident	Pradhān Mantrī प्रधान मंत्री
Progress	progrès	Fortschritt/Entwicklung	pragatī/tarakkī प्रगति/तरक्की
Promise	promesse	Versprechen	vachan/waidā वचन/वायदा
(to) purchase	acheter	kaufen	kharidnā खरीदना
		Q	
Question	question	Frage	prashna/sawāl प्रश्न/सवाल
		R	
Rain	pluile	Regen	varshā/bārish वर्षा/बारिश
Rare	rare	selten	bahut kam बहुत कम
Rate	taux	Mass/Preis/kurs	dar/bhāo दर/भाव
Raw	cru	roh	kacchā कच्चा
Razor	rasoir	Rasiermesser	raizar/ustrā रेज़र/उस्तरा
Ready	prët	fertig	tayyār तैयार
(to) recover	récupérer	wiedererlangen/genesen	vasūl karnā वसूल करना
(to) remove	enlever/éloigner	beseitigen/entfernen	hatānā हटाना
Request	requête/demande	Bitte	prārthnā/darkhwāst प्रार्थना/दरख्वास्त
Rest	repos	Ruhe	ārām आराम
Result	résultat	Ergebnis	phal/natījā

ENGLISH	*FRANCAIS*	*DEUTSCH*	*HINDI/ROMAN*
			फल/नतीजा
(to) return	rendre/retourner	zurückgeben	lautanā /vapas jānā लौटना/वापस जाना
Reward	récompense	Belohnung	inām इनाम
Rice	riz	Reis	chāwal चावल
Rich	riche	reich	dhanwān/amīr धनवान/अमीर
Right	correct/exact	recht/richtig	thīk/sahī ठीक/सही
Ring	bague	ring	angūthī अंगूठी
Ripe	mûr	reif	pakkā पक्का
(to) rise	se lever	aufstehen	uthnā उठना
River	fleuve/rivière	Fluss	nadi/dariyā नदी/दरिया
(to) roast	rôtir	braten	bhūnanā भूनना
Room	chambre/pièce	Zimmer/Raum	kamrā कमरा
Rose (flower)	rose (fleur)	Rose (Blume)	gulāb ka phūl गुलाब का फूल
Rupee	roupie	Rupie	rupayā रुपया
		S	
Safe	sûr/à l'abri	sicher	surakshit / hifāzat se सुरक्षित/हिफाज़त से
Salary	salaire	Lohn/Gehalt	vetan/tankhwāh वेतन/तनख्वाह
Salt	sel	salz	namak नमक
Sample	échantillon	Muster	namūnā नमूना
Sand	sable	Sand	ret/bālu रेत/बालू
Satisfactory	satisfaisant	befriedigend	thīk ठीक
Sauce	sauce	Sosse	chatnī चटनी
Saucer	soucoupe	Untertasse	tashtarī/rakabī

ENGLISH	*FRANCAIS*	*DEUTSCH*	*HINDI/ROMAN*
			तश्तरी/रकाबी
(to save)	sauver	sparen/retten	bachāna बचाना
(to) say	dire	sagen	kahnā कहना
Scene	scène/vue	Szene	drishyā/nazzārā दृश्य/नज़ारा
Scissors	ciseaux	Schere	kainchī कैंची
Sea	mer	See/Meer	samudra समुद्र
Season	saison	Jahreszeit	ritu/mausam ऋतु/मौसम
(to) see	voir	sehen	dekhnā देखना
(to) sell	vendre	verkaufen	bechnā बेचना
(to) send	envoyer/expédier	senden	bhejnā भेजना
(to) send (for a person)	faire chercher (quelqu'un)	ausschicken/fragen bitten	bulānā बुलाना
(to) send (for things)	aller chercher (quelque chose)	schicken/holen lassen/ bestellen	mangānā मंगाना
Servant	serviteur	Diener	naukar नौकर
Shampoo	shampooing	Shampoo	shampū शैम्पू
Shawl	châle	Schal	shāl शाल
Shoe	soulier/chaussure	Schuh	jūtā जूता
Shop	magasin/boutique	Laden	dukān दुकान
Short	court/petit	kurz	chhotā छोटा
(to) show	montrer	zeigen	dikhānā दिखाना
(to) shut	fermer	schliessen	band karnā बन्द करना
Sick	malade	krank	bimār बीमार
Silent	silencieux	still	chup

ENGLISH	*FRANCAIS*	*DEUTSCH*	*HINDI/ROMAN*
			चुप
Silk	soie	Seide	resham रेशम
Silver	argent	Silber	chāndī चांदी
Simple	simple	einfach	sādā सादा
Single	seul	einzein	akelā/ek अकेला/एक
Sister	soeur	Schwester	behan बहन
(to) sit	s'asseoir	sitzen	baithnā बैठना
Skirt	jupe	Rock	ghagrā/lehngā घाघरा/लहंगा
Sky	ciel	Himmel	akāsh/asmān अकाश/आसमान
(to) sleep	dormir	schlafen	sonā सोना
Slow	lent	langsam	dhīrey/ahistā धीने/आहिस्ता
Small	petit	klein	chhotā छोटा
(to) smile	sourire	lächeln	muskarānā मुस्कराना
Soap	savon	Seife	sābun साबुन
Soft	doux	weich	mulāyam मुलायम
Some	un peu/quelque	etwas/ein wenig/einige	kuchh/thorā कुछ/थोड़ा
Son	fils	Sohn	putra/betā/larkā पूत्र/बेटा/लड़का
Song	chant, chanson	Lied	gīt गीत
Soon	bientôt	bald	jaldī जल्दी
Soup	soupe	Suppe	ras/shoruā/sūp रस/शोरबा/सूप
South	sud	Süden	dakshin दक्षिण
(to speak)	parler	sprechen	bolnā

ENGLISH	*FRANCAIS*	*DEUTSCH*	*HINDI/ROMAN*
			बोलना
(to) spend	dépenser	ausgeben	kharch karnā खर्च करना
Stairs	l'escalier	Stufen/Treppe	sīrhī/zīnā सीढ़ी/जीना
(to) stand	être debout/se tenir debout	stehen	khare honā खड़े होना
Star	étoile	Stern	sitārā सितारा
Statue	statue	Statue	mūrtī मूर्ति
Stone	pierre	Stein	patthar पत्थर
Story	histoire	Geschichte/Erzählung	kahānī कहानी
Street	rue	Strasse	galī/saṛak गली/सड़क
Strong	fort/solide	stark	mazbūt मज़बूत
Successful	plein de succès/ réussi	erfolgreich	saphal/kāmyāb सफल/कामयाब
Sugar	sucre	Zucker	chīnī चीनी
Suit	costume	Anzug	sūt सूट
Sun	soleil	Sonne	sūraj सूरज
Surprise	surprise	Überraschu-ng	ascharyā/tājjaub आश्चर्य/ताज्जुब
Sweet	doux/sucré	süss	mīthā मीठा

T

ENGLISH	*FRANCAIS*	*DEUTSCH*	*HINDI/ROMAN*
Table	table	Tisch	mēz मेज़
Tailor	tailleur	Schneider	darzī दर्जी
(to) take	prendre	nehmen	lenā लेना
(to) talk	parler	reden	bāt karnā बात करना
Tall	grand	gross	lambā लम्बा
Tank	bassin/étang	Tank	tālāb

ENGLISH	*FRANCAIS*	*DEUTSCH*	*HINDI/ROMAN*
			तालाब
Tea	thé	Tee	chai चाय
Telegram	télégramme	Telegramm	tār तार
(to) tell	dire	erzählen	kahnā कहना
Temple	temple	Tempel	mandir मंदिर
Thanks	remerciements/merci	Dank	dhanyawād/shukriyā धन्यवाद / शुक्रिया
That	ce, cela	jene	woh वह
Theatre	théâtre	Theater	nātak/drāmā नाटक / ड्रामा
Theft	vol	Diebstahl	chorī चोरी
Thin	mince/maigre	dünn	patlā/dublā पतला / दुबला
(to) think	penser	denken	sochnā सोचना
Thirsty	assoiffé	durstig	pyāsā प्यासा
This	ce, ceci	dies	yeh यह
Thread	fil	Faden	dorā/dhāgā डोरा / धागा
Thumb	pouce	Daumen	angūthā अंगूठा
(to) tie	nouer/attacher	binden	bāndhnā बाँधना
Tiffin (packed lunch)	collation	eingepacktes Mittagessen	tiffin/dophar kā khānā टिफिन / दोपहर का खाना
Tiger	tigre	Tiger	bāgh/cheetā बाघ / चीता
Tight	serré	dicht/fest/knapp	kasā/sakht कसा / सख्त
Time	temps (l'heure, la durée)	Zeit	samay/waqt समय / वक्त
Tired	fatigué	müde	thakā थका
Tobacco	tabac	Tabak	tambākū

ENGLISH	*FRANCAIS*	*DEUTSCH*	*HINDI/ROMAN*
			तम्बाकू
Today	aujourd'hui	heute	āj आज
Together	ensemble	zusammen	sāth साथ
Tomb	tombeau	Grabmal	maqbarā मकबरा
Tomorrow	demain	morgen	käl कल
Tooth-brush	brosse à dents	Zahnbürste	dānt burush दांत बुरुश
Total	total	total/zusammen	kul कुल
Tour	tournée/voyage	Tour	yātrā/daurā/pariyatan यात्रा/दौरा/पर्यटन
Tourist	touriste	Tourist	Pariyatak पर्यटक
Towel	essuie-mains	Handtuch	tauliyā तौलिया
Town	ville	Stadt	nagar/shahar नगर/शहर
Track	piste/allée	Fährte/Weg/Geleise	rāstā रास्ता
Traveller	voyageur	Reisende	yātrī यात्री
Tree	arbre	Baum	perh/darakht पेड़/दरख्त
Trousers	pantalon	Hose	pajāmā/patlūn पजामा/पतलून
Turban	turban	Turban	pagrī/sāfa पगड़ी/साफा
		U	
Umbrella	parapluie	Schirm	chhātā छाता
Uncle	oncle	Onkel	chāchā चाचा
(to) understand	comprendre	verstehen	samajhnā समझना
Uneasy	mal à l'aise	unruhig/unbequem	bechen बेचैन
		V	
Vacant	vacant/libre/vide	unbetzt	khālī

ENGLISH	*FRANCAIS*	*DEUTSCH*	*HINDI/ROMAN*
			खाली
Valuable	de valeur/précieux	kostbar/teuer	qīmtī कीमती
Vegetable	légume	Gemüse	tarkārī/sabzī तरकारी/सब्ज़ी
Verbal	verbal	wörtlich	zabānī जबानी
Village	village	Dorf	gāon गांव
Vinegar	vinaigre	Essig	sirkā सिरका
		W	
(to) wait	attendre	warten	intazār karnā इंतजार करना
(to) wake	reveiller	aufwachen/wecken	jāganā जागना
Wall	mur	Wand	dīwār दीवार
(to)want	désirer/vouloir	bedürfen / wünschen	chāhnā चाहना
(to) warm	chauffer	wärmen	garam karnā गर्म करना
Washerman	blanchisseur	wäscher	dhobī धोबी
Water	eau	wasser	pānī पानी
Waterfall	cute d'eau	wasserfall	jharnā झरना
(to) watch	regarder/veiller	bewachen behüten	dekhnā/nigrānī rakhnā देखना/निगरानी रखना
Wax	cire	Wachs	mom मोम
Weak	faible	schwach	kamzōr कमजोर
Weather	temps (atmosphèrique)	Wetter	mausam मौसम
Wedding	mariage	Hochzeit	viwāh/shādi विवाह/शादी
(to) weigh	peser	weigen	tolnā तोलना
Well-done	bien fait	gut gemacht	bahut achchā kiyā

ENGLISH	*FRANCAIS*	*DEUTSCH*	*HINDI/ROMAN*
			बहुत अच्छा किया
Well-known	connu/celebre	bekannt	mashuūr मशहूर
West	ouest	Westen	pashchim पश्चिम
Western	occidental	westlich	pashchimī पश्चिमी
Wet	mouille/humide	nass	gīlā गीला
White	blanc	weiss	safed सफेद
Wick	mèche	Docht	battī बत्ती
Wife	femme (épouse)	Gattin/Gemahlin	patnī/bīwī पत्नी/बीवी
Wild	sauvage	wild	janglī जंगली
Window	enêtre	Fenster	khīrkī खिड़की
Wine	vin	Wein	sharāb शराब
Wise	sage	weise	buddhimān/ akalmand बुद्धिमान/अक्लमन्द
(to) wish	souhaiter	wünschen	ichchhā/khwāhish karnā इच्छा/ख्वाहिश करना
Within	dans/a I'interieur de	innerhalb/darin	bhītar भीतर
Without	dehors/sans	ohne/ausserhalb	bahār बाहर
Woman	femme	Frau	aurat औरत
Wool	laine	Wolle	ūn ऊन
Woollen	de laine/en laine	wollig	ūnī ऊनी
(to) work	traveiller	arbeiten	kām karnā काम करना
World	monde	Welt	sansār/duniyā संसार/दुनिया
(to) wrap	envelopper	einwickeln	ordhnā/lapetnā

ENGLISH	*FRANCAIS*	*DEUTSCH*	*HINDI/ROMAN*
			ओढ़ना / लपेटना
(to) write	écrire	schreiben	likhnā लिखना
		Y	
Yacht	yacht	Jacht	nāo/yāch नाव / याच
Yard	yard (91 cm)	Yard (91 cm)	gaz गज़
Year	année	jahr	varsh/sāl वर्ष / साल
Yes	oui	ja	hān हां
Yesterday	hier	gester	kal कल
Young	jeune	jung	tarun/jawān तरुण
		Z	
Zero	zéro	null	shūnyā/sifar/zēro शून्य / सिफर / ज़ीरो
Zoo	zoo	Tiergarten	chiriyāghar/zū चिड़ियाघर / जू

Appendix 'A'

Hospitality-Reception Terminology

Advance Payment

Money requested by the receptionist at the check-in from a guest who has not made an advance reservation and who is unable to produce any of the credit cards accepted by the Hotel.

Amenity

A gift for the guest with compliments of the Hotel.

American Plan (AP)

A type of room rate that includes the price of the room, breakfast, lunch, and dinner. Also known as full pension.

Apartment Hotel

Accommodation in apartment-style units rather than rooms: with minimum or expanded in-suite cooking facilities. Defined by legislation for licensing and classification purposes.

ARR

Hotel revenue divided by the number of rooms sold. Hotels use this measure to calculate the average price at which they are booking hotels each night. So, if a hotel made ₹ 5,00,000 and sold 200 rooms, its ARR would be ₹ 5,00,000 / 200 = ₹ 2,500. ARR is also known as Average Daily Rate, and Average rate per occupied room.

ATR (Average Transient Rate)

Hotel revenue divided by the number of paying rooms (number of rooms sold - complimentary rooms - house use rooms). So, if a hotel made ₹ 5,00,000 and sold 200 rooms but had 10 complimentary rooms and 30 house use rooms, its ATR would be 5,00,000/(200 - 10 - 30) = ₹ 3,125.0

Authorization Approval Code

A code given by credit card company to the hotel to indicate that they have extended credit limit for one of its cardholder.

Available Rooms (suites, beds)

The number of rooms normally available on a day-to-day basis, less those permanently used for some purpose other than guest occupancy.

Average Daily Rate (ADR)

The total room revenue for a given period (day, month to date, month, year to date), divided by the number of rooms occupied for the same period. Frequently used as a measure of economic performance.

Average Transient Rate

Average rate per occupied room.

Bed and Breakfast (B&B)

A type of room rate, which includes the price of the room and breakfast. Also known as Continental Plan.

Boutique Hotel

Historical, classic buildings, remodeled into boutique hotels with usually have less than 30 rooms.

Cash Basis

The guest pays for the room, service and tax for the duration of his stay upon checking into the hotel. No facilities are provided by the hotel for charging other items to his account i.e. restaurant, laundry bills etc. If the guest wishes to charge items to his account, he will have to put down as extra deposit to cover his incidental charges.

Check-in

Guest arrives and registers in.

Check-out

Guest departs and settles the bill.

Check-out Print Out

A print out of bills for the guest perusal before he settles the amount stated either by cash or credit card.

Central Reservation System (CRS/CReS)

The ability of guests to make a reservation for one out of a number of hotels by contacting one agency, contracted by the hotels acting as a group, to operate this "central" reservation service.

Complimentary Room

An occupied guest room for which no price is charged. This may include a room occupied by a hotel employee.

Condominium Hotels

Customers purchase fee-simple equity in the units - the hotel's guestrooms. Unit owners may live in the hotels permanently or use them as second and third homes. Depending on the hotel's policy, unit owners may rent their units independently or through the management company's rental program and derive income through a revenue-sharing arrangement. Unit owners also incur budgeted maintenance and operating expenses. Depending on the management company, unit owners have varying degrees of access to their hotel's amenities and services.

Credit Card Commissions

A fee paid to credit card companies based upon a contracted percentage of credit card charges accepted.

Daily Reports

A set of reports prepared for Management by the mid-night shift daily. Management uses these reports on hotel statistics in their daily planning; forecasting and marketing.

Destination Clubs

The newest entrant to lodging, this niche most closely resembles country clubs in ownership structure. While developers of destination clubs expect to branch out into other price segments, for now this niche targets the most affluent of travelers. Customers pay initiation fees, for example, that can run as high as ₹ 25,00,000 and annual dues running as high as ₹ 1,25,000. In return, customers get to stay for weeks at a time in multi-million dollar residences and villas in prime urban and resort locations and enjoy a full range of amenities and services.

D. N. A.

Did not arrive when accommodation was reserved.

D. N. D.

A special request by guest who did not wish to be disturbed.

Double Locked

Door is secured from inside by guest and cannot be opened by room attendant supervisor. It can be double locked by assistant manager and security office for a special reason.

Double Rooming

When two unrelated guests are mistakenly accommodated in the same room.

Downgrade

Moving a guest to a lower category room and decreasing his rate.

Duplicate Folio

Folio that has several copies duplicated for control purpose i.e. guest folio, deposit receipt, room bills etc.

Due in

Numbers of expected guests/rooms for the day.

Due out

Room expected to be vacated.

Drop Safe

A safety deposit box usually located at the General Cashier's Office, where all outlet cashiers and service associates could remit their day's collection.

Early Arrival

Refers to guest checking in before 12 noon. Early morning arrival is subject to space availability (6.00am start of day). If a client informs the hotel that he is arriving early, he must be informed that check-out time is not until 12.00 noon and the hotel cannot guarantee the room before then. We will, however, do our utmost to have a room ready as soon as possible. If the client wishes, he can reserve and pay for the room the night before to ensure immediate occupancy on arrival.

Early Departure

Guest who checked out earlier than the expected departure date (See "Unexpected Departure").

Express Check-Out

A condition whereby guest leaves the hotel without having to check-out at the Front Desk. However, guest needs to furnish his credit card details on the "Express Check-Out" form, prior to his departure. This arrangement could also apply to city ledger settlement.

Extend Stay

An in-house guest who is expected to check-out, extends his stay for a day or more depending on the room's availability.

Extension of Stay

Authorized change of departure dates.

Extra Bed

See Rollaway Bed (R.W.B.)

Extra Rate

Applies to third person in room and not extra bed. Extra person/bed rate to be waived for suite occupants.

Facilities

Core physical features: accommodation, restaurants, bars, and meeting rooms.

Family Plan

No additional charge for children under 18 years occupying the same room as their parents or guardian.

Franchise

The right to market a service and/or product often exclusive for a specified area, as granted by the manufacturer, developer or distributor in return for a fee: prevalent in the fast food industry but increasingly adopted within the hotel community.

Frequent Independent Traveler (FIT)

Designation which applies to visitors who arrive on their own as opposed to being a part of an organized group.

Front Office

An office usually situated in the lobby, always located inside the main entrance, whose primary function is to control the sale of guest rooms, provide keys, mail, information service for guests, maintain guest accounts, render bills, receive payments as well as providing information to other departments within the hotel.

Golden Circle Program

Guest recognition program that provides uniform delivery of value-added individual services, features and amenities to high valued guests, across all Shangri-La Hotels & Resorts.

Guaranteed

Refers to a reservation that has been guaranteed. This means that the guest plans on arriving after 4.00 pm and has guaranteed to pay should he fail to arrive. The hotel will hold the room all night, and if the guest does not arrive, he will be charged. In the event that the guest has guaranteed and the hotel does not have space when he arrives, the hotel will find alternative accommodation at a similar hotel and pay for it.

Guest Account

An itemized record of a guest's charges and credits, maintained in the front office until departure. Also referred to as a guest bill, guest folio, and/or guest statement.

Guest Amenities

Not to be confused with "amenities", this is the term given to the range of disposable items provided in guest room bathrooms and includes such items as shampoo, lotion, conditioner, soap, toothpaste, toothbrush, shower caps, etc... The costs of these items are built into room rate.

Guest Check (Restaurant)

The invoice presented to restaurant and bar patrons for food and beverage consumed during a visit. Also referred to as a waiter's check or restaurant check.

Guest History

A record maintained for each guest who has stayed at the hotel with a separate entry for each visit and details of pertinent preferences. This is a valuable reference tool for reservations, marketing, and credit departments. Guest histories are now more readily available through the increased utilization of computers and technology.

Guest House

A personal residence with a small amount of overnight accommodation sometimes limited by legislation and residence constraints. Typically provides breakfast, which is included within the room rate but no other meals. Not licensed to provide alcoholic beverages commercially.

Guest Folio

A statement of the guest's hotel charges.

Guest Service Directory

A document listing all of features of a hotel together with general and pertinent information about the community within which the property is located. Directories are usually provided within each guest room.

Guest Name Record (GNR)

This is the guest's reservation record which includes guest name, hotel accommodations, arrival information, rate, address and any other pertinent information.

Half Day Charge

A charge of 50% off folio rate for late check-out at 6.00pm (50% off rack for "wholesale" guests who wish to extend late check-out on their own account).

High (Peak) Season/Shoulder Season

The period of consecutive months during which optimum revenues, room/suite occupancy and average room rates are generated. For example in the state of Rajasthan this is generally October through March.

Hotel

Minimum number of available rooms, services, and amenities, usually defined by legislation for licensing and classification purposes as well as eligibility for fiscal incentives in some jurisdictions. May provide food and beverage services on site but not always within the accommodation building(s): usually by in-house staff but occasionally through an outside food and beverage contractor. May or may not provide a range of recreation and other amenities on site or by arrangement with others off site. Includes motor hotel, resort hotel or resort, and commercial hotel.

Hold for Arrival

Holding the items that arrived in advance before the guest check-in.

Hot Card

A credit card which has been reported lost or stolen.

House Count/Status

This term indicates the occupancy of the hotel at any time of the day, expressed in either actual rooms or percentage.

Hotel Representative

An individual or firm with the responsibility to facilitate market accessibility to the hotel property by the travel trade.

Ingress and Egress

Ingress/Egress relates to the Civil Authority coverage part of the Business Income/EE forms. If one is unable to enter or exit by direction of civil authority.

In-House Guest

All guests that are registered with the Hotel.

Intelligent Hotels

Hotels that are identified because they have state of the art technology systems for their operations. These hotels have replaced the traditional systems to reduce their energy cost and usually have integrated systems that join analog and digital systems to achieve an effective communication in their hotels. The return on investment is reflected in the energy-cost savings and the comfort they provide to their guests.

Innkeepers Statutes

Statutes that limit the common law liability of innkeepers.

Incognito Stay

See "Confidential Stay".

Joiner

Guest to check into room with already registered guest requiring a separate account.

Key Permit

An in-house guest authorizes another non-registered guest to gain access to his room.

Key Rack

A rack that is used to placed the room keys.

Key Request

In-house guest requests for a second room key or another key to replace his/her lost key.

Late Check-Out

Additional time allotted by the hotel after normal check-out time with or without extra charge. Free-of-charge is subject to space availability or as promised, e.g. Value Rate (Rack).

Limited Service Hotels

Brand hotels with franchise memberships of recognized hotels, built within limited areas without a restaurant. These hotels are located near business areas such as industrial parks, cities, and airport terminals.

Limousine

Hotel vehicle used to transport guests to or from the airport/train station/pier or hourly bookings.

Locator message

Guest advises that he/she may be contacted at a specific location when he/she is not in the room for a period of time.

Lockout

Denying the guest access to the room, usually because of unpaid bill.

Logbook

Book for inter department communication.

Log Printer

Printer dedicated to printing critical computer transactions i.e. Creation of Reservation, Guest Check-in, Post to Folio, Status Reports, Telephone Charges, etc.

Loss of Attraction

"Loss of Attraction" falls under the Business Income and Extra Expense coverage form although coverage is rarely included as it is hard to prove. For example, if a fire occurred at a hotel in a particular locality, there may be other hotels in the surrounding area that will have lost income as a result of the reduction in tourism. For those hotels that have not suffered direct damage to the property, Business Income claims would fall under "Loss of Attraction." Loss of Attraction coverage is not common and can be difficult to identify the loss resulting from a disaster and that, which could have resulted from poor management or other uninsured factors.

Physical damage to insured property is the primary trigger for business interruption claims; however, additional triggers of coverage outside of physical damage include acts of civil authority, ingress/egress, contingent business interruption and loss of attraction.

Low (off-peak) Season

The consecutive months during which the lowest revenues, room/suite occupancy and average room rates are generated. For example, in the Rajasthan this is generally April to September.

Luggage Claim Check

A tag that indicates the belongings of the guest that are kept with the Concierge.

Market Share

That percentage of the hotel market (in terms of units, rupee, or any other index) which is captured by a given segment.

Mini Bar

A specially designed small floor mounted refrigerator containing a variety of beverages and snacks located in guest rooms, with individual guest room key access. This amenity serves as a more credible and profitable substitute for room service.

M.O.D.

Manager On Duty.

Motel

Overnight accommodation originally targeted to automobile travelers and therefore, situated at roadside locations. A more contemporary definition would be the provision of accommodation only, with no other amenities and services provided by the motel.

Net Rate

A non-commissionable rate or rate inclusive of taxes and service charge.

Night Manager

Evening Manager.

Night Safe

See "Drop Safe".

Non In-House Guest

Guest that are not registered with the Hotel.

No-Show

Guest who did not arrive when accommodation was reserved. Guaranteed no-shows are not to be checked into the PMS to capture occupancy. The Front Office Manager in consultation with the Director of Marketing is to advise the Credit Manager the following day which guaranteed no-shows to be charged. All relevant correspondences are to be attached to the no-show report and submitted to Credit Manager for proper billing.

Occupancy (Occ. %) (Occ Rate)

The percentage of available rooms occupied for a given period of consecutive time. This figure is calculated by dividing the number of rooms occupied for a period by the number of rooms available for the same period and is expressed as a percentage.

On Request

Situation whereby the hotel is expecting high occupancy and certain room categories are placed on request basis to travel agents, sister hotels and Central Reservations Offices.

Out Of Order Rooms

Rooms removed from saleable inventory due to major (O.O.O.) repair works e.g. renovation or refurbishment.

Out Of Service Rooms

Rooms temporarily blocked off for minor repair works((O.O.S.) e.g. servicing of air-conditioners, general cleaning; or rooms temporarily closed off due to low occupancy. (These O.O.S. rooms do not affect the occupancy forecast).

Overbooking

A situation in which a hotel has taken more room reservations than what the hotel is able to accommodate. Hotels that use overbooking as a policy are increasingly being targeted by tour wholesalers and operators in an attempt to better control and minimize the serious adverse marketing effects which overbooking has for all stakeholders.

Package

The name given to an assembly of components under a one price system. Typically, the core package price would include: return transportation, ground transfers, baggage handling, accommodation, one or more meals per day, and applicable taxes. Car rentals, recreation and entertainment and gratuities may also be included, but are more often supplementary to the core package price.

Percentage of Occupancy

Occupancy determined by dividing the total occupied rooms (including complimentary rooms) by the total available rooms (excluding O.O.O. rooms).

Permanent Folios

Room types defined in Fidelio beginning with “P” are considered pseudo or “dummy” room types. The system provides all normal functionality available in Fidelio for “P_” room types, such as creating reservations, attachment of Travel Agent or Company profiles, charge routing, check-in, posting, settlement by all payment methods, check-out, etc. These rooms are not included in the daily rooms statistics, but revenue and payment figures are taken in as part of the hotel total. This flexibility allows these “dummy” rooms to fulfill a variety of functions for the hotel. In order to segregate the functions and easily identify the purpose of each “P” room type, it is recommended to use the following designations:

Pledge Relocates

Rooms for guests housed at another hotel, but paid for by the hotel as a result of the hotel not being able to honour a guaranteed reservation.

PMS

Property Management System (Fidelio/Opera)

POS

Point of Sales (Micros)

Pre-Assigning/Block

Setting aside rooms for reservations with specific requests for a service, feature, amenity and early arrivals.

Pre-register

Process whereby guests' full particulars are obtained prior to arrival and only guests' signatures are obtained upon check-in.

Profile

A master record of details of a guest/company/travel agent e.g. name, address, telephone number, guest history and etc.

Quoted Rate

On the Shangri-La Hotels & Resorts confirmation, we are honour bound to provide the guest with the room and/or rate specified on the confirmation, regardless of availability.

Rate Change

An occupied room, which rate, is changed due to certain reason.

Rack Rate

The full, undiscounted published room rate (price).

Rebate

An adjustment made to the guest folio (bill). This is always a negative figure and is an adjustment due to unsatisfactory services or for a posting error.

Register

Process of filling in the registration card at check-in.

Registration Card (Reg. Card)

A form on which arriving guests record their names, addresses, and other details including mode of transportation used, nationality, purpose of visit (usually business or pleasure), method of payment, and length of stay. A space is also provided for signature, room rate and room number. Additional questions may be included as a part of the hotel's market research platform.

Resort Hotels & Spas

A hotel that caters primarily to vacationers and tourist and typically offers more recreational amenities and services, in a more aesthetically pleasing setting, than other hotels. These hotels are located in attractive and natural tourism destinations and their clientele are groups and couples that like adventure with sophistication and comfort. The attractions vary depending on the region and some might offer golf, tennis, scuba diving and, depending on the natural surrounding, may also arrange other recreational activities.

Revenue Per Available Room (REVPAR)

Revpar is the key measure in the performance of the core business of hotels-selling rooms. Revenue per available room (revpar) is the key indicator of performance for hotels and can be broken down into two parts reflecting occupancy and rates:

Revpar = occupancy (percentage of available rooms occupied) × average room rate per night.

Room revenue divided by the number of room nights that are available (can be mathematically derived from occupancy rate multiplied by average daily rate).

Trends in revpar are very important. Revpar can be used to compare companies but only if they have broadly similar hotels - i.e. similarly priced in similar locations. This is less unlikely than it may seem as most hotels companies give regional breakdowns of revpar and this can be compared.

Rollaway Bed (R.W.B.)

A portable single bed which can accommodate an additional guest.

Rooming

The entire procedure by which the desk greets and assigns new arrivals and the bellman directs them and brings their luggage to their rooms.

Room Block

A pre-determined number of rooms reserved in advance for group (conference, tour) use.

Room Change

When a guest moves from one room to another during his stay.

Room Count

The number of occupied rooms.

Room Service

Food and beverage delivered and served in a guest room.

Rooming (a guest)

The entire procedure by which the desk greets and assigns new arrivals and the bellman directs them and brings their luggage to their rooms.

Room Discrepancies

Rooms reported by Housekeeping when the physical status of the rooms do not tally the Front Office PMS status.

Room Rate

This rate which is designated for a specific room.

Rooming List

A list of guest names provided by a travel agent or group organizer to the hotel to inform names of persons occupying the block booking.

Round Trip Transfer

Two way transfer from airport/train station/pier to hotel; and from hotel to airport/train station/pier.

Routing Instructions

Process whereby billing instructions are set in guests' reservations.

Run Of House (ROH)

A term used for travel agent's contracted rate for the lowest room category and when this category is not available upon guest's arrival, the guest must automatically be upgraded to the next available category at no extra cost.

Safety Deposit Boxes

Individual boxes provided for the safekeeping of guest valuables. Located either in a central, secure, and supervised location or in individual guest rooms.

Share With

Two or more guests occupying the same room but with separate accounts or folios.

Shift

The number of hours worked by a member of staff in one day.

Shoulder Season

The period between peak and low season.

Skip Room

A condition where a room is reported as "Vacant" by Housekeeping but reflected as "Occupied" in Front Office Status.

Sleep Out

When a guest keeps the room but does not stay in.

Stay over

An anticipated checkout but remains beyond his departure date or any guest who stays overnight.

Star Ratings

Five Star Hotel

Luxury hotels

Most expensive hotels/resorts in the world; numerous extras to enhance the quality of the client's stay (for example: some have private golf courses and even a small private airport).

Four Star Hotel

First class hotels; expensive (by middle-class standards); has all of the previously mentioned services; has many "luxury" services (for example: massages or a health spa).

Three Star Hotel

Middle class hotels; moderately priced; has daily maid service, room service, and may have dry-cleaning, Internet access, and a swimming pool.

Two Star Hotel

Budget hotels; slightly more expensive; usually has maid service daily.

One Star Hotel

Low budget hotels; inexpensive; may not have maid service or room service.

No Category Hotels

These hotels include motels, cottages, bungalows and others with limited services. Nevertheless, these hotels represent 41% of the total hotel market share.

Suite

Accommodation consisting of one or two bedrooms and a connecting sitting room (parlor).

Suite Presidential

The highest suite category

Suite – Specialty

One of the more elegant suites.

System Up

When computer is operational.

System Down

The duration of time when the computer is shut.

Travel Agent Voucher

Document used by the travel agent to instruct the Hotel to provide accommodation or meals and payment is to the travel agent.

Timeshare (Vacation Ownership)

A marketing and equity-financing concept, which permits participants to enjoy vacation accommodation for a fixed, one time amount for life, or shorter contracted period. According to the American Resort Development Association (ARDA), timeshare consumers make a one-time purchase of furnished resort accommodations, at a fraction of whole ownership costs, and pay an annual maintenance fee. Each condominium, or unit, of a vacation ownership resort is divided into intervals, either by the week or points equivalent, which are sold separately.

The accommodations are priced according to a variety of factors, including size of the unit, resort amenities, location, and season. The purchaser owns the vacation accommodations, but only for the amount of time he or she plans to use it - typically one or two weeks each year. With time-share, the owner has all the benefits of a vacation home without the year-round costs. From its origin, the idea behind time-sharing was to give people the ability to purchase their future vacation - at current prices.

Fractional are a variation of timeshare in which the purchaser owns longer intervals, from four to 12 weeks a year. Costs of fractional are significantly higher, ranging to more than $600,000. Major branded hotel companies participate in fractional timeshare, though not to the extent of independent operators.

Tour Operator

An organization or individual who actively manages and escorts tours and tour packages to FIT and group visitors.

Traditional Lodging

Guests pay nightly rates for single rooms or suites and have full access to the hotels' range of amenities and services. Rates begin at "rack," but vary widely, based on time of week and season and nearby events and attractions.

Transfer

This refers to the transportation of visitors between their point of arrival and selected hotel, and back again on departure day.

Tour Group

A group booked by a travel agent or association, etc.

Tour Group Concession

Complimentary rooms accorded as per the contract signed with the travel

Trace

A message/instruction left in the PMS for the relevant department to follow up.

Travel Agent

Represents guests to arrange travel and hotel bookings.

Travel Agent Voucher

Document used by the travel agent to instruct the Hotel to provide accommodation or meals and payment is to the travel agent.

Unexpected Departure

See "Early Departure".

Upgrade

Situation where a guest is given a higher priced room at a lower rate, usually for business promotions or out of goodwill. This must be approved as per Delegation of Authority.

Upsell

Moving a guest into a higher priced room in the hotel with a rate increase.

Vacant Room

Room available for sale but not occupied during the period.

VIP

A person designated by management to receive special treatment.

Voucher

Document used to record debits or credits posted to a room account.

Wake Up call

A call made by front office, usually by telephone, to a guest room at the time requested by a room guest to be wakened.

Walk In Guest

One who checks-in without an advance reservation.

Walked Guests

When a hotel is overbooked and a guest room is not available for a confirmed guest, the hotel has "walk the guest" to a nearby hotel. This usually includes paying for transportation to the hotel and covering any difference in the room rate at the hotel the guest was "walked" to.

Appendix 'B'

Bibliography

A Century of Hospitality by *Educational Institute* of AH&LA

Basic Hotel and Restaurant Accounting, by *Raymond Cote*, CPA, CCP

Ethics in the Hospitality and Tourism Industry, by *Bruce Nissen, Karen Lieberman*

Guide to Best Practices in Tourism and Destination Management, by *Rich Harrill,* Ph.D.

High Performance Hospitality: Sustainable Hotel Case Studies by *Educational Institute of AH&LA*

Hospitality 2015: The Future of Hospitality and Travel by *Frederick J. Demicco, Marvin J. Cetron*

Hospitality Industry Financial Accounting, by *James W. Damitio, Raymond S. Schmidgall* Ph.D., CPA

Hospitality Sales and Marketing by *James R. Abbey*

Hospitality Today: An Introduction, by *Andrew N. Vladimir,* CHE, *Rocco M. Angelo,* CHA

Hotel Asset Management: Principles & Practices, by *Educational Institute of AH&LA*

International Hotels: Development and Management, by *Chuck Yim Gee*

Managing Beverage Service, by *Lendal H. Kotschevar,* Ph.D., *Ronald F. Cichy,* Ph.D., CHA, CFBE, CHA

Managing Beverage Operations, by *Lendal H. Kotschevar,* Ph.D., *Ronald F. Cichy,* Ph.D., CHA, CFBE, CHA

Management of Food and Beverage Operations, by *Jack D. Ninemeier*

Managing Front Office Operations, by *Educational Institute of AH&LA*

Managing Front Office Operations, by *Michael L. L. Kasavana, Richard M. Brooks*

Managing Housekeeping Operations, by *Aleta Nitschke, William D. Frye*

Managing Service in Food & Beverage Operations, by *Philip J. Hickey, Jr*

Managing Technology in the Hospitality Industry, by *John J. Cahill, Michael L. L. Kasavana*

Preventive Guestroom Maintenance, by *Educational Institute of AH&LA*

Planning and Control for Food and Beverage Operations, by *Jack D. Ninemeier*

Professional Hotel Management, by *Dr. Jagmohan Negi*, S. Chand & Co, New Delhi, India

Revenue Management: Maximizing Revenue in Hospitality Operations, by *Gabor Forgacs*

Sales Tactics in a Tough Economy, by *Educational Institute of AH&LA*

The Lodging and Food Service Industry, by *Gerald W. Lattin*, Ph.D, CHA

The Lodging and Food Service Industry, by *Educational Institute of AH&LA*

The Spirit of Hospitality (including Enhanced Training Program), by *Educational Institute of AH&LA*

Understanding Hospitality Law, by *Banks Brown, Jack P. Jefferies*

World of Resorts: From *Development to Management by Educational Institute of AH&LA*